What Can I Bring?

Yvonne Baker
What Can I Bring?

Fleming H. Revell
Old Tappan, New Jersey

Scripture quotations are taken from King James Version of the Bible.

Interior illustrations © 1988 by Laura Prill

Library of Congress Cataloging-in-Publication Data

Baker, Yvonne G.
   What can I bring?

   1. Cookery.   2. Quantity cookery.
I. Title.
TX652.B313   1988   641.5'7   88-4528
ISBN 0-8007-1577-2

Copyright © 1988 by Yvonne Baker
Published by the Fleming H. Revell Company
Old Tappan, New Jersey 07675
Printed in the United States of America

This book is dedicated to all of my relatives in Nebraska who gave me my earliest memories of community meals filled with love and great food.

Acknowledgments

It is almost impossible to properly acknowledge the sources of this book. Though all of the recipes have been rewritten, standardized, and updated, they originated from many people, many countries, many sources. They were found on scraps of paper, in old books, on photocopies from friends; they were handwritten, typed, and scrawled. Some were recently given to me; some I had from when I was a child. The following list contains the names attached to some of the recipes, but unfortunately the names have been lost from many others. To these people and to those I'm not able to name personally, I gratefully acknowledge your contribution. Recipe and idea sharers: Amelia Stock, Debby Gloyd, Dorothy Oswald, Bernie Erb, Agatha Eickelberger, Evelyn Schantz, Mary Erb, Marilyn Schantz, Kay Marshall, Pat Newsome, Mae Page, Evie Nall, Jane Sheffer, Nancy Sidner, Joanna Stone, Catherine Volan, Sherrie Haffer, Willie Stock.

Some recipes previously appeared in *Today's Christian Woman*.

Contents

**Part One
The Community Meal**   **15**

The Tradition of the Community Meal   **17**

Organizing a Successful Community Meal   **20**

Planning, Planning, and More Planning   21
    Basic Decisions   21
    Menu Planning   23
Into Action   27
    Reconnaissance   27
    Shopping   28
    Setting Up   30
    Serving   32
    Cleanup   33
Miscellaneous Tips   34

Menus and Special Meals   **36**

Guidelines for Using These Menus   36
Thirty Menus for Community Meals   37
Quantities for 25, 50, and 100 Servings   43
Special Meals   48
    Pancake Suppers   48
    Spaghetti Dinners   51
    Barbecuing and Grilling   53

Part Two
Recipes

57

Appetizers   **59**
  Party Starters   59
  Spreads and Dips   68
  Hot Stuff   76
  Nibbles   78

Main Dishes   **81**
  Beef   81
  Poultry   108
  Ham, Pork, and Lamb   122
  Fish and Seafood   130
  Eggs and Cheese   135
  Soups and Stews   140

Vegetables and Side Dishes   **160**
  Vegetables   160
  Side Dishes   183

Salads   **193**
  Vegetable Salads   193
  Pasta and Grain Salads   203
  Green Salads   206
  Molded Salads   213
  Slaws   222
  Fruit Salads   224
  Fluff Salads   229
  Salad Dressings and Toppings   231

Breads   **237**
  Quick Breads   237
  Coffee Cakes   248
  Batter Breads   257
  Yeast Breads   260
  Biscuits, Rolls, and Muffins   268
  Special Butters   278

Desserts   **281**
  Cakes   281
  Frostings   297

Pies   302
Special Desserts   320
Cookies and Bars   330

Beverages   **340**
  Hot Beverages   340
Cold Drinks   347

Common Equivalents   **353**

Index   **361**

What Can I Bring?

Part One
The Community
Meal

The Tradition
of the Community Meal

"What can I bring?"

Hear these words and the imagination begins to dance with the anticipation of delicious food. No matter the name—potluck dinner, community meal, covered-dish supper—the magic is the same. Many contributors, many offerings, each one adding to the creation of a feast.

And so it has always been. The history of food isn't made up of solitary individuals who eat their meals hidden away in corners or closets. It is rather people sharing meals:

- Early Hebrew families sharing a lamb in commemoration of Passover.
- Jesus using a child's simple lunch to feed five thousand hungry people.

- Monks in the Middle Ages extending a welcome to all hungry and weary travelers.
- Indians and Puritan settlers, together, feasting and giving thanks for a much needed harvest.
- An Independence Day community picnic with fireworks, fried chicken, and homemade strawberry ice cream.
- A city neighborhood block party gathering many peoples and many foods from many cultures.

A community meal goes by many different names. In some parts of the country, it's called a *covered-dish supper* or a *hot-dish supper*, because each contribution is transported in a covered casserole dish. In areas with Scandinavian influences, such a meal is called a *smorgasbord*. The community meal is part of the fabric of the local church, with the entire congregation (and fortunate guests) turning out for a *church supper* or a *Sunday school picnic*. But undoubtedly the most popular name for this type of meal is *potluck*.

The very word *potluck* conjures up memories of tables groaning with an endless variety of meat loaf and chicken, baked beans and corn bread, fruit pies and layer cakes. You stand in line with your friends, first on one foot, then the other, waiting with agonizing anticipation for the grown-ups to hurry up and ask the blessing. Your brother, who secretly scouted out the tables, reports happily that Mrs. Taylor did indeed bring her special lasagna.

These memories are not far removed from the original meaning of the word *potluck*. To be invited for potluck means that you are served a meal for which no special preparations are made; it is standard fare, a regular meal. In other words, you get the luck of the pot. And obviously, you take your chances when you accept such invitations!

But to be invited for potluck also means that you are considered family. You are a person for whom no pretense is necessary, someone who shares both good times and bad. Potluck carries with it a fundamental sense of hospitality and belonging.

Madeleine L'Engle observes ". . . there has always been a sacramental aspect to a shared meal." A meal is one of the most universal human experiences. And the sharing of meals offers every person the opportunity to develop and exercise the finest disciplines of life.

In sharing a meal, we learn service. We discover the satisfaction of completing a good work, of serving those we love and those who need.

We learn compassion. Feeding the hungry is in every culture and in every age an act of compassion. We show compassion when we share a meal with someone who would otherwise not eat.

We learn hospitality, that wonderful quality that makes every guest welcomed and honored. When real hospitality is extended, a guest will only remember how welcome he or she felt, never the untidy bathroom or the dusty windows.

We learn peace. By sharing a meal or breaking bread, we make peace with those who share our table. To share a meal is a sign of trust and honor.

We learn fellowship and companionship. When we share a meal with people, we experience a sense of celebration and enjoyment. Our commitments are deepened; our bonds are strengthened.

We need potluck. It's time to make shared meals a part of our lives once more. Any occasion can become an opportunity to share a meal. Start with a small group of friends or perhaps a family reunion. Many communities celebrate holidays such as Shrove Tuesday or Fourth of July with a community-wide meal. Some communities and churches have even begun regular programs for feeding the homeless and hungry of the community, with various members of the community contributing cooked dishes on a scheduled basis.

It needn't be elaborate or fancy or expensive. It should simply be a shared meal. As Madeleine L'Engle promises, "If there is a sense of sacrament about the meal, then it can spread out to all areas of life."

Organizing a Successful Community Meal

Far too often, potluck dinner means not only potluck menu, but potluck everything else.

Imagine a meal where nobody knows who is bringing what or if table service is being provided. No one knows who will do the setup or cleanup or any serving in between. People don't know where to put their food when they arrive—the refrigerators are full and there aren't enough tables set up. When the meal is over, used paper plates and cups threaten to overrun the room because someone forgot to buy trash bags. In the name of informality, chaos reigns.

Fortunately, it doesn't have to be this way.

Planning, Planning, and More Planning

Planning is the key to a carefree, smoothly run, fun-for-all-involved community meal. It's rather ironic that a community meal, which sounds like it should be less work, actually needs considerable attention ahead of time to be a real success. The truth is that the more effortless an event appears, the more planning went into it.

Planning is important whether the event is large or small, whether it's "just family" or the entire community. No matter what the size of the event, the same principles of planning apply. If you take the time to plan, you will save time and energy by consolidating tasks like shopping and errands, you will avoid mistakes (that take extra time to correct), and you will save yourself tremendous wear and tear on your nerves, allowing you to *enjoy* yourself.

Basic Decisions

Planning involves making some basic decisions.

1. Who's in charge?
2. Purpose and theme of meal
3. Number of guests
4. Budget
5. Location
6. Decorations
7. Menu
8. Personnel

1. Who's in charge? Democracy notwithstanding, every event needs to have one person to act as overseer, someone who will take the responsibility for organizing people, for making decisions, for following up on the little details. Even if this meal is being planned by a committee, the committee needs someone to be in charge. So don't be shy; pick a leader.

2. Decide on the purpose and theme of the meal. Is the purpose a family reunion, a bridal tea, or a traditional Christmas party? Your choice of *theme* depends on the purpose of the event. Informal church suppers or family reunions don't usually need a theme, but you may wish to choose a theme for more special events, such as birthdays, anniversaries, homecomings, retirements, and other milestones of life. For example, the theme for a pastor's retirement dinner could be a journey down memory lane with a memory quilt as the visual focus in the room.

3. Determine how many guests will be present. Try to get an accurate count of the number of people you expect to serve. Sign-up sheets can be used in most situations. Deadlines for signing up or responding are quite helpful to planning, with reminder telephone calls to those folks who forget to respond. And don't forget to include all the workers in your count!

4. What is the budget? Even the most informal potlucks require an outlay of money for things like condiments, beverages, paper goods, decorations, supplies, and so on. Expenses add up quickly, so it is good to determine ahead of time exactly what your budget restrictions are. If you have absolutely no budget at all, the non-cooks can contribute some of these things. But in order to ask someone to supply them, you must anticipate the need.

5. Select a location. For a small potluck with close friends, a living room can be quite comfortable. A graduation celebration with a hundred guests will need a hall or picnic shelter. Make sure that the location will comfortably hold the number of guests you expect to serve.

6. Decide on decorations. In addition to all of the obvious considerations (such as the purpose and theme of the event), make certain that you find out all you can about the location before you finalize decoration decisions. Many meeting rooms have fire codes and other regulations that may influence decorating decisions. For example, are you permitted to use thumbtacks or tape on the walls?

Also, the decor of some locations will sometimes determine the decorating for you. We once held a Christmas appetizer buffet at a mansion that is opened to the public. The beautiful interior of the mansion, with its crystal chandeliers, carved wood furniture, scarlet poinsettias, and ropes of fresh pine boughs made any extra decorating seem silly.

Decorations needn't only be crepe paper streamers and balloons; flowers, antiques, baskets of fruit and vegetables, quilts and weavings, almost anything can be used to create a special feeling and mood in a room. Small touches often make the biggest difference.

7. Choose a menu. Selecting an appropriate menu involves two things. First, know what style of community meal will be served. Will this be a traditional potluck menu, an arranged menu, or a prepared-on-site menu? Second, the menu should complement the occasion. The menu that is appropriate for a high school post-game party would not work for a businesswomen's luncheon.

(For help in planning your menu, see the Menu Planning section of this chapter, as well as the chapter entitled "Menus and Special Meals.")

8. Finally, line up your personnel. Determine who will help shop, set up, cook, serve, and clean up. One way to do this is to ask folks to volunteer for those tasks that they enjoy doing. But if that doesn't work, draft them, promising them the first choice of dessert.

Note: The best way to keep a handle on your planning is to keep a notebook in which you keep your schedule, the menu, a list of your co-workers (and their phone numbers), shopping lists, guest list, plus any other helpful information and checklists. This keeps all your planning conveniently at hand. Then after the event is over, make notes about what worked and what didn't. Put a checkmark or plus sign beside the things that worked and make comments about how things can be improved or changed. Don't forget to note the people and the suppliers who were especially helpful. These notes become invaluable when it's time to plan another community meal.

Menu Planning

Menus for community meals generally fall into one of three categories: the Traditional Potluck Menu, the Arranged Menu, and the Prepared-on-Site Menu. Each style has its own strengths and charms; the occasion and your preferences will determine which style is most suitable. And because each style is flexible and easy to manage, different features from the three menu styles may be combined for special situations.

As you consider which style of menu to use, remember the menu should be coordinated with the event and the season. Just as Sloppy Joes would not be appropriate for a formal banquet, Chicken Baked in Cream is unsuitable for a post-game party.

The Traditional Potluck Menu

This is the type of menu you think of when you remember a covered-dish supper or a Sunday school picnic. Everyone involved brings a dish or two, usually their specialty. All of the dishes are laid out buffet style, and then the feasting begins.

This is a wonderfully informal and adventurous sort of meal. Depending on the group, the meal can range anywhere from just this side of heaven to just this side of edible. The key, obviously, is knowing the group and their cooking capabilities.

Although this sounds like a rather freewheeling sort of meal, general guidelines are still necessary to ensure success. People need to know what kind of dish or dishes they are expected to bring, whether it's an appetizer, an entrée, a salad, a dessert, or whatever.

Planning a Traditional Potluck Menu involves five steps.

1. Decide what type of potluck this will be.
2. Determine the types of food needed.

3. Determine the quantities of food needed.

4. Develop a system for food assignments.

5. Assign the food.

1. What type of potluck are you planning?

A full meal potluck would include: meat/main dish, vegetable, salad, bread, and dessert.

A light meal potluck may include: meat/main dish, salad, and dessert.

A specialty potluck would be a menu featuring a specific food such as a salad buffet, a dessert buffet, or a soup and bread buffet.

Most potluck meals will fall into these three categories, but don't limit yourself. Use your imagination to create your own potluck.

2. What types of food do you want? This will become evident once you've determined what kind of potluck menu you are planning.

3. What quantities of food will you need? Using the menu guidelines on page 36, make a general list of the quantities of various dishes needed to feed the number of people expected to attend. Adjustments should be made according to the group. Men and boys eat more food than women. People will generally eat more in the evenings than at noontime, and will want more in the winter than in the summer. When in doubt, a good rule of thumb is to plan for a little extra food.

4. How will the food be assigned? There are many ways to do this. If you know your group well, you can simply make *general assignments.* For example, if this is a supper for families, you may ask each family to bring one meat/main dish plus two other items of their choice. If this is a meal that will include a wide range of people, you may ask each family to bring a meat/main dish and a dessert, each single person to bring a salad, and each couple to bring a vegetable and a bread. For a salad buffet, each household should simply bring one salad.

A *sign-up sheet* is the most common system used. Across the top of the sheet, list the categories of food and how many items you want each family to bring. Each household then writes their name on the right side and checks what items they will be bringing under the food categories.

Another effective method is to have a *drawing.* Each item needed is written on a slip of paper and placed in a large basket or box. Each household selects one or two (or however many you determine). Or each household could be asked to bring one meat or main dish and then draw slips to determine what else they will bring: salad, vegetable, dessert, or bread.

The best system for a very large group is the *alphabet* system. Assignments are made according to the first letter of the participant's last name. For example:

A–F - bring a main dish and a salad
G–L - bring a vegetable and a dessert
M–S - bring a vegetable and a dessert
T–Z - bring a side dish and a bread

or

A–L - bring a main dish, salad, and vegetable
M–Z - bring a main dish, bread, and dessert

Experiment with your own breakdowns, based on what kind of meal you are planning.

5. Assign the food. Using whichever system you've chosen, see that food and people are matched up. Follow-up is a major part of this task. While there are lots of folks who will go out of their way to sign up, many others need to be reminded and encouraged to participate. Don't be afraid to make calls to folks to ask them to participate. This not only represents a wonderful opportunity to extend a welcome, it is a necessary part of maintaining control of the meal. It's important to have an accurate idea of what foods you can expect to be contributed. Call those who haven't volunteered; extend a personal invitation and be prepared to give them specific suggestions on what they can bring, just in case they are short on ideas. And call key people, those who have been regulars in the past, to make certain they will attend. If they won't be there, you will need to fill in the food gaps.

The Arranged Menu

In this style of community meal, a set menu is determined and many people individually prepare portions of the food in their own kitchen and then bring them to the event. This style of meal has many of the advantages of a large meal prepared in one central kitchen, but it is actually much easier because the majority of the work, from the shopping to the cooking, is shared.

This style of community meal is excellent for more structured or formal situations. It is great for those occasions when you want to honor a member of your group or celebrate special events such as graduations, anniversaries, retirements, special achievements, homecomings, and birthdays. It is also great for holiday gatherings such as an Easter brunch or a Christmas dinner. The Arranged Menu has all the advantages of a catered banquet, with the added attractions of being far more personal and far less costly.

The Arranged Menu must be planned more carefully than the Traditional Potluck. These are the considerations:

1. Decide on the menu.
2. Determine the amounts of food needed.
3. Copy the recipes along with details of the event
   and any special instructions.
4. Assign the recipes.
5. Follow up.

1. Decide on the menu. The host or hostess or committee should decide on the overall menu. The menus in this book have been arranged to indicate how many contributions of each recipe must be made to feed various numbers of people. Use these menus as guides to determine the best menu for your event. Feel free to make your own selections and substitutions, based on your experience and the tastes of your community.

2. Determine the amounts of food needed. This means you must decide how many times each recipe should be prepared in order to serve the number of people attending. For example, you are planning to serve the Beef Pot Roast menu to fifty people. The menu indicates how many times each recipe must be made in order to serve fifty people.

Sunday Dinner Pot Roast	5
Fancy Potatoes	4
Cheese Scalloped Carrots	6
Waldorf Salad	5
All-Purpose Rolls	2
Apple Pie	8

You can ask thirty people to each make one batch of recipe (five to make Beef Pot Roast, four to make Fancy Potatoes, etc.) or you may want to combine some of the tasks, asking some folks to make both a vegetable and a salad.

3. Copy the recipes along with details of the event and any special instructions. Recipes should always be clearly written, with accurate instructions. If you have special concerns like serving instructions or where to deliver the dish on the day of the event, be sure to write these out as well. Include the names and phone numbers of the organizers and the facility where the event will be held so that last-minute questions may be answered easily.

4. Assign the recipes. You may ask people to volunteer to make certain dishes or you may ask them to draw one or two of the recipes out of a hat.

5. Follow up. Call each contributor one week before the event to remind them of the event and to answer any questions that may have come up. This also gives you a chance to anticipate any problems such as transportation, schedule

conflicts, and so on. Follow up on anyone who seems to need some extra help.

The Prepared-on-Site Menu

This menu is just like the Arranged Menu meal except, as the name implies, this meal is prepared in just one kitchen, usually at the site of the event. This is the most difficult way to prepare a community meal, mostly because it takes experienced personnel. It should be planned and run by someone who not only has experience in cooking food in large quantities, but who also is able to organize and supervise lots of volunteers (who may or may not be experienced).

For this style of menu, these are the steps:

1. Decide on a menu.
2. Determine the amounts of food needed.
3. Check out the kitchen for equipment and supplies.
4. Make out a shopping list.
5. Line up your help and assign tasks.
6. Set up a schedule.
7. Follow through.

Into Action

Now that most of your planning is done, it's time to get moving. There are five major areas of concern in preparing for a community meal: Reconnaissance, Shopping, Setting Up, Serving, and Cleaning Up.

Reconnaissance

1. Take time to review the hall and kitchen facilities well in advance. Meet the people who take care of the facility; they are an invaluable resource. Ask about entrances and exits, fire extinguishers, emergency kits, mops, brooms, cleaning supplies, and trash areas. Also make arrangements to see that you can have access to the kitchen and hall when you need it for setup and preparation. There's nothing worse than needing to get into a building when the custodian is out on an errand.

2. Get acquainted with the kitchen and check for the following:

> Refrigerator and freezer space
> Oven and stove top space
> Counter space

Automatic dishwasher available?
Cooking and baking utensils
Special pieces of equipment, such as coffee makers,
    microwave ovens, steam tables, and warming trays
Kitchen tools
Supplies, such as towels, pot holders, aprons

3. Check the dining area or hall for:

Tables (for dining and for food and beverage setup)
Chairs
Lighting
Accessibility to the kitchen
Available decorations, such as candles or tablecloths
Available help (sometimes a facility will have
    custodial help who will help set up and clean up.
    Of course, always offer them a meal!)

Shopping

1. Review the entire menu and your Basic Decisions worksheet.

2. Determine which parts of the meals will be prepared by contributors and which parts of the meal (if any) will be supplied by the host group. (Sometimes the host group will supply beverages and bread, sometimes hot dogs, hamburgers, and buns, sometimes the main course.) Assemble any recipes to be prepared by the host group, then make a shopping list of all ingredients (with the amounts) and supplies needed.

3. Organize your shopping list into four categories:

Nonperishable items   This includes canned and frozen foods, condiments, paper goods, supplies, and decorations. These may be purchased any time in advance of the event.

Rental supplies   Any equipment and services that must be specially arranged. A local rental agency can be a lifesaver to anyone involved in a community meal, supplying tables and chairs, special equipment such as coffee makers and warming trays, as well as serving pieces and utensils. Be sure to reserve needed pieces well in advance; during peak entertaining seasons, such as November and December or May and June (graduation and weddings), agencies often run out of equipment.

Special order foods and items   This could include ingredients that are not always available in your area, as well as anything that you may need in large quantities, such as meats. If you need to have anything prepared in a particular manner (such as having the meat sliced or specially cut), it should be specially ordered. Most grocers and markets will handle such orders without extra charge. Flower arrangements, tanks of helium (for balloons), and bakery goods are examples of other things that should be ordered in advance. Special orders should be placed at least a week in advance.

Perishable foods   This includes all fresh foods: meats, fruits, vegetables, baked goods, and so forth. These should be purchased no more than one or two days in advance of cooking.

4. Take inventory. Using the shopping list as a guide, determine if any of the needed foods and supplies are on hand before you shop. Also check the kitchen and the hall for equipment and furniture.

The shopping list is an important part of maintaining control. As items are purchased or supplied, they should be marked off the list. It is also important that receipts be collected and totaled for control purposes and to help plan future events.

Basic Items for a Shopping List

Paper goods
napkins (allow three to five per person)
hot drinking cups
cold drinking cups
paper plates (large for main courses, smaller for desserts)
plastic flatware (allow for clean flatware for each course)
tablecloths (for food tables and dining tables)

Condiments
salt and pepper
butter or margarine
cream and sugar
ketchup, mustard, and bottled sauces
relishes, pickles, olives, etc.

Kitchen supplies
aluminum foil
plastic wrap
trash bags
paper towels, dish towels
food storage bags

Decorations
flowers

Setting Up

Setting up a community meal involves orchestrating a number of details.

1. Dining Arrangements

Provide enough tables and chairs to seat everyone with plenty of room for free movement.

Determine what tableware will be used. Some people prefer everything disposable: plates, cups, flatware. Others prefer the real thing. Some prefer a combination. Whatever you decide, make sure that the tableware is suitable for the menu. Everyone has at least one memory of a thin paper plate filled with hot food buckling halfway between the food table and the dining table. Or trying to cut a slice of roast beef with a plastic fork.

Decorate and set the tables, if necessary. Some community meals have plates, flatware, and napkins set up with the food tables. Other times, the flatware and napkins are set up on the dining tables and the plates are with the food tables. Or, the entire place setting is arranged on the dining tables, and guests carry their own plates to the buffet tables. You decide which arrangement works best for you.

Just before the meal begins, supply each table with a set of salt and pepper shakers, butter, condiments, relishes, and pitchers of ice water.

2. Food Service Arrangements

Provide an adequate number of food tables. Don't underestimate the amount of space needed to set out the food; casserole and baking dishes are quite bulky. And contributors are not pleased if there is no room for their special dish.

Arrange the tables so that traffic flows smoothly and comfortably. Sample Table Arrangements are shown on page 31.

Arrange the tables so that like foods may be grouped together. For example, all salads should be together, all main dishes, all breads, and so on. Small signs on the tables indicating where certain foods go may also be helpful.

Consider setting up dessert tables in an area separate from the main food tables. Many folks prefer to set up dessert near the beverage service.

3. Beverage Service Arrangements

Set beverage tables up well away from the food tables, out of the flow of food table traffic. This way people are less likely to spill their drinks. This is especially important when children are present.

A beverage service area should include the following:

> Hot Beverages
>> regular coffee
>> decaffeinated coffee (brewed or instant)
>> hot water (for tea)
>> tea bags

BUFFET TABLES

Buffet tables should be arranged so guests are served quickly and easily. A general rule of thumb is to allow one serving table for every 75 to 100 guests.

Below are some suggestions for arranging buffet tables.

To serve up to 100 guests: One Table
(8 feet by 30 inches)

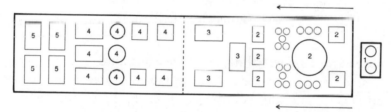

To serve 100 to 200 guests: Two Tables
(End to end, 16 feet by 30 inches)

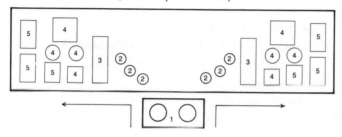

To serve 200 to 350 guests: Four Tables
(arranged by twos, end to end, then pushed together to form a table measuring 16 feet by 5 feet)

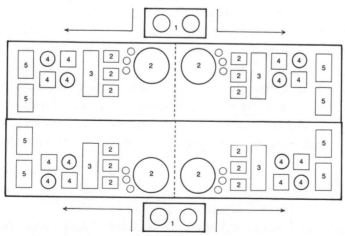

1. Plates   2. Salads   3. Breads   4. Vegetables and side dishes   5. Main dishes

Desserts and Beverages should be arranged on separate tables away from the flow of traffic of the main food tables.

Cold Beverages
    ice water
    a selection of cold beverages (including
       soft drinks, milk, and/or punch)
    ice cubes

lemon slices
sugar
artificial sweetener
cream or coffee lightener (half-and-half,
   milk, and/or non-dairy creamer)
hot water cups
cold water cups
spoons and stirrers
paper napkins

Keep a wastepaper basket near the beverage table so that people can discard used cups, empty sugar packets, and so on.

Serving

Helpers are needed for everything: to arrange furniture, to decorate, to set the dining tables, to set up the food and beverage tables, to greet guests, to serve, and to clean up. The people who help are in effect the hosts and hostesses of the event. And their presence is invaluable.

This becomes particularly apparent in the few hours before and during the meal.

Every community meal needs a crew of hosts and hostesses on hand to greet arriving guests. It is, first of all, a gracious act of hospitality. Hosts and hostesses should make every arrival feel welcome and appreciated for their contribution. Second, hosts and hostesses can keep things from getting out of control by seeing that questions are answered and guests are helped. The hosts and hostesses should direct traffic: either direct the guests to the appropriate food table with their contribution or take it from them as they enter. A host or hostess can also see that foods are kept cold or warm during a pre-meal program, if necessary. In other words, hosts and hostesses can mean the difference between calm and chaos.

During the meal, the hosts and hostesses can make the meal run smoothly and pleasantly.

They should:

• see that water pitchers are filled
• oversee the food tables to see that empty food dishes are removed and replaced with new ones

- be aware of any guests with special needs, such as children, the handicapped, or the elderly. Offer help to anyone who needs help filling or carrying a plate of food. And don't forget food refills and beverages!
- know where to find rags and mops for spills
- know what to do in an emergency: how to get the first-aid kit, where to find a telephone, and so forth.
- help clear the tables after main course, if necessary, and direct guests to the dessert tables.

In other words, hosts and hostesses make everything seem easy and fun.

Cleanup

Cleanup is cleanup. There's simply no way around it. But it can be easier than you think.

1. Put together a cleanup crew, people whose only responsibility is cleaning up. Try not to ask the folks who set up or served as hosts and hostesses.

2. Have large trash cans with liners. Place them around so that they are convenient yet out of sight of food and dining tables.

3. In some situations, guests can throw out their own refuse and pick up after themselves.

4. Contributors should each be responsible for collecting their own food dishes and taking them home to be washed.

5. All rented and borrowed equipment should be washed immediately following the meal and returned. Be sure to assign one member of the cleaning crew to return any rented supplies.

6. Be prepared for leftovers. Have self-sealing food bags on hand, in case guests wish to share or swap food. Singles, retirees, and others who cook for one are often pleased to take home a few extra leftovers. Don't forget local shelters and soup kitchens which may be pleased with usable contributions.

7. Remove all of the decorations. Flowers may be given to the sick and shut-ins.

8. See that all of the tables and chairs are folded and stacked.

9. Sweep the floor and mop, if necessary.

10. Make sure the kitchen is clean. It never hurts to leave a place cleaner than you found it.

11. Check the kitchen and hall the day after the event, in case things are left behind.

Miscellaneous Tips

• Line up more helpers than you think you will need. Somebody always gets sick or cancels out at the last minute.

• Have stickers (or masking tape) and markers on hand to label baking dishes, casseroles, serving platters, and their accompanying lids.

• Some groups place tags beside each dish on the food tables, naming the cook who made the dish. This allows everyone to receive the proper credit. It also lets you know who to ask for the recipe!

• Be sure to include noncooks in the festivities. Ask them to bring food from the deli or the bakery. Or ask them to help set up or to be a host or hostess. Often the cooks are simply too harried to be good hosts and hostesses.

• If the group is large, name tags and a few people assigned to make introductions can make a community meal run more smoothly.

• Let your guests know what to wear to a community meal. Most community meals are informal, but sometimes they're more formal. Hospitality means that your guests know what is expected of them.

• Make mealtime definite. Guests and help alike should always know precisely what time the meal will begin.

• If you are short on ovens or refrigerator space, ask contributors to bring their food in an ice chest with ice to keep food cold. Hot food will stay hot if it's wrapped in a towel and several layers of newspaper then put into a plastic foam cooler (without ice, of course). And don't forget that slow cookers, warming trays, and electric frying pans are all able to keep food warm.

• Always say thank you. Many people contribute to make a community meal a success, and each one deserves a thank you for what they brought or how they helped.

• Send thank you notes to businesses or individuals who helped make the event a success.

• Set aside sometime soon after the event to sit down with the people who helped. Evaluate the meals, and write down any notes, comments, or ideas about how to make the next one better.

- Above all, enjoy yourself. Margorie Kinnan Rawlings once wrote: "Two elements enter into successful and happy gatherings at a table. The food, whether simple or elaborate, must be carefully prepared; willingly prepared; imaginatively prepared. And the guests—friends, family, or strangers—must be conscious of their welcome." Sharing a meal is about grace and welcome and hospitality. Put your guests before all else, and your meal will taste of heaven.

Menus and Special Meals

Guidelines for Using These Menus

1. The following menus have been devised to help you plan your community meal. Most of these menus are designed for a specific event and each one balances taste and texture to give the meal a sense of wholeness. Feel free to make substitutions in any of these menus. Certain foods may be out of season or certain tastes may be preferred above others. The menus are not rules, but guidelines. So have fun!

2. If you are having a small potluck for friends or family, you will want to ignore the amounts given in the menus. Simply select the menu you wish to use and, based on the serving amounts indicated on the individual recipes, determine how many times to repeat the recipe for your event. In some cases, you may need to plan on leftovers.

3. The menus indicate how many times you will need to repeat a particular *recipe* in order to serve *25 people*, *50 people*, and *100 people*.

4. If a menu calls for five batches of a particular dish, *do not* attempt to make only one batch by simply multiplying all the ingredients by five. It won't work unless you've had considerable experience in cooking food in large quantities because the seasonings and ingredients need to be carefully adjusted. It is usually safe to double a recipe, except in the case of baked goods.

5. When a recipe is doubled, the actual yield is more than double the servings of a single recipe. This is why some of the menus indicate 3 recipes to serve 25 people, but 5 (not 6) to serve 50.

6. Unless a specific beverage is mentioned, it is assumed that water, milk, juice, soft drinks, coffee, and/or tea will be served with each menu. The instructions for beverages for large groups are in the section called "Beverages."

7. Appetizers have not been included in the menus, as community meals generally do not offer appetizers. Feel free to add one or more appetizers to your menu.

8. Don't forget those wonderful store-bought standbys like fresh bakery breads, ice cream, fresh fruits, applesauce, popcorn. These make wonderful additions or substitutions to any menu when you're short on time or energy. Some folks even throw potluck suppers where all of the food is purchased—deli, Chinese takeout, gourmet ice creams. Perfect for working people who stop on their way home from work, pick up some goodies, and head over to a friend's house for potluck.

Thirty Menus for Community Meals

Menu	25 servings	50 servings	100 servings
Covered-Dish Suppers			
Beef			
Sunday Dinner Pot Roast	3	5	10
Fancy Potatoes	2	4	7
Cheese Scalloped Carrots	3	6	11
Waldorf Salad	3	5	10
All-Purpose Rolls	1	2	4
Apple Pie	4	8	16

Menu	25 servings	50 servings	100 servings
Ham			
Baked Ham with Raisin Sauce	1	2	4
Broccoli and Tomatoes	3	6	12
Easy Scalloped Potatoes	2	4	8
Sunshine Salad	1	2	4
All-Purpose Rolls	1	2	4
Cherry Pie	4	8	16
Meatloaf			
Traditional Meat loaf (or try a variety)	3	6	12
Nebraska Corn Pudding	3	6	12
Potluck Green Beans	3	6	12
Five-Cup Salad	4	8	16
Six Weeks Bran Muffins	1	2	4
Carrot Cake	1	2	4
Chicken			
Chicken Baked in Cream	4	8	16
Carrots and Walnuts	3	6	11
Tossed Salad	1	2	4
Dill Bread	2	3	6
German Chocolate Cake	1	2	4
Regional and Ethnic Favorites			
Great Plains Chicken Pie Supper			
Chicken Potpie	4	8	16
Tossed Salad	1	2	4
All-Purpose Rolls	2	4	8
Apple Crisp	2	4	8
New England Baked Bean Supper			
Boston Baked Beans	2	4	6
Tangerine or Granny Smith Cole Slaw	3	5	10
Boston Brown Bread	1	2	4
Apple Pie with Cheddar Cheese Slices	4	8	16
Greek Islands Feast			
Moussaka	2	4	8
Tossed Salad	1	2	4

Menu	25 servings	50 servings	100 servings
Holiday Greek Bread	2	4	8
Baklava	1	2	4
Mexican Fiesta			
Chicken Enchiladas Supreme	3	6	11
Spanish Rice With Beef	3	6	11
Jicama Salad	3	5	9
Strawberry-Topped Flan	4	8	16
Hearty German Supper			
Yorkville Sauerbraten With Gingersnap Gravy	2	4	8
Red Cabbage Side Dish	3	6	11
German Potato Salad	2	4	7
Swedish Rye Bread	1	2	7
German Chocolate Cake	1	2	4
Soups and Breads			
Heartlands Soup and Salad Luncheon			
Hungarian Goulash Soup	1	2	3
New England Clam Chowder	2	4	8
Salad Bar	1	2	4
Herb-Onion Bread	1	2	4
Apple Crisp	2	4	8
Quartet of Soups Buffet			
Minestrone à la Genovese	1	2	3
Cauliflower Cheese Soup	4	8	16
Crab Gazpacho	1	2	3
French Quarter Mushroom Soup	2	4	7
Challah	2	4	8
Cherry Pie	4	8	16
Fireside Soup Supper			
German Beef and Noodle Stew	2	4	6
All-Day Lentil Soup	3	6	12
Salad Bar	1	2	4
Homemade Oat Bread	1	2	4
German Chocolate Cake	1	2	4

Menu	25 servings	50 servings	100 servings
Saturday Night Chili Supper			
Rio Grande Chili Con Carne	2	4	8
Granny Smith Cabbage Slaw	3	6	12
Cheesy Corn Bread	4	8	16
Oatmeal Cake	2	4	8
Picnics			
Old-Fashioned Church Picnic			
Country Fried Chicken	5	9	17
Deviled Eggs	1	2	4
Granny Smith Cabbage Slaw	3	6	12
Country Potato Salad	2	4	7
All-Purpose Rolls	1	2	4
Amish Sugar Cookies	1	2	3
Lemonade	2	4	8
Western Barbecue Picnic			
Evie's Barbecued Brisket	3	6	12
Boston Baked Beans	1	2	4
Sour Cream and Cucumbers	3	6	12
or			
Tangerine Cole Slaw	3	6	12
Cheesy Corn Bread	4	8	16
Apple Crisp	2	4	8
Luncheons			
Ladies' Luncheon			
Perch With Crab-Mushroom Topping	5	10	20
Spinach Carambola Salad	3	5	9
Apple-Cinnamon Puffs	2	4	8
Chocolate Mint Pie	4	8	16
Ladies' Luncheon			
Hot Chicken Salad	2	4	7
Pineapple-Orange Spinach Salad	3	5	10
Angel Biscuits	1	2	3
Frozen Fruit Salad (for dessert)	3	6	11

Menu	25 servings	50 servings	100 servings
Men's Luncheon			
Wild Rice and Mushroom Chicken	4	8	16
Broccoli and Tomatoes	3	6	12
Spicy Aspic Salad	3	6	12
Homemade Oat Bread	2	4	8
Royal Cheesecake	2	4	7
Men's Luncheon			
Pork Chops Italiano	3	6	12
Italian Green Bean Salad	3	6	12
Potatoes With Rosemary	3	6	12
Angel Biscuits	1	2	3
Easy Peanut Butter Pie	4	8	16
Youth Favorites			
Hot Sandwich Supper			
Barbecued Beef	2	4	6
or			
Sloppy Joes	3	6	12
Granny Smith Cabbage Slaw	3	5	10
Potato Chips (pounds)	1	2	4
Chocolate Chip Cookies	1	2	4
Ranger Cookies	1	2	3
Super Taco Lunch			
Super Taco Platter	3	6	11
or			
Acapulco Delight	3	5	10
Salad Bar	1	2	4
Carrot Cake	1	2	4
Gridiron Feast			
Gridiron Casserole	3	6	11
Sunshine Salad	1	2	4
Potluck Green Beans	3	6	12
All-Purpose Rolls	1	2	3
Frozen Banana Split Dessert	1	2	4

Menu	25 servings	50 servings	100 servings
Special Events			
Summer Salad Fest			
Pasta Salad Primavera	1	2	3
Waldorf Salad	2	3	5
Confetti Cole Slaw	2	3	5
Five-Cup Salad	4	8	16
Copper Pennies Carrot Salad	2	4	7
Ambrosia Salad	3	6	11
Salad Bar	1	2	4
Blueberry Cream Mold	1	2	4
Angel Biscuits	1	2	3
English Tea Party			
Poppy Seed Bread	2	4	6
Orange Scones	1	2	4
Lemon Squares	2	4	8
Strawberry Breakfast Bread	1	2	4
(optional: Cheese and Onion Pie)	1	2	4
Hot Spiced Afternoon Tea	1	2	4
Community Breakfast			
Sausage Quiche	3	6	12
Shrimp Quiche	3	6	12
Strawberry Breakfast Bread	1	2	4
Sunshine Muffins	2	4	8
Mixed Fruit Bowl	1	2	4
Mocha Punch	1	2	4
Easter Brunch			
Mushroom and Asparagus Brunch Munch	3	6	12
Baked Ham with Raisin Sauce	1	2	4
Hot Cross Buns	1	2	4
Overnight Coffee Cake	2	4	8
Mixed Fruit Bowl	1	2	4
Mocha Punch	1	2	4
Holiday Buffet			
Cranberry-Cherry Mold	3	5	10
Whipped Sweet Potatoes	3	5	10

Menu	25 servings	50 servings	100 servings
Garden State Vegetable Medley	3	5	10
Honey-Butter Baked Turkey (20–25 pounds each)	1	2	4
Apple-Chestnut Stuffing	2	4	7
All-Purpose Rolls	1	2	4
Maple Pumpkin Pie	3	5	10
Harvest Pie Social			
Buttermilk Custard Pie	2	4	8
All-American Apple Pie	2	4	8
Pecan Pie	2	4	8
Easy Peanut Butter Pie	2	4	8
Raisin Cream Pie	2	4	8
Mississippi Sweet Potato Pie	2	4	8
Creamy Spiced Tea	3	6	12
Dessert Buffet			
Royal Cheesecake	1	2	3
Lemon Squares	1	2	3
German Chocolate Cake	1	2	3
Fresh Strawberry Pie	2	4	6
Baklava	1	2	3

Quantities for 25, 50, and 100 Servings

	Approximate size of each serving	25 servings	50 servings	100 servings
Appetizers and Snacks				
Potato chips	1 oz.	24 oz.	48 oz.	96 oz.
Raw vegetables	2½ oz.	4 lbs.	8 lbs.	12 lbs.
Dips	1 oz.	3 cups	6 cups	12 cups
Popcorn (popped)	1 cup	6 qts.	12 qts.	24 qts.
Nuts	1 oz.	24 oz.	48 oz.	96 oz.

	Approx-imate size of each serving	25 servings	50 servings	100 servings
Main Dishes				
Bacon	2 slices	3 lbs.	6 lbs.	12 lbs.
Beef, rolled rib roast	3 oz. (cooked)	13 lbs. (before boning)	25 lbs. (before boning)	45 lbs. (before boning)
Beef, ground (for hamburgers)	2½–3oz. cooked	6½–8 lbs.	12½–15 lbs.	25–30 lbs.
Chicken (for roasting)	¾ lb.	18–20 lbs.	35–40 lbs.	70–80 lbs.
Chicken, stewing (for cut-up cooked chicken)	½ lb.	10–12 lbs.	20–25 lbs.	40–50 lbs.
Fish (fillets)	5 oz.	7½ lbs.	15 lbs.	30 lbs.
Frankfurters	2	50	100	200
Ham, canned (boned)	¼ lb.	7 lbs.	13 lbs.	25 lbs.
Ham, to bake (with bone)	¼ lb.	12lbs.	22–25 lbs.	50 lbs.
Ground meat (for meatloaf)	2–3 oz. cooked	6 lbs.	12 lbs.	24 lbs.
Sausage (bulk or links)	2–3 oz. cooked	7 lbs.	12½ lbs.	25 lbs.
Soup	1 cup	1½ gals.	3 gals.	6 gals.
Turkey (for dishes using cut-up cooked turkey)		8–9 lbs.	16 lbs.	30–32 lbs.
Turkey (for roasting)	½–⅔ lb.	18–20 lbs.	35–40 lbs.	70–80 lbs.
Vegetables & Side Dishes				
Baked Beans	½ cup	¾ gal.	1½ gals.	2½ gals.
Canned vegetables	½ cup	7 1-lb. cans	14 1-lb. cans	28 1-lb. cans
Carrots	⅓ lb.	8 lbs.	16 lbs.	30 lbs.

	Approx-imate size of each serving	25 servings	50 servings	100 servings
Cauliflower (flowerets only)	¼ lb.	8 lbs.	15 lbs.	30 lbs.
Corn on the cob	1 ear	25 ears	50 ears	100 ears
Frozen vegetables	½ cup	4 16–24 oz. packages	7–8 16–24 oz. packages	14–16 16–24 oz. packages
Noodles or pasta	½ cup cooked	24 oz. un-cooked	3 lbs. un-cooked	6 lbs. un-cooked
Potatoes (to mash)	½ cup	13 lbs.	25 lbs.	48 lbs.
Potatoes (to scallop)	½ cup	7 lbs.	12½ lbs.	24 lbs.
Rice	½ cup cooked	1¾ lbs. un-cooked	3½ lbs. un-cooked	8 lbs. un-cooked
Sweet potatoes (glazed)	6–8 oz.	13 lbs.	25 lbs.	48 lbs.

Salads & Condiments

	Approx-imate size of each serving	25 servings	50 servings	100 servings
Applesauce	½ cup	7 20-oz. cans	14 20-oz. cans	28 20-oz. cans
Cabbage (for slaw)	⅓ cup	6–8 lbs.	12–15 lbs.	24–30 lbs.
Chili sauce	1 tbsp.	2–5 12-oz. bottles	4–5 12-oz. bottles	8–9 12-oz. bottles
Cranberry sauce (jellied)	½-inch slice	3 1-lb. cans	6 1-lb. cans	12 1-lb. cans
Ketchup	1 tbsp.	1 20-oz. bottle	3 14-oz. bottles	4 20-oz. bottles
Lettuce (for salad)	2–3 leaves	3 heads	6 heads	12 heads
Mayonnaise or salad dressing	1 tbsp.	2 cups	1 qt.	2 qts.

	Approximate size of each serving	25 servings	50 servings	100 servings
Olives	2 olives	1 qt.	2 qts.	4 qts.
Pickles	2 small	1 qt.	2 qts.	4 qts.
Potato salad	½ cup	3 qts.	6¼ qts.	3¼ gals.
Tuna (for salad)	½ cup salad	8 6½-oz. cans	16 6½-oz. cans	32 6½-oz. cans
Tomatoes (for salad)	3 slices	16 medium	30 medium	60 medium
Breads				
Butter or margarine	½ tbsp.	½–¾ lb.	1½ lbs.	2–2½ lbs.
Crackers	2	½ lb.	1 lb.	2 lbs.
Loaf bread	1½ slices	2½ loaves	5 loaves	10 loaves
Rolls, biscuits, or muffins	1½	3½ doz.	6½ doz.	13 doz.
Jams, jellies, or spreads	1 tbsp.	1½ lbs.	3 lbs.	6 lbs.
Desserts				
Cupcakes	1 cupcake	25	50	100
Cookies	2 cookies	4½ doz.	8½ doz.	17 doz.
Heavy cream (for whipping)	1 rounded tbsp. for topping	1 pt.	1 qt.	2 qts.
Ice cream	½ cup	1–1½ gals.	2–3 gals.	4–5 gals.
Layer cakes	1-inch slice	1½ 9-inch cakes	3 9-inch cakes	6 9-inch cakes

	Approx- imate size of each serving	25 servings	50 servings	100 servings
Pies (9″)	3-inch slice	4	7	13
Sheet cakes	2½- by 3-inch square	2	4	8
Watermelon	1½ lbs.	40 lbs.	75 lbs.	150 lbs.
Beverages				
Coffee	6 oz.	¾ lb.	1¼ lbs.	2½ lbs.
Cream (half-and-half)	2 tbsp.	1½ pts.	1½ qts.	3 qts.
Fruit juice concentrates	4 oz.	7 6-oz. cans	13 6-oz. cans	26 6-oz. cans
Fruit or vegetable juices (canned)	½ cup	2 46-oz. cans	4 46-oz. cans	8 46-oz. cans
Lemon (for tea)	1 slice	3 large	5 large	9 large
Milk	8 oz.	3½ qts.	7 qts.	3½ gals.
Punch	6 oz.	1 gal.	2 gals.	4 gals.
Soft drinks	8 oz.	6 liters	12 liters	24 liters
Sugar		¾ lb.	1½ lbs.	3 lbs.
Tea	¾ cup	2 oz.	¼ lb.	½ lb.

Special Meals

Pancake Suppers

The French arrived in America with their crepes, the Russians with blini, the Germans with Pfannkuchen, but whatever their origin, the final American result we all love is the buttermilk pancake.

Who hasn't waited impatiently on a weekend morning with fresh butter and hot maple syrup poised until the pancakes were ready? Who hasn't stood in line at a pancake supper waiting for a turn at those hearty, satisfying treats served with bacon or ham and orange juice? Shrove Tuesday, the last day before Lent, has been a traditional time for pancake suppers. This is a time of feasting and celebration prior to the austerities of Lent. What better food to feast with than piles of pancakes?

Tips for Making Pancakes:

- Don't overstir pancake batter. A few lumps are not harmful and overstirred batter will produce tough pancakes.
- Pancake batter may be made several hours ahead and refrigerated. It tends to thicken up when it sits, so you may need to add milk or water to thin it before using it.
- Test your griddle to see if it is hot enough by sprinkling on a few drops of water. If they sizzle and dance, it is ready.
- Always make a trial pancake first to see if the griddle is the right temperature. Break the pancake open to make sure it is cooked through.
- Keep a cup of cooking oil and a brush on hand to lightly regrease the griddle.
- Use a small ladle (about $\frac{1}{4}$ cup) to dip out pancake batter.
- Turn pancakes only once. Turn them when there are bubbles around the edges, with a few starting to form in the center.
- It takes a pancake about half as long to cook on the second side.

Pancakes for a Crowd

The number one rule of pancake suppers is: Make lots of pancakes. The ingredients are not expensive and most of the fun of a pancake supper is that it is "all you can eat."

Be assured if you plan an "All You Can Eat" pancake supper that at least a few people will show up whose appetites will amaze you. Plan on about 4 4-inch pancakes per person for starters and then adjust according to what else you will be serving and according to the makeup of the group.

For example, if you are also serving a fruit mixture and a meat such as sliced ham, you won't need lots of seconds. But if you are serving only pancakes and a beverage and your audience is primarily teenagers, you probably should double the amount per person.

When cooking pancakes for a crowd, it's best to cook and serve them immediately. This is possible if you rent several portable grills. At other times, you might simply have to make the pancakes ahead of time and keep them warm in a 200° oven. Don't cover them and avoid overlapping the pancakes so they don't get soggy.

All-American Pancakes

3 cups flour
$1\frac{1}{2}$ teaspoons salt
$\frac{1}{4}$ cup sugar
1 tablespoon baking powder
$\frac{1}{3}$ cup oil or melted butter or margarine
3 eggs, beaten
2 to $2\frac{1}{2}$ cups milk

In one bowl stir together the flour, salt, sugar, and baking powder. In another bowl, combine the oil or melted butter or margarine, the eggs, and the milk. Stir until just barely combined. Add additional liquid if necessary. Cook as directed above. Makes 24 to 28 4-inch pancakes.

Variations
- Buttermilk Pancakes: Substitute buttermilk or sour milk for the milk and 2 teaspoons baking soda for the baking powder.
- Buckwheat Pancakes: Use $1\frac{1}{2}$ cups buckwheat flour and $1\frac{1}{2}$ cups white flour.
- Nutty Cakes: Add $\frac{1}{2}$ to 1 cup of chopped pecans or walnuts to the batter.
- Chocolate Chip Pancakes: Add $\frac{1}{2}$ to 1 cup of miniature chocolate chips to the batter.
- Rocky Road Pancakes: Add $\frac{1}{2}$ cup miniature chocolate chips and $\frac{1}{2}$ cup nuts to the batter.
- Apple Pie Pancakes: Add 1 cup grated apple and $\frac{1}{2}$ teaspoon nutmeg to the batter.
- Orange Spice Pancakes: Add $\frac{1}{2}$ teaspoon cinnamon and 1 teaspoon grated orange peel to the batter, and substitute orange juice for half of the liquid.

- Blueberry Pancakes: Toss 1 cup or more fresh blueberries with the flour, then proceed as directed above.
- Banana Pancakes: Thinly slice several bananas. Top each pancake with one or two slices of banana immediately after batter is poured onto the griddle.
- Vanilla Pancakes: Add $\frac{1}{2}$ teaspoon vanilla to the batter.

Pancake Toppings

Pancake toppings are very personal. Some people prefer the mere hint of flavor or sweetness. Others feel that pancakes are to be tolerated only as an excuse to eat toppings. A variety of butters and toppings can make a pancake supper a very special event (though not especially slimming!).

Determining how much of any topping to have on hand can be confusing. The most important thing is not to run out.

Syrups: Allow approximately 2 to 4 tablespoons *per pancake.* If you want to stretch the syrup, heat it up: Warm syrup goes further than room temperature or cold syrup.

If you serve more than one flavor of syrup, remember that a maple-flavored syrup will be the most popular.

Butters: Allow 1 to 2 tablespoons *per serving.* A batch of 24 pancakes will serve 6 to 8 people. One cup of plain or flavored butter should be enough.

Fruit or Honey Toppings: Allow approximately 2 to 4 tablespoons *per serving.* Again warm toppings will go further than cool ones.

- Maple Syrup With Nuts: Add $\frac{1}{2}$ cup chopped pecans to maple syrup. Serve warm or at room temperature, stirring to distribute nuts just before serving.
- Cinnamon Maple: Heat maple syrup over low heat for about 10 minutes with a couple of cinnamon sticks in it. If you serve the syrup in small- to medium-sized pitchers, leave the sticks in as stirrers.
- Fruit and Honey: Combine 2 cups of light-flavored honey with 3 cups of fresh or frozen berries such as blueberries, blackberries, strawberries, or raspberries. Or add 3 cups of finely chopped fruit such as peaches or apricots. Heat over low heat for about 10 minutes, stirring constantly, never allowing it to come to a boil. Serve hot or at room temperature.
- Fried Fruit: This is really delicious. Melt 2 to 3 tablespoons of butter in a skillet. Add 2 cups of sliced fruit. You can use either apples, bananas, or peaches. Sprinkle on top 1 teaspoon lemon juice and 2 tablespoons either granulated sugar, powdered sugar, or honey. Sauté, stirring frequently until fruit is soft. If desired you can add either $\frac{1}{4}$ cup sliced almonds or raisins. Makes about $1\frac{1}{2}$ cups.

Simple Toppings
- whipped butter
- powdered sugar (in a sifter)
- sweetened whipped cream
- freshly made applesauce
- applesauce mixed with crushed pineapple
- any sweetened or fruit butter

Spaghetti Dinners

Piles of spaghetti heaped with a fragrant sauce, hot garlic bread, and a crisp green salad—can you imagine a more wonderful community meal?

Pasta

One package (16 ounces) of spaghetti or other pasta will serves 6 to 8 people. Try other pasta shapes besides regular spaghetti. For example, rigatoni, shells, and elbow macaroni are delicious and easier to eat than regular spaghetti.

The most important cooking tool for cooking pasta for a crowd is a large colander. You can cook the pasta in any sort of large kettle, but if you don't have a large colander, you can't drain the pasta properly, and improperly drained pasta tastes gummy. If the kitchen you are using doesn't have a large colander, either rent or purchase one.

To cook the pasta, bring the water to a full boil, add salt and oil, add the pasta, and allow water to return to a boil. Stir frequently while it is boiling.

To cook
1 pound pasta, use $3\frac{1}{2}$ quarts water and 2 teaspoons each salt and oil
2 pounds pasta, use $6\frac{1}{2}$ quarts water and 1 tablespoon each salt and oil
3 pounds pasta, use $7\frac{1}{2}$ quarts water and $1\frac{1}{2}$ tablespoons each salt and oil
4 pounds pasta, use $8\frac{1}{2}$ quarts water and 2 tablespoons each salt and oil
5 pounds pasta, use 10 quarts water and $2\frac{1}{2}$ tablespoons each salt and oil

Cook the pasta until it is tender, but still slightly firm. When pasta is cooked, pour immediately into a colander and rinse well with warm water.

To keep pasta from sticking together, add about 2 tablespoons to $\frac{1}{4}$ cup of oil while pasta is warm and in the colander. Toss to distribute well. This also enables you to store the pasta for serving later.

After you have oiled the pasta, you may place it in steam table pans or large baking dishes. Cover with foil. It may be kept warm in a 150° to 200° oven if it will be served within the hour. Or it may be chilled and reheated just before serving. To reheat, place in a 250° oven 20 to 30 minutes or until heated through. Reduce heat until ready to serve.

Perfect Pasta Sauce

It's fun to provide a pasta bar of sauce choices at a spaghetti supper. If you do that, make more than the regular amount because people tend to eat more when they have a variety of choices.

4 pounds ground beef
1½ pound bulk Italian sausage
3 onions, chopped
6 cloves garlic, minced
2 cans (28 ounces each) tomatoes, pureed
5 cans (6 ounces each) tomato paste
14 cups water
1¼ tablespoon basil
1 tablespoon sugar
1 tablespoon marjoram
2½ teaspoons oregano
½ teaspoon rosemary
  salt and pepper to taste

In a large pan, sauté the ground beef, Italian sausage, onions, and garlic until meat is browned and onions are golden. Break up ground beef and Italian sausage while cooking. Drain off fat. Add tomatoes, tomato paste, and water. Stir to combine. Simmer for 30 minutes. Add basil, sugar, marjoram, oregano, rosemary, salt, and pepper. Simmer for another 30 minutes. Adjust seasonings.
  Serves 16. Serve with grated Parmesan cheese.

Variations
- Mushroom Spaghetti Sauce: Replace the ground beef and Italian sausage with 4 pounds of fresh mushrooms, thickly sliced. Sauté the onions and garlic until soft in 2 tablespoons of olive oil. Then add the mushrooms with the tomatoes and proceed as directed with the recipe.
- Italian Sausage Sauce: Reduce ground beef to 1 pound. Replace the bulk Italian sausage with 3 pounds of link Italian sausage that has been sliced. Gently sauté it with the ground beef and proceed as directed with the recipe. *Warning:* this is a very tangy sauce.

• Red Clam Spaghetti Sauce: Replace the meat with 10 cans (6 ounces each) clams, drained. Sauté the onions and garlic until soft in 2 tablespoons of olive oil. Add the clams with the tomatoes and proceed as directed with the recipe.

Barbecuing and Grilling

Food that has been cooked outside tastes extra special. Maybe there is a bit of the pioneer in each of us that enjoys food fresh from an open fire.

Outdoor cooking is a fun option for community meals. Outdoor cookouts may be as plain or as fancy as you desire. The main dish may be anything from hot dogs to steaks. Don't limit your menu to meat only. Grilled corn on the cob, vegetable kabobs, or roasted potatoes may complete your meal.

Tips for Outdoor Cooking
• Be sure you have enough grills. For a large group, renting one or two large grills might be the perfect answer. The rental company can deliver and pick them up and can tell you exactly how much charcoal you will need. This can save a tremendous amount of confusion.
• Be sure you have the proper tools: long-handled forks, spatulas, and tongs. These may be rented as well. Have plenty of pot holders and paper towels on hand. And as with cooking indoors, always have a fire extinguisher and a first-aid kit with burn medication on hand.
• Follow the manufacturer's or rental company's instructions on how much charcoal to use with the grill you are using. Light the charcoal at least 45 to 60 minutes before you intend to start grilling. The charcoal should be white-hot.
• For additonal flavor, add wood chips to the coals after they are hot. Fruit woods are delicious with chicken. Hickory and mesquite are wonderful with steaks and sausage. For an exotic and different flavor, sprinkle rosemary or thyme on the coals—the aroma is tantalizing.
• To prevent burnt food, do not allow the coals to flame up. To avoid this, never start grilling until the coals are glowing and trim excess fat from the meat. Keep a spray bottle of water on hand to douse flames if they flare up.
• Make sure all of your food is done at the same time by consulting the following procedures for various kinds of grilled foods. Designate either one grill or portion of a grill for each type of food and cook it for the proper time. For example, if you plan to grill corn and hot dogs, the corn takes about 25 minutes and the hot dogs less than 10 minutes. Put on the corn, wait about 15 minutes, and then add the hot dogs.
• It is a good idea not to be overly ambitious. For a large group, limit your menu to no more than two kinds of grilled food.

• One final note: Never forget that grills are open fires. Always keep children well away from the grills. Be especially watchful during the time the coals are heating up, when you are tempted to leave the grills unattended. Thoroughly extinguish the coals as soon as the cooking is completed. Safety should never be forgotten.

Recipes for Grilling

Hamburgers   Allow a $\frac{1}{4}$ pound of ground beef for each person. Shape the ground beef into patties, with pieces of waxed paper between the patties. Grill the patties 5 to 6 minutes on one side, then turn and grill 5 to 6 minutes on the second side. The grilling time depends on how well done people prefer their meat.

Variations:
• For every pound of meat, add: *2 tablespoons chopped onion, 1 teaspoon garlic salt, 1 tablespoon Worchestershire sauce, 1 tablespoon ketchup, dash of pepper.*
  Shape into patties and grill.

• Enclose a slice of Cheddar cheese or American cheese inside each patty before grilling. Or for more sophisticated tastes, try 1 tablespoon crumbled blue cheese.

Hot dogs or sausages   Use the precooked variety, which needs only 5 to 10 minutes of grilling. For variation wrap each in a slice of bacon and grill until the bacon is crisp. Or cut a selection of hot dogs and sausages into chunks and make kabobs.

Steaks   Steaks should be at least 1-inch thick. Allow the meat to come to room temperature before grilling. Slash the fat of the meat at intervals so it will lie flat. For medium rare, grill 8 to 10 minutes on one side, turn over, add salt and pepper, and then grill an additional 5 to 7 minutes.

Corn on the cob   Strip the husk back and remove the corn silk. Pull the husk back over the corn. Cover with water and soak the ears about 15 minutes. Place on the grill and cook for about 20 to 25 minutes or until the husks are browned. If you are grilling corn for a large group, fill a coffee can with melted butter or margarine. As the corn is taken off the grill (with oven mitts on your hands), quickly pull the husk back and dip the corn into the melted butter—oh, is that good!

Vegetable Kabobs Vegetable kabobs are great accompaniments to a picnic. On bamboo skewers, alternate any of the following:

- cherry tomatoes
- squares of green or red pepper
- small onions, parboiled 5 minutes
- whole mushrooms
- zucchini or summer squash, cut into bite-size pieces
- pineapple chunks

Brush with vegetable oil and grill for two minutes on each side.

Vegetable packets Potatoes, carrots, onions, mushrooms, cauliflower, and summer squash may all be cooked in foil packets. Prepare vegetables by cleaning (paring, if necessary) and cutting into bite-sized pieces. Assemble $\frac{1}{2}$ cup or more of vegetables in heavy-duty aluminum foil. Add herbs or butter if desired. Sprinkle on a few drops of water. Close up the foil packet, sealing tightly, and place on the grill. Cook about 45 to 60 minutes or until tender.

Fruit packets Cut up or core either apples or pears and place on squares of heavy-duty aluminum foil. Either fill the core or sprinkle over slices some butter, brown sugar, and cinnamon. You may also add nuts, raisins, or mincemeat. Fold up packet, sealing tightly, and grill for about 45 minutes.

Part Two
Recipes

Appetizers

··· Party Starters ···

All sorts of simple appetizers can be created from a dip or spread served with bread: French bread cut in thin slices and served with whipped sweet butter; pita bread cut in quarters and served with a garbanzo bean dip; whole wheat crackers with an assortment of nut butters. If you don't have time to make special breads, purchase an assortment of breads and crackers: bread sticks, whole wheat crackers, melba rounds, party pumpernickel, lahvosh cracker bread.

If you do have time to make your own, here are a few easy, tasty ideas.

Rye-Garlic Rounds

Great by themselves, these are also tasty with a fairly mild dip or cream cheese with a sliver of ham on top.

2 loaves thinly sliced party rye bread
¾ cup melted butter or margarine
  garlic salt

Brush party rye slices with melted butter or margarine. Arrange on ungreased cookie sheets. Sprinkle garlic salt lightly on top. Toast in a 400° oven for 10 minutes. May be served hot or cold.
  Makes about 24 servings.

Cheese Straws

These can be made with any firm cheese such as Cheddar or Swiss. Try making them with smoked Gouda or pepper cheese for a tangy change of taste.

3 tablespoons butter or margarine, softened
¾ cup flour
  dash of salt
½ pound grated cheese
  dash of liquid hot-pepper sauce (optional)

Mix all ingredients together to form a dough. Roll out on a floured board until ¼ inch thick. Cut into strips ¼ inch wide and 2 to 3 inches long. Arrange pieces on an ungreased baking sheet so they don't touch one another. Bake in a 400° oven for 10 to 12 minutes or until lightly browned.
  Makes about 48 pieces.

Baked Tortilla Chips

Bake your own chips and avoid the heavy, greasy taste of prepared chips. Most supermarkets carry prepackaged tortillas in the dairy section. If you are fortunate enough to live in an area where you can get fresh corn tortillas, so much the better!

10 corn or flour tortillas
  corn oil
  salt (optional)

Brush each tortilla with corn oil. Cut each into eight pie-shaped wedges and place on lightly greased cookie sheets. If desired, sprinkle with a little salt. Bake in a 350° oven for 10 minutes or until lightly browned.

Makes 80 chips, enough for 4 to 6 people.

Cold Vegetable Platter

This is the most popular appetizer at any group occasion, whether a formal dinner or a chili supper. Cold vegetables are universally liked, tremendously versatile, colorful, and easy to prepare. They can be very filling when served with crackers and hearty dips, and when nibbled alone, they satisfy the most diet-conscious person. Follow the tips below to construct a successful vegetable platter.

• Choose only the freshest, most tender vegetables that can be served raw.
• Cut or break large vegetables into sticks, slivers, flowerets, or other easy-to-dip sizes.
• To crisp the vegetables after cutting and cleaning them, place them in covered containers or plastic bags, with water to cover, and refrigerate. Several hours before serving, drain and arrange on serving platters, then wrap tightly with plastic wrap or aluminum foil. Refrigerate, if possible. The mois-

No Time to Cook?
Your appetizer contribution could be:
· *an antipasto selection from an Italian deli*
· *Chinese take-out dumplings, noodles, egg rolls*
· *nuts: smoked almonds, macadamias, peanuts, mixed nuts*
· *a selection of cheeses and crackers*
· *cheese and fruit*
· *snack mixes, such as oriental snack mix or sesame sticks*

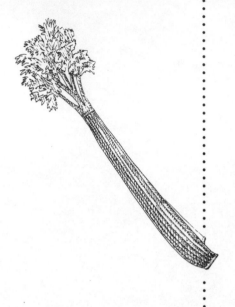

ture inside the wrapping will keep the vegetables fresh and crisp.

- When arranging the platter, use fancy lettuce, parsley, and edible flowers for garnishes.
- Try combining fruits with vegetables for something different. For an all-orange tray, use carrot sticks, cantaloupe slices, and orange wedges. An all-red tray could include cherry tomatoes, radishes, and strawberries, while a green tray could consist of celery sticks, cucumber slices, broccoli flowerets, and green grapes. A variety of fruit and vegetable platters makes quite an impression at large buffets.
- To serve 25 people, you need approximately 4 pounds of prepared vegetables and, if you like, 4 cups of assorted dips.
- Some good vegetables to include on your platter are:

celery sticks
carrot sticks
green onions
cucumber slices or spears
zucchini squash spears
yellow squash spears
cherry tomatoes
broccoli flowerets
cauliflower flowerets
whole mushrooms
snow peas
fresh green beans with the ends cut off and strings
  removed
Belgian endive leaves
green or red pepper slices or chunks
turnip slices
jicama slices
radishes

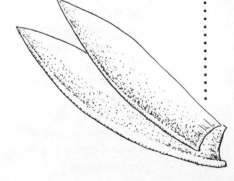

Antipasto Platter

A wonderful way to start an Italian meal. In addition, an antipasto platter is great food for any community meal: It is easy to make, portable, delicious. With lots of fresh Italian bread and sweet butter, it even makes a great meal.

Antipasto is also versatile, since it may feature a huge variety of ingredients. Keep some canned ingredients on hand, then add whatever else you may have available.

The list below is a starting point; add and subtract ingredients as you feel inspired. The most important element of an antipasto platter is presentation: The food should look beautiful! Arrange the food to delight all the senses. Use any of the following, arranged in alternating rows radiating from the center of a large platter.

Canned antipasto ingredients

- caponata (an eggplant relish)
- marinated artichoke hearts, drained
- Italian pepperoncini (small, green pickled peppers)
- pickled hot cherry peppers
- sweet fried peppers with onions
- pickled hot pepper rings
- sardines
- anchovy fillets
- marinated mushrooms
- black and green olives

Cheeses
- mozzarella slices
- feta cheese chunks

For a special appetizer presentation, use bamboo skewers and appetizer picks to skewer fruits, cheese, vegetables, meats . . . you name it. Skewers save messy fingers and make any party seem more special.

Other ingredients
- cherry tomatoes
- green onions
- hard-boiled egg wedges
- Italian salami slices
- prosciutto or boiled ham, thinly sliced and rolled
- radishes
- pimiento strips

Cucumbers Stuffed With Feta Cheese

This appetizer is refreshing and cool, a good complement to highly spiced foods.

4 medium cucumbers, peeled
½ cup crumbled feta cheese
1 or more tablespoons mayonnaise
    dash of Worcestershire sauce
    fresh chopped dill weed or parsley

Cut cucumbers in half lengthwise, then scrape out and discard the seeds. In a small bowl, mix together the feta cheese, Worcestershire sauce, and mayonnaise, adding just enough mayonnaise to make the mixture creamy. Fill the cucumber shells with the mixture and sprinkle with dill weed or parsley. Chill for 1 hour, then cut into $\frac{3}{4}$-inch slices.

Serves 6 to 8.

Deviled Eggs

The traditional potluck appetizer. The basic filling of mayonnaise and mustard can be dressed up with an assortment of additions and/or toppings.

6 hard-boiled eggs, cooled and peeled
3 tablespoons mayonnaise
1 teaspoon prepared mustard
   dash of salt

Slice eggs in half lengthwise. Carefully removed the yolks and mash them in a small bowl with the mayonnaise, mustard, and salt until smooth and creamy. Spoon into the hollows of the whites. Garnish, if desired. Chill until serving time.
   Serves 6.

Variations: Add any of the following to the egg-yolk mixture.
- 1 teaspoon drained pickle relish
- $\frac{1}{4}$ to $\frac{1}{2}$ teaspoon drained prepared horseradish
- $\frac{1}{2}$ teaspoon chopped green onion
- 1 teaspoon crumbled blue cheese
- $\frac{1}{4}$ teaspoon curry powder
- 1 tablespoon chopped smoked salmon

Garnishes:
- chopped green onion
- green or black olive slices
- a sprinkling of paprika
- a sprinkling of caviar
- finely chopped chutney
- chopped chives
- fresh dill weed

For fancy deviled eggs, use a pastry bag with a rosette tip to fill the eggs.

Scotch Eggs

A traditional British snack, Scotch eggs are perfect buffet fare. They are also delicious for picnics or any occasion requiring food that travels well.

This method removes most of the fat from the sausage. To lower the fat and calorie count still further, you may use turkey sausage instead of pork (*see* recipe below).

To keep the yolks centered in hard-cooked eggs, gently stir the eggs every few minutes while they are cooking. They will be perfect for deviled eggs.

1 pound ground turkey or pork sausage
4 peeled hard-boiled eggs
1 cup flour, seasoned with salt and pepper
$\frac{3}{4}$ cup milk
1 beaten egg
1 cup dry bread crumbs
  oil for frying

Divide the sausage into four parts. On a floured surface, pat each piece of sausage into a circle about 5 inches across. Beat together the milk and egg. Dip one hard-boiled egg at a time into the flour, then into the egg-and-milk mixture and back into the flour. Place one flour-covered egg in the center of each sausage circle, bringing up the edges of the sausage, and pat together to seal the sausage around the egg. Dip each sausage-covered egg into the egg-and-milk mixture and then into the bread crumbs.

Heat 4 to 5 inches of oil in a deep skillet or saucepan to 375°. Fry the eggs one at a time until deep brown—about 10 minutes.

To remove additional fat from the sausage, after frying, bake in a 350° oven for 30 minutes. Cut in half, then serve at room temperature. Salt and hot mustard may be served alongside.

Makes 4 servings.

To Bake Scotch Eggs:

If you wish to avoid frying your Scotch Eggs, simply place them on an ungreased baking sheet and bake in a preheated 350° oven for 45 to 60 minutes or until well browned.

Turkey Sausage

Just the thing when you want a sausage but don't want the fat.

1½ teaspoons fennel seed
½ teaspoon ground allspice
¼ teaspoon pepper
½ teaspoon chili powder
2 teaspoons oregano
1 tablespoon dried sweet pepper flakes
2 cloves garlic, minced
2 pounds ground turkey

Using a mortar and pestle or blender, grind spices together. Mix spices and minced garlic into the ground turkey. Cover and place in refrigerator overnight. To bake sausage, shape into 12 patties and place on an ungreased cookie sheet. Bake in 350° oven for 20 to 25 minutes or until browned.

Makes 12 patties.

New dishes beget new appetites.
Thomas Fuller

When measuring shred-
ded cheese, do not pack
the cheese in the meas-
uring cup.

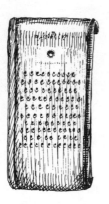

··· **Spreads & Dips** ···

Three-Cheese Torte

Rich and elegant, a cheese torte makes a wonderful centerpiece for a buffet. Serve with an assortment of crackers, fresh grapes, apple and pear slices.

First cheese combination:
$\frac{1}{2}$ cup butter, softened
2 ounces cream cheese, softened
$\frac{1}{2}$ cup crumbled blue cheese
$\frac{1}{2}$ cup grated Monterey Jack cheese

Second cheese combination:
$\frac{1}{2}$ cup butter, softened
2 ounces cream cheese, softened
1 cup grated Cheddar cheese
$1\frac{1}{2}$ cups finely chopped walnuts

In a medium bowl, combine butter, cream cheese,
blue cheese, and Monterey Jack cheese. Set aside.

In another bowl, combine butter, cream cheese,
and Cheddar cheese. Set aside.

Prepare the mold for the torte. You may use an
8-inch springform pan, an 8-inch soufflé dish, or
another dish with straight sides. Line the dish with
several layers of aluminum foil, so the foil completely covers the sides of the dish and overhangs
the edges. (This is so the torte can be removed
from the dish.)

Assemble the torte in alternating layers: half of
the first cheese combination, a layer of chopped
walnuts, half of the second cheese combination, a
layer of walnuts. Repeat until the cheese and
walnuts are used up. Gently press the layers together and cover. Refrigerate at least 4 hours (or
overnight) until serving time.

At serving time, turn the torte upside down on a
serving platter and carefully remove the aluminum
foil.

Makes 24 servings.

Great Northern Salmon Cream Cheese Ball

More refreshing than many cheese balls, this is a perfect complement to fruit salads or a fruit platter.

1 can (15½ ounces) salmon, bones removed
1 package (8 ounces) cream cheese, softened
1 tablespoon prepared horseradish
1½ tablespoons lemon juice
1 tablespoon mayonnaise
½ teaspoon dried dill weed
1 tablespoon dried parsley flakes
  dash of salt

Combine all ingredients and shape into a ball. Chill at least 8 hours before serving. Serve with an assortment of crackers.
Makes one medium-size ball.

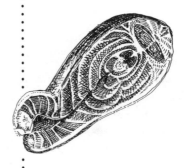

American Cheese Ball

Everybody loves these, and they couldn't be easier to make.

1 package (8 ounces) cream cheese, softened
1 cup crumbled blue cheese
1 cup grated Cheddar cheese
1 tablespoon Worcestershire sauce
1 tablespoon grated onion
1 teaspoon seasoned salt
½ cup chopped walnuts or pecans

Blend all ingredients except the walnuts or pecans in a food processor or with your hands. Form into a ball or log and roll in chopped nuts. Chill well. Serve with an assortment of crackers.
Serves 15 to 20.

Salinas Valley Artichoke Spread

Small slices of dark pumpernickel bread or rye crackers are the perfect accompaniment for this spread.

4 hard-boiled eggs, chopped
1 jar (6 ounces) marinated artichoke hearts, drained
    and finely chopped
⅓ cup sour cream
¼ teaspoon curry powder
    salt and pepper to taste
    capers (for garnish)

Mix together the chopped eggs and chopped artichoke hearts. Add sour cream, curry powder, salt, and pepper. Stir together and adjust the seasonings. Chill before serving. To serve, mound on a plate or serving dish and garnish with capers.
    Makes about 1½ cups.

Capers are the unopened flower buds of the caper bush, which grows wild on the mountain slopes around the Mediterranean Sea. Especially good with tomatoes and eggplant, capers are widely used in Mediterranean cuisine. Capers may be found in most markets packed in salt or in vinegar.

Roquefort Cheese Dip

2 cups (1 pint) sour cream
1 cup crumbled Roquefort (or blue) cheese
    dash of liquid hot-pepper sauce
    dash of Worcestershire sauce
    dash of garlic powder
1 tablespoon finely chopped green onion

Combine all ingredients with a fork. If possible, refrigerate at least 8 hours before serving.
    Makes 2 cups.

Nantucket Clam Dip

1 package (8 ounces) cream cheese, softened
1 tablespoon ketchup
1 teaspoon Worcestershire sauce
1 clove garlic, minced
2 cans (6½ ounces each) minced clams, drained.
   Reserve the juice from one can.

Mix together the cream cheese, ketchup, Worcestershire sauce, and garlic. Add the clam juice and mix well. Stir in the drained clams.
   Makes about 1½ cups.

Dill Dip

1 cup mayonnaise
1 cup sour cream or plain yogurt
1 tablespoon dried dill weed
1 teaspoon onion salt

Stir together. Chill several hours or overnight before serving.
   Makes about 2 cups.

*Sit down and feed, and
welcome to our table.*
   William Shakespeare

Pacific Crab-Avocado Dip

This dip is particularly nice with an assortment of green and white vegetables: celery, broccoli, cauliflower, and zucchini.

2 ripe avocados, peeled
1 cup sour cream
2 tablespoons lemon juice
1 clove garlic, minced
1 teaspoon prepared horseradish
1 can (6 ounces) white crabmeat, drained and flaked

Mash avocados with a fork. Blend in sour cream, lemon juice, garlic, and horseradish. Stir until well combined; add crabmeat. Chill several hours.

Makes about 2 cups.

An avocado is ripe when it yields to gentle pressure. Allow avocados to ripen at room temperature. Storing them at too cold a temperature can result in brown streaks in the fruit.

Kansas City Hot Beef Dip

Hearty and warm, this dip is perfect for a post-football-game buffet.

1 package (8 ounces) cream cheese, softened
$\frac{1}{2}$ cup sour cream
3 tablespoons chopped green onion, tops included
$\frac{1}{4}$ cup finely chopped green pepper
2 tablespoons finely minced pimiento
*   dash of pepper*
2 jars (2$\frac{1}{2}$ ounces each) sliced dried beef

In a medium bowl, cream together the cream cheese and sour cream until smooth. Stir in green onions, green pepper, pimiento, and pepper. Chop sliced dried beef into small pieces. Stir into the mixture. Spoon mixture into an ovenproof casserole and bake at 350° for 15 to 20 minutes. Serve immediately with crackers or reheat later.

Makes about 2$\frac{1}{2}$ cups.

Georgia Bacon-Pecan Spread

This is a great starter for a men's luncheon. Serve with rye crackers and crisp celery sticks.

5 slices bacon, fried until crisp
1 package (8 ounces) cream cheese, softened
1 cup sour cream
¼ cup finely minced onion
⅓ cup finely chopped pecans
   dash of salt

Crumble bacon and set aside. In a medium bowl, mix the cream cheese and sour cream until well blended. Stir in the onion, pecans, salt, and crumbled bacon. Refrigerate covered until serving time.

Makes about 2 cups.

Layered Tostada Dip

This is wonderful! And it is hearty enough to make a meal of, if you can fight off your friends.

2 cans (16 ounces each) refried beans
1 teaspoon chili powder
3 ripe avocados, peeled and mashed
2 tablespoons chopped onion
5 tablespoons mayonnaise
2 tablespoons lemon juice
1 cup chopped tomatoes
½ cup sliced black olives
1 can (4 ounces) chopped green chiles, drained and
   seeds removed
1 cup grated Monterey Jack cheese
½ cup sour cream
   tortilla chips

Mix together refried beans and chili powder. Spread the mixture on a 12-inch round serving platter. Blend together the avocados, onions, mayonnaise, and lemon juice. Spread this mixture over the layer of refried beans. Set aside a few chopped tomatoes and sliced olives for garnishing, then spread a layer of chopped tomatoes, a layer of sliced black olives, a layer of green chiles, and a layer of grated Monterey Jack cheese. Before serving, top with dollops of sour cream and garnish with chopped tomatoes and sliced olives.

Variation: For a heartier dip, add a layer of ground beef or *chorizo* which has been browned and drained of all fat.

Chorizo (cho-ree-soh) is spicy hot Mexican smoked-pork sausage. Seasoned bulk-pork sausage may be used as a substitute.

Easy Guacamole

Guacamole, a staple of the Southwest, makes a delicious dip for tortilla chips. It is also a great condiment for any Mexican food.

2 or 3 ripe avocados, peeled
1 ripe tomato, chopped
1 medium onion, chopped
2 tablespoons lemon juice
2 tablespoons salsa (bottled or see Santa Fe Salsa, recipe follows
1 clove garlic, minced

Mash the avocado with a fork. Stir in remaining ingredients. For a smoother dip, puree the avocados in a food processor or blender.

Makes about $1\frac{1}{2}$ cups.

Santa Fe Salsa

Salsa is the traditional dip for tortilla chips. It is also delicious as a condiment for any Southwestern or Mexican food. Don't hesitate to vary the flavorings to suit your own taste.

1 can (16 ounces) whole tomatoes, juice included
1 fresh tomato, finely chopped
$\frac{1}{3}$ cup finely chopped onions
2 to 4 tablespoons canned, chopped green chiles, drained and seeds removed
1 tablespoon lemon juice
1 tablespoon olive oil
    dash of salt and pepper
1 teaspoon chopped fresh cilantro (or chopped parsley)

Puree the canned tomatoes in the blender. Stir in the remaining ingredients. Allow to sit for at least 1 hour before serving.
Makes about 3 cups.

Cilantro is a leafy herb that looks similar to parsley and, in fact, is often called Chinese parsley. It is more popularly known in this country as fresh coriander. Cilantro is widely used in Mexican, Chinese, and Indian cooking. Cilantro has a distinctive lemon flavor which cannot be duplicated by substituting other types of parsley or even coriander seeds.

Nacho Cheese Dip

A hot, spicy cheese dip, good with chips or raw vegetables. This dip is also great when poured over a platter of tortilla chips to make nachos.

2 tablespoons butter or margarine
3 green onions with tops, chopped
2 cans (4 ounces each) chopped green chiles, drained and seeds removed
1 can (14$\frac{1}{2}$ ounces) whole tomatoes, chopped, with juice
2 pounds processed American cheese, cut into chunks
1 cup (about $\frac{1}{4}$ pound) grated Cheddar cheese

In a large saucepan, melt the butter or margarine. Add the green onion, chiles, and tomatoes. Sauté, stirring frequently, until onions are soft and liquid is reduced. Add cheeses and stir over medium heat until smooth. Serve warm in a chafing dish with chips or vegetables alongside for dipping, or pour over tortilla chips.

Makes 4 to 5 cups.

Variations
- Add $\frac{1}{4}$ to $\frac{1}{2}$ pound of spicy sausage which has been browned and drained of all fat.
- Instead of chopped mild chiles, add 1 or 2 jalapeño peppers which have been seeded and finely chopped.

··· Hot Stuff ···

Spicy Chicken Wings

In the West, this is one of the most popular appetizers for casual suppers. The amount of hot sauce you use depends upon your palate's courage.

4 pounds chicken wings, cut apart at joints, with the wing tips discarded
4 cups vegetable oil
$\frac{1}{3}$ cup butter or margarine
2 to 5 tablespoons liquid hot-pepper sauce
1 tablespoon cider vinegar
  buttered French bread slices

Pat chicken wings dry. Place oil in a deep-fat fryer or deep skillet. Heat oil to 375°. Fry $\frac{1}{3}$ of the

There is an emanation from the heart in genuine hospitality which cannot be described but is immediately felt, and puts the stranger at once at his ease.

Washington Irving

wings at a time for 10 minutes, until brown and crispy. Remove and drain well.

In a small pan, melt the butter or margarine, add the liquid hot-pepper sauce and vinegar. Pour the sauce over the hot chicken wings. Serve with buttered slices of French bread.

Serves 4 to 6.

Chinese Chicken Wings

½ cup light soy sauce
1 teaspoon sherry flavoring
1 clove garlic, crushed
1 teaspoon grated fresh ginger or ½ teaspoon ground
* ginger*
2 teaspoons sugar
30 chicken wings, cut apart at joints with wing tips
* discarded*

Place the soy sauce, sherry flavoring, garlic, ginger, and sugar in a small saucepan. Heat and stir until the sugar dissolves, then cook 10 minutes over low heat. Allow sauce to cool.

Place the chicken wings in a bowl and pour the cooled sauce over them. Marinate at least ½ hour (or overnight). Remove wings from marinade and place on an ungreased cookie sheet. Bake in a preheated 350° oven for 35 to 40 minutes. If desired, baste with the marinade once or twice during the baking.

Makes 60 pieces, enough for 10 to 12 servings.

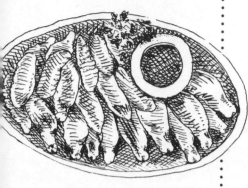

Gilroy Chicken Wings

Don't let the garlic in this recipe frighten you away. Its flavoring is delicious, not overwhelming.

2 garlic cloves, crushed
$\frac{1}{2}$ cup melted butter or margarine
30 chicken wings, cut apart at joints with wing tips
    discarded
pepper
1 cup bread crumbs

Add crushed garlic to melted butter or margarine. Dip chicken wings in butter or margarine, sprinkle with pepper. Roll in bread crumbs and place on an ungreased cookie sheet. Bake in a preheated 350° oven for 35 to 40 minutes until lightly browned.

Makes 60 pieces, enough for 10 to 12 people.

··· Nibbles ···

Nuts and Bolts

Stores now carry a ready-made version of this ever-popular appetizer, but nothing beats the homemade variety.

7 ounces of Cheerios
7 ounces of Wheat Chex
7 ounces of pretzel sticks
1 cup shoestring potatoes (optional)
1 pound mixed salted nuts or peanuts
1 pound butter or margarine
1 tablespoon garlic salt
$\frac{1}{2}$ teaspoon onion salt
3 tablespoons Worcestershire sauce

In a large bowl, toss together the cereals, pretzel sticks, shoestring potatoes, and nuts. In a medium saucepan, melt the butter or margarine. Add garlic salt, onion salt, and Worcestershire sauce to the melted butter or margarine. Stir together. Pour this mixture over the cereal mixture and toss to coat. Spread out on 2 cookie sheets or jelly-roll pans. Bake at 250° for 2 hours, stirring every 25 minutes. Cool on paper towels and store in containers to retain crispness.

Makes 8 quarts.

Chili Toasted Nuts

2 cups raw Spanish peanuts
2 tablespoons butter
1 tablespoon chili powder
1 teaspoon garlic salt

Place the peanuts in a medium mixing bowl. Melt the butter and stir in the chili powder and garlic salt. Pour melted butter and seasonings over the peanuts and toss to coat. Spread coated nuts on a cookie sheet and bake in a 300° oven 15 to 20 minutes, stirring a couple of times during baking. Remove from oven, cool on paper towels, and store.

Makes 2 cups.

Serve appetizers in unusual containers to spice up a party. Baskets, antique bowls and plates, unusual tins, even clay flowerpots add festivity and color to any table. Toy trucks make great serving bowls for a baby shower.

Curried Pecans

1 cup pecan halves
1 teaspoon curry powder
1½ teaspoons vegetable oil

Place the nuts in a small bowl. Stir the curry powder into the oil. Toss the pecans with the seasoned oil, spread in a baking pan, and bake for 20 minutes at 300°. Stir once or twice during baking.
Makes 1 cup.

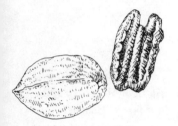

Garlic Nuts

2 cups walnuts or almonds
1 teaspoon garlic salt
⅛ teaspoon onion salt
1 tablespoon vegetable oil

Place the nuts in a small bowl. Stir the garlic salt and onion salt into the oil. Gently toss the nuts with the seasoned oil. Spread on a baking pan and bake for 20 minutes at 300°. Stir once or twice during baking.
Makes 2 cups.

Main Dishes

· · · Beef · · ·

Sunday Dinner Pot Roast

This recipe calls for long, slow cooking, producing fork-tender meat and savory gravy at the same time. Pot roast works well for a community meal: You slice it, arrange the vegetables around the meat, spoon the gravy on, and have a dish everyone will love.

$\frac{1}{3}$ cup flour
1 teaspoon salt
$\frac{1}{2}$ teaspoon pepper
1 5- to 6-pound beef rump roast
$\frac{1}{4}$ cup vegetable oil
3 cups beef stock or bouillon

2 tablespoons Worcestershire sauce
2 tablespoons wine vinegar
1 clove garlic, crushed
1 tablespoon soy sauce
2 onions, sliced
4 large potatoes, quartered
8 carrots, each peeled and cut into 3 or 4 pieces
3 tablespoons flour
$\frac{1}{2}$ cup water

Combine the flour, salt, and pepper. Coat the beef on all sides with the flour mixture. Heat the oil in a Dutch oven over medium heat, then brown the roast well on all sides. When the beef is browned, add the bouillon, Worcestershire sauce, wine vinegar, garlic, and soy sauce. Lay the sliced onions on top of the meat. Cover and bake in a 275° oven for 6 to 8 hours.

When meat is tender, add the potatoes and carrots and bake for one more hour, or until vegetables are done. Remove beef and vegetables from the Dutch oven and place them on a serving dish. Keep warm.

Skim the fat from the broth in the Dutch oven. Measure the liquid to be sure you have at least $2\frac{1}{2}$ cups. If you have less than $2\frac{1}{2}$ cups of liquid, add beef stock or bouillon or water as needed. Return the liquid to the Dutch oven. In a small bowl, combine 3 tablespoons flour with $\frac{1}{2}$ cup of water. Stir into the liquid in the Dutch oven and cook, stirring constantly, until thickened. Season to taste.

Serves 8 to 10.

No Time to Cook?
Your contribution could be:
- *platters of cold cuts*
- *barbecued chicken*
- *barbecued ribs*
- *a selection of Chinese dishes (from your local take-out restaurant)*

Evie's Barbecued Brisket

This recipe requires a lot of marinating and cooking time, but produces incredibly tender, flavorful meat.

1 4-pound beef brisket
1 bottle (4 ounces) liquid smoke
1 bottle (5 ounces) Worcestershire sauce
1 bottle (18 ounces) barbecue sauce
$\frac{1}{4}$ cup molasses
  dash of garlic powder
  dash of onion powder
$\frac{1}{4}$ cup water

Marinate the brisket in the liquid smoke and Worcestershire sauce for 24 hours. After marinating, place the brisket in a 9- by 13-inch baking pan. Cover the pan with aluminum foil and bake in a 250° oven for 6 hours (or overnight). When cooked, refrigerate in the baking pan. When cold, pour off the sauce, remove the grease, and slice the brisket. Mix together the barbecue sauce, molasses, garlic powder, onion powder, and water; pour over the brisket and cover. Bake in a 325° oven for 40 minutes.
Serves 8.

Food imaginatively and lovingly prepared, and eaten in good company, warms the being with something more than the mere intake of calories. I cannot conceive of cooking for friends or family, under reasonable conditions, as being a chore.
Majorie Kinnan Rawlings

Baked Brisket With Fruit

1 4- to 5-pound brisket of beef
1 teaspoon garlic powder
1 teaspoon rosemary
1 teaspoon thyme
3¼ cups Concord grape juice or 3 cups beef stock, divided
½ pound dried apricots
½ pound dried prunes
2 teaspoons cornstarch
¼ cup water

Place the brisket in a 9- by 13-inch glass baking dish (do not use a metal dish). Sprinkle with the garlic powder, rosemary, and thyme. Pour juice or beef stock over the meat until the meat is half covered, reserving ¼ cup of juice. Bake uncovered in a 450° oven for 30 minutes.

Turn the oven down to 300° and cover the meat with aluminum foil. Bake 4 hours or until meat is fork tender, basting occasionally with pan juices. Mix together the remaining juice and the dried prunes, and apricots. Spoon on top of roast and bake another 30 minutes.

Drain off the sauce and place it in a saucepan. Mix together the cornstarch and water and add to the sauce. Cook over medium heat, stirring constantly until the sauce thickens and clears.

Serves 6 to 8.

To remove the leftover odor of onion or garlic, rub your hands with a cut lemon, then wash with soap and water.

Yorkville Sauerbraten With Gingersnap Gravy

3 cups water
2 cups red wine vinegar
2 onions, sliced
1 lemon, sliced
15 cloves
6 bay leaves
10 peppercorns
2 tablespoons sugar
1 tablespoon salt
$\frac{1}{2}$ teaspoon ground ginger
1 5-pound beef rump roast
$\frac{1}{4}$ cup vegetable oil
1 cup finely crushed gingersnaps
$\frac{1}{2}$ cup water

Place the water, red wine vinegar, sliced onion, sliced lemon, cloves, bay leaves, peppercorns, sugar, salt, and ginger in a large nonmetal bowl. Stir until the sugar and salt are dissolved. Add the beef roast to the marinade, cover, and refrigerate for 24 to 48 hours, turning the meat several times a day.

At the end of that time, remove the meat from the marinade and pat dry. Heat the oil in a Dutch oven. Brown the roast on all sides and cover with strained marinade. Cover and bake in a 325° oven for 5 hours.

When done, remove the meat, slice, and place it on a platter. Add the crushed gingersnaps and $\frac{1}{2}$ cup of water to the pan drippings. Cook, stirring and scraping the bottom of the pan, until the gravy is thick. Pour the gravy over the sliced meat and serve immediately (or reheat with gravy on meat).

Serves 10 to 12.

Barbecued Beef

This may be served as is for a buffet or may be served in buns. Either way, its Western flavor makes it a perennial favorite.

3 pounds stew beef
  vegetable oil
1 bottle (14 ounces) ketchup
2 tablespoons brown sugar
2 tablespoons vinegar
$\frac{1}{2}$ cup water
1 chopped onion
2 cloves garlic, minced finely
1 can (4 ounces) taco sauce
2 tablespoons Worcestershire sauce
$\frac{1}{2}$ teaspoon dry mustard
$\frac{1}{2}$ teaspoon chili powder
  dash or two of liquid hot-pepper sauce (optional)
  dash of salt and pepper
16 hamburger buns (optional)

In an ovenproof baking dish or Dutch oven, brown the beef in just enough oil to keep it from sticking. Combine remaining ingredients in a bowl and pour over beef. Bake, covered, in a 325° oven for 4 to 5 hours. Stir occasionally.

Serves 12 as a main dish or makes 16 sandwiches.

Barbecued Ground Beef:

Substitute 3 pounds of ground beef for the stew beef. As you brown the ground beef, break it into small pieces with a spoon or fork. Proceed with recipe.

Beef Stroganoff

$\frac{3}{4}$ cup butter or margarine
3 pounds beef sirloin, cut into thin 1- by $2\frac{1}{2}$-inch strips
4 cups sliced onion
2 garlic cloves, minced
1 teaspoon salt
2 teaspoons Worcestershire sauce
1 pound fresh mushrooms, sliced
2 cans (8 ounces each) tomato sauce
4 teaspoons instant beef bouillon powder
2 cups boiling water
2 cups sour cream
12 cups cooked noodles, buttered

Melt the butter or margarine in a large saucepan. Add the beef; brown over medium heat. Add the sliced onions and minced garlic and cook until the onions are translucent. Stir in the salt, Worcestershire sauce, mushrooms, and tomato sauce. Dissolve the beef bouillon powder in 2 cups of boiling water and add. Cover and simmer for about 40 minutes. Just before serving, stir in the sour cream, but do not allow it to boil. Serve over hot noodles.
Serves 12.

Swiss Steak

This recipe allows approximately $\frac{1}{4}$ pound of meat per serving. If you want larger servings of up to $\frac{1}{3}$ pound, you may add more meat without changing any other ingredients. Have the butcher cut the meat into serving portions for you.

$\frac{3}{4}$ cup flour
1 teaspoon salt
$\frac{1}{2}$ teaspoon pepper
$\frac{1}{4}$ teaspoon garlic salt

3 pounds ¾-inch-thick beef round or sirloin, cut into 12
   serving portions
3 tablespoons vegetable oil
2 cans (14½ ounces each) stewed tomatoes, cut into
   chunks
½ cup ketchup
1 tablespoon Worcestershire sauce
2 cups sliced celery
1 cup sliced onion
1 cup sliced carrots

Mix flour, salt, pepper, and garlic salt together.
Pound the seasoned flour into the meat. Heat the
oil in a skillet; brown each piece of meat well.
Place meat into a 9- by 13-inch baking pan.

Stir together the tomatoes, ketchup, and Worcestershire sauce. Pour over the meat, then add the
celery, onions, and carrots. Cover with aluminum
foil and bake in a 325° oven for 2 hours.

Serves 12.

Pineapple Beef

Slightly sweet and sour, this dish provides an
Oriental flavor suited for American taste buds.

2 pounds round steak, cut into 1- by 2-inch strips
1 can (6 ounces) pineapple juice, plus juice drained
   from pineapple tidbits (below)
½ cup soy sauce
2 teaspoons dried onion flakes
2 tablespoons sugar
1 teaspoon finely minced fresh ginger
1 clove garlic, minced
   vegetable oil for frying
2 tablespoons cornstarch
2 cans (8 ounces each) pineapple tidbits drained, juice
   reserved

*Fresh ginger is gener-
ally peeled before minc-
ing, grating, or slicing.
Don't be afraid to experiment with this extraordi-
nary spice. Try ginger
in:*

· *marinades for grilled
  meat, fish, and
  chicken*
· *soups, stews, and
  sauces*
· *Chinese stir-fry dishes*
· *steamed vegetables,
  such as tomatoes,
  squash, onions, and
  sweet potatoes*

2 packages (10 ounces each) frozen snow peas, barely thawed
6 cups cooked rice

Marinate the beef in the pineapple juice, soy sauce, dehydrated onion, sugar, ginger, and garlic for at least 3 hours (preferably overnight). Drain and reserve marinade. Place the meat in a large wok or skillet with a little oil and brown briefly.

Dissolve the cornstarch in a little of the marinade and add to the reserved marinade, mixing in well. Return the marinade to the wok or skillet with the beef and cook, stirring constantly, until thickened. Add pineapple tidbits and snow peas and heat through. Place the rice in a 9- by 13-inch pan and spoon the beef-pineapple mixture over it. May be reheated in an oven, if needed.

Serves 12.

Oven Stew

This is so easy—just pile everything in a roasting pan and put in the oven. Start it before work or church, and when you come home, you'll have a thick, rich stew.

3 pounds beef stew meat
1 large onion, sliced
4 large potatoes, cut into chunks
6 carrots, cut into chunks
5 ribs celery, sliced
½ pound fresh mushrooms, halved
2 teaspoons salt
½ teaspoon pepper
5 tablespoons sugar
5 tablespoons tapioca
2 tablespoons Worcestershire sauce
4 cups canned vegetable juice

Talk of joy: there may be things better than beef stew and baked potatoes and homemade bread——there may be.

David Grayson

Place the stew meat in a large roaster or Dutch oven with the onion, potatoes, carrots, celery, and mushrooms on top. Sprinkle the salt, pepper, sugar, tapioca, and Worcestershire sauce on top, then pour in vegetable juice. Cover tightly and bake in a 250° oven for 5 hours (or in a 225° oven for 8 to 10 hours).

Serves 6 to 8.

Sloppy Joes

2 pounds ground beef
½ cup minced onion
½ cup minced green pepper
3 tablespoons chili sauce
½ cup ketchup
*   salt and pepper to taste*
8 sandwich buns

Sauté the ground beef, onion, and green pepper until the beef is done and the onion is translucent. Drain off the grease. Stir in the chili sauce and ketchup; salt and pepper to taste. Cook until warmed through. Serve on sandwich buns.

Serves 8.

Sloppy Joe Variations:
You may add any of the following to the basic recipe.
• 2 cans (3 ounces each) mushroom pieces
• 1 can (15 ounces) pinto beans
• 1 can (12 ounces) corn
• liquid hot-pepper sauce

Sloppy Josés

A Southwestern casserole version of the ever-popular Sloppy Joes.

1 pound ground beef
1 chopped onion
1 can (6 ounces) tomato paste
1 can (14½ ounces) stewed tomatoes
2 cans (15 ounces each) pinto beans or kidney beans
1 can (4 ounces) chopped mild green chiles, drained
    and seeds removed
½ teaspoon garlic powder
1 or 2 teaspoons chili powder
    salt and pepper to taste
1½ cups grated Cheddar cheese
2 cups corn chips

In a medium, ovenproof skillet, sauté the ground beef and onion until done, breaking up the ground beef while it cooks. When done, pour off the grease and place the meat into a 2-quart casserole. Stir in the tomato paste, stewed tomatoes, beans, chiles, garlic powder, chili powder, salt, and pepper. Sprinkle grated cheese on top. Place in a preheated 350° oven for 10 to 15 minutes, until cheese melts. Just before serving, top with corn chips.

Serves 6 to 8.

Danish Meatballs

These meatballs have an extremely rich taste and are good served over plain, buttered noodles. You may also make them about half the size described in this recipe and serve them as an appetizer.

Meatballs:
3 slices bacon, cooked and finely crumbled
1 pound ground beef
½ cup seasoned bread crumbs
2 tablespoons grated onion
½ teaspoon nutmeg
½ teaspoon salt
1 cup butter or margarine
2 cups unsweetened 100% white grape juice
1 cup water
1 bay leaf
   salt and pepper

Sauce:
2 tablespoons butter or margarine
2 tablespoons flour
¼ teaspoon nutmeg
1 tablespoon Dijon-style mustard
2 cups of the broth used to cook the meatballs
1 egg yolk

Mix together thoroughly the bacon, ground beef, bread crumbs, onion, nutmeg, and salt. Form into about 20 1-inch meatballs.

In a large saucepan, melt 1 cup butter or margarine. Add the white grape juice, water, bay leaf, salt, and pepper, and bring to a simmer. Gently add meatballs and cook until done, about 20 to 30 minutes. Remove the meatballs and place in a casserole. Reserve 2 cups of broth.

Make a sauce for the meatballs by melting

Fasting and feasting are universal human responses, and any meal, shared with love, can be an agape.
                    Elsie Boulding

2 tablespoons of butter or margarine in a small saucepan. Add flour and stir together for a few minutes. Add the reserved broth and stir until thick. Season with nutmeg and Dijon-style mustard. Put a little bit of the sauce in a cup, stir the egg yolk in, and return the mixture to the sauce. Stir to combine, then pour over the meatballs.

Serves 6 to 8.

Swedish Meatballs

You may make these tiny to serve as an appetizer or larger for a main dish.

1 cup finely chopped onion
2 tablespoons butter or margarine
4 eggs, slightly beaten
2 cups milk
1 cup fine, dry bread crumbs
2½ pounds ground beef
⅓ pound ground pork
2 teaspoons salt
½ teaspoon dill weed
¼ teaspoon allspice
¼ teaspoon nutmeg
¼ teaspoon ground cardamom
3 tablespoons butter or margarine
⅓ cup flour
2 cans (10¾ ounces each) condensed beef broth, undiluted
1 cup half-and-half
1 teaspoon dill weed

In a small skillet, sauté the chopped onion in the butter or margarine until soft. Place into a bowl and add the eggs, milk, and bread crumbs. Stir to combine. Add ground beef, ground pork, salt, dill weed, allspice, nutmeg, and cardamom. Combine well with your hands. Chill for one hour.

Remove from refrigerator and shape into about 72 meatballs. Melt 3 tablespoons butter or margarine in a skillet. Sauté meatballs, about $\frac{1}{4}$ at a time, until lightly browned all over. Remove from the skillet and place in 2 2-quart casseroles.

Remove skillet from heat and pour off fat, returning $\frac{1}{2}$ cup to the skillet. Add the flour and cook, stirring, for about five minutes. Add beef broth and cook, stirring constantly, until the mixture thickens. Reduce heat, add half-and-half and the dill weed. Pour this sauce over the meatballs in the casseroles. Bake, covered, in a 325° oven for 30 minutes.

Makes 24 servings.

Porcupines √

1$\frac{1}{2}$ *pounds ground beef*
1 onion, finely chopped
1 green pepper, finely chopped
$\frac{1}{3}$ *cup uncooked long-grain rice*
1 teaspoon salt
$\frac{1}{4}$ *teaspoon pepper*
1 egg
  vegetable oil for browning
2 cans (10$\frac{3}{4}$ ounces each) tomato soup, undiluted or mushroom
1 cup water

Combine the ground beef, onion, green pepper, rice, salt, pepper, and egg in a medium mixing bowl. Form into meatballs and brown in a skillet.

Mix together the tomato soup and water. Pour over meatballs, bring to a simmer, cover, and cook for 1 hour.

Serves 6 to 8.

Lasagna

A classic for community meals. If you don't know what to make, this is always a favorite.

2 tablespoons olive oil
1 pound ground beef
1 pound ground Italian sausage
1 large onion, chopped
3 cloves garlic, minced
2 cans (6 ounces each) tomato paste
2 cans (16 ounces each) pureed tomatoes
2 teaspoons basil
1 teaspoon sugar
　dash of salt and pepper
1 pound cooked lasagna noodles
1 pound ricotta cheese
1 pound mozzarella cheese, grated
$\frac{1}{4}$ cup grated Parmesan cheese

In a large skillet, place the olive oil, ground beef, Italian sausage, onion, and garlic. Sauté until meats are cooked. Drain off grease. Add tomato paste, tomatoes, basil, sugar, salt, and pepper to taste.

Layer the lasagna in a 9- by 13-inch baking dish: sauce, lasagna noodles, ricotta cheese, mozzarella cheese. Repeat until all the ingredients are used up, then top with a generous sprinkling of Parmesan cheese. Bake in a preheated 350° oven for 30 to 45 minutes or until heated through.

Serves 12.

Variations:

- You don't need to cook the lasagna noodles. Simply add $\frac{1}{2}$ cup of water to the sauce and layer the uncooked noodles in the casserole as if they were cooked. They will cook as the lasagna is baked.
- To make vegetarian lasagna, instead of using ground beef and Italian sausage, sauté 3 cups of chopped eggplant and 3 cups of chopped fresh

To cut the acidity of canned tomatoes, add a grated carrot: It not only improves the flavor, but adds texture and nutrition.

mushrooms in olive oil until tender. Proceed with the recipe as above.

- Try spinach noodles instead of the regular white noodles.

Zucchini Lasagna

Using zucchini instead of noodles makes a lighter, but tasty and satisfying lasagna.

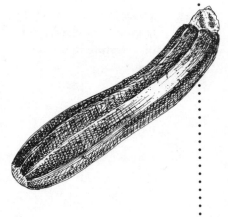

2 tablespoons olive oil
½ pound ground beef
1 onion, chopped
2 cloves garlic, minced
½ pound mushrooms, chopped
1 can (16 ounces) pureed tomatoes
1 can (6 ounces) tomato paste
2 cans (8 ounces each) tomato sauce
1 teaspoon oregano
2 teaspoons basil
½ cup ricotta cheese
1 egg
¼ cup minced fresh parsley
2 cups grated mozzarella cheese
8 medium zucchinis, sliced lengthwise into ½-inch slices
¼ cup grated Parmesan cheese

Place the olive oil in a large skillet. Sauté the ground beef, onion, and garlic until the meat is browned. Drain off the grease. Add the mushrooms and sauté a few minutes more. Stir in the tomatoes, tomato paste, tomato sauce, oregano, and basil. Simmer for 20 minutes.

In a bowl, combine the ricotta cheese, egg, and parsley. When the sauce is done, put a thin layer on the bottom of a 9- by 13-inch baking pan. Cover that with a layer of sliced zucchini. Top the zucchini with a thin layer of ricotta cheese, a thin layer of mozzarella cheese, then sauce. Repeat this layering until all the ingredients are used up. Top with Parmesan cheese. Bake in a 350° oven 40 minutes or until heated through.

Serves 10 to 12.

Traditional Meat Loaf

$1\frac{1}{2}$ pounds ground beef
3 slices of bread, torn into small pieces
2 eggs, slightly beaten
1 can (8 ounces) tomato sauce
$\frac{1}{3}$ cup chopped onion
1 teaspoon salt
1 teaspoon basil
  dash of marjoram
$\frac{1}{4}$ teaspoon pepper
$\frac{1}{4}$ cup ketchup

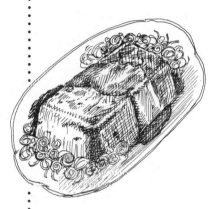

Place all the ingredients except the ketchup in a bowl and combine well. Shape into a loaf and place in a loaf pan. Pour the ketchup over the meat loaf and bake in a 350° oven for about $1\frac{1}{4}$ hours.

Serves 6 to 8.

Cheesy Meat Loaf

A meat loaf is great for a community meal. It's easy to make, it's easily served, and it tastes good at any temperature. A variety of meat loaf recipes makes a nice men's luncheon or father-son banquet.

2 pounds ground beef
$\frac{1}{2}$ cup chopped onion
1 cup diced Cheddar cheese
1 cup soft bread crumbs
2 eggs, slightly beaten
1 can (8 ounces) tomato sauce
$\frac{1}{4}$ teaspoon thyme
1 teaspoon salt

In a large mixing bowl, combine all ingredients with your hands. Shape into a loaf and bake in a 9- by 9-inch baking pan. Bake in a 350° oven for $1\frac{1}{2}$ hours.

Serves 8 to 10.

Beef-Mushroom Meat Loaf

Stay is a charming word in a friend's vocabulary
                                    A.B. Alcott

2 cans (3 ounces each) chopped mushrooms, drained
$\frac{1}{4}$ cup ketchup
$\frac{1}{4}$ cup milk
1 egg, slightly beaten
2 teaspoons Worcestershire sauce
1 teaspoon salt
$\frac{1}{2}$ teaspoon dry mustard
$\frac{1}{4}$ teaspoon pepper
2 pieces of bread, torn into small pieces
$1\frac{1}{2}$ pounds ground beef

Set aside one can of chopped mushrooms and the ketchup. Place all of remaining ingredients in a large bowl and combine. Shape into a loaf and bake in a 350° oven for 1 hour. Remove from the oven, brush on the ketchup, and place the remaining can of mushrooms on top. Return to the oven and bake an additional 15 minutes.

Serves 6.

Berry-Glazed Meat Loaf

1 pound ground beef
$\frac{1}{2}$ pound ground pork sausage
$\frac{1}{3}$ cup quick-cooking rolled oats
$\frac{1}{3}$ cup milk
1 egg, slightly beaten

2 tablespoons chopped onion
½ teaspoon salt
  dash of pepper
1 can (16 ounces) whole cranberry sauce
⅓ cup firmly packed brown sugar
1 tablespoon lemon juice

In a large bowl, combine the ground beef, pork sausage, oats, milk, egg, onion, salt, and pepper. Shape into a loaf and place in a loaf pan. Combine the cranberry sauce, brown sugar, and lemon juice in a small saucepan and heat slowly until the brown sugar dissolves. Spoon over the meat loaf. Bake in a 350° oven for 1¼ hours. Baste with the glaze several times during baking.

Serves 6.

South Side Stuffed Cabbage Rolls

Part of the hearty food heritage of Poland and its neighboring countries, stuffed cabbage is at home at any community meal.

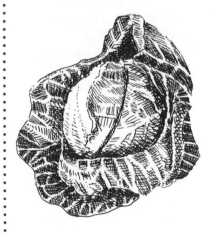

1 large head of green cabbage
2 pounds ground beef
1 onion, chopped
2 cups cooked rice
1 tablespoon paprika
1 teaspoon salt
¼ teaspoon pepper
1 cup tomato juice
1 cup ketchup
½ cup firmly packed brown sugar

Core the cabbage and plunge it into a large kettle of boiling water for 3 to 5 minutes. Remove the cabbage and allow it to cool enough to be handled. Peel off 12 good-sized leaves and set aside.

Sauté the ground beef and onion; drain. In a bowl combine the beef, rice, paprika, salt, and pepper.

Take a generous spoonful of this mixture and place it on a cabbage leaf. Fold over the sides of the leaf and roll it up. Place it, seam side down, in a 9-by 13-inch baking pan. Repeat until all the mixture and cabbage leaves are used up.

Combine the tomato juice, ketchup, and brown sugar. Pour over the cabbage rolls. Bake uncovered in a 350° oven for 20 to 30 minutes, or until heated through.

Serves 6 to 12.

Rio Grande Chili Con Carne

Chili powder is a combination of the ground pods of several varieties of Mexican peppers with other herbs and spices such as cumin, garlic, and oregano.

2 tablespoons vegetable oil
2 large onions, diced
2 cloves garlic, minced
2 pounds ground beef
2 cans (8 ounces each) tomato sauce
1 can (16 ounces) stewed tomatoes
½ cup ketchup
1 tablespoon chili powder (increase, if desired)
1 cup water
2 cans (13 ounces each) kidney beans

Place the oil in a large kettle. Sauté the onion and garlic over medium heat until the onion is soft. Add the ground beef and break it up as it browns. Drain.

Combine the tomato sauce, stewed tomatoes, ketchup, chili powder, and water with the beef and simmer for one hour.

Add the kidney beans, heat through, and serve.
Serves 12.

Spanish Rice With Beef

This is a good dish for a Mexican buffet.

2 pounds ground beef
1 medium onion, chopped
1 green pepper, chopped
1 cup uncooked long-grain rice
2 cans (8 ounces each) tomato sauce
1 can (6 ounces) tomato paste
1 teaspoon chili powder
2 cups water
$\frac{1}{2}$ teaspoon salt
  dash of pepper
1 cup grated Cheddar cheese

Place the ground beef, onion, and green pepper in a large skillet. Sauté until the meat is browned, then drain grease. Add the rice, tomato sauce, tomato paste, chili powder, water, salt, and pepper. Heat to boiling, then reduce to a simmer and cover. Cook for 30 minutes on low heat. Uncover and top with grated Cheddar cheese before serving.
  Serves 8.

Gridiron Casserole

One of the classic ground beef-and-noodle casseroles—great American eating.

2 pounds ground beef
2 onions, chopped fine
2 cans ($10\frac{3}{4}$ ounces each) tomato soup, undiluted
1 cup water
1 teaspoon salt
$\frac{1}{2}$ teaspoon pepper

1 package (6 ounces) elbow macaroni cooked
   according to package directions
1 can (17 ounces) creamed corn
1 cup grated Cheddar cheese

Place the ground beef and onion in a large skillet. Brown the meat, then drain. Combine and add the tomato soup, water, salt, and pepper. Add cooked macaroni and creamed corn. Spoon into a greased casserole and sprinkle the Cheddar cheese over the top. Bake in a 350° oven for 30 minutes.
Serves 8.

Texas Beans

This may be served as a main dish with corn bread and cole slaw or it can be a hearty side dish to serve with barbecued chicken.

2 pounds ground beef
2 onions, chopped
2 green peppers, chopped
3 cans (16 ounces each) pork and beans
$\frac{3}{4}$ cup ketchup
$\frac{1}{3}$ cup molasses
$\frac{1}{4}$ cup firmly packed brown sugar
1 tablespoon dry mustard
   salt and pepper to taste
1 tablespoon liquid smoke (optional)

Put the ground beef, chopped onion, and chopped pepper in a large skillet to brown. Drain grease. Stir the beef in a casserole with the pork and beans, ketchup, molasses, brown sugar, dry mustard, salt, and pepper. If desired, mix in liquid smoke. Bake in a 350° oven for 1 hour, uncovered.
Serves 8 as a main dish, 12 as a side dish.

Calico Beans With Beef

This recipe gets its name from the various beans used in it. If you want to substitute a different kind of bean, go ahead—that's part of the fun of making it.

$1\frac{1}{2}$ pounds ground beef
$1\frac{1}{2}$ cups chopped onion
$\frac{3}{4}$ pound bacon, cut into small pieces
2 cans (16 ounces each) pork and beans
1 can (16 ounces) kidney beans
1 can (16 ounces) lima beans
1 cup ketchup
$\frac{1}{3}$ cup firmly packed brown sugar
2 tablespoons cider vinegar
1 teaspoon dry mustard

Brown the beef and onions, then drain off the fat. Remove the beef and brown the bacon pieces. Combine the ground beef mixture and cooked bacon with the remaining ingredients, place in large casserole, and bake in a 350° oven for $1\frac{1}{2}$ hours.
Serves 8.

Acapulco Delight

A great American version of a Mexican casserole.

2 pounds ground beef
1 package taco seasoning mix
2 cans (4 ounces each) green chiles, minced, drained, and seeds removed
6 corn tortillas
2 cups grated Cheddar cheese

Be very careful when working with chilies in Mexican cooking (California, jalapeno or serrano) and Chinese cooking (cayenne chilies or Chinese dried chilies). If the oils from the seeds and membrane get onto your fingers and fingernails, they are quite difficult to wash away. These oils will burn eyes, lips, anything they touch . . . sometimes for many days. The hottest parts of a chile are the seeds and the inner membrane and these should always be removed before using them in any dish. Simply slit open the chile and scrape away the seeds and the membrane. If possible, wear rubber gloves.

1 can (17 ounces) refried beans
1½ cups sour cream
½ cup chopped green onion
1 can (2¼ ounces) sliced ripe olives
½ cup Monterey Jack cheese
1 cup chopped lettuce
1 cup chopped tomatoes
½ cup sour cream

Brown the beef and drain off the excess fat. Stir in the taco seasoning mix, adding water according to the package directions. Add green chiles and simmer 5 minutes.

Place 2 tortillas in the bottom of a buttered 9- by 13-inch baking dish. Spread half of the meat mixture over the tortillas and sprinkle with ½ cup Cheddar cheese. Top with 2 more tortillas. Spread with refried beans. Cover with 1½ cups of sour cream. Sprinkle with green onion and sliced olives. Place 2 remaining tortillas over the mixture and cover with the remaining meat mixture and Cheddar cheese. Top with Monterey Jack cheese. Bake in a 350° oven for 20 to 30 minutes until bubbly. Remove from oven and top with lettuce, chopped tomatoes, and sour cream.

Makes 8 to 10 servings.

Seven-Layer Hot Dish

1 cup uncooked long-grain rice
1 can (8¾ ounces) whole-kernel corn, drained
2 cans (8 ounces each) tomato sauce
½ cup water
¼ cup chopped onion
¼ cup chopped green pepper
1 pound uncooked ground beef
¼ cup water
4 strips bacon

In a 2- to 3-quart casserole, layer the ingredients in the following order: rice, corn, one can of tomato sauce, $\frac{1}{2}$ cup water, chopped onion, chopped green pepper. Over this, crumble the uncooked ground beef. Add $\frac{1}{4}$ cup water and second can of tomato sauce. Lay the 4 strips of bacon on top. Cover and bake in a 350° oven for 1 hour, then uncover and bake an additional 30 minutes.

Serves 6 to 8.

Super Taco Platter

1 pound ground beef
$\frac{1}{3}$ cup water
1 package taco seasoning mix
1 package (3 ounces) cream cheese, softened
$\frac{1}{3}$ cup milk
1 can (4 ounces) mild green chiles, drained and seeds removed
1 cup shredded lettuce
1 cup diced tomatoes
$\frac{1}{4}$ cup chopped onion
1 jar (4 ounces) mild salsa or $\frac{1}{2}$ cup Santa Fe Salsa
$\frac{1}{2}$ cup sliced ripe olives
$\frac{1}{2}$ cup grated Cheddar cheese
2 tablespoons sour cream
  corn chips

Brown the ground beef and drain off excess fat. Add $\frac{1}{3}$ cup water and taco seasoning mix to the skillet; stir to combine.

Mix together the cream cheese and milk until smooth. Line a large platter with the mixture as a base for the taco filling.

Place the ground beef on top of the cream cheese, then add the green chiles, lettuce, tomato, and onion. Pour the salsa over the top. Add the ripe olives, Cheddar cheese, and sour cream as the final layer.

Frugality is one of the most beautiful and joyful words in the English language, and yet it is one that we are culturally cut off from understanding and enjoying. The consumption society has made us feel that happiness lies in having things, and has failed to teach us the happiness of not having things.

Elise Boulding

Serve with tortilla chips for scooping up the filling.

Serves 12 to 16 as an appetizer or 6 to 8 as a main dish.

Shepherd's Pie

This is a wonderful way to use up leftovers. Substitute any available meat or vegetables for the ones called for below. If you want, you may also substitute a tomato sauce for the gravy.

3 cups chopped leftover cooked beef
1 can (16 ounces) green beans, drained
1 can (17 ounces) corn, drained
$\frac{1}{2}$ cup chopped onion
$\frac{1}{2}$ cup chopped celery
2 tablespoons butter or margarine
2 cups leftover gravy or 1 can (16 ounces) beef gravy
$\frac{1}{2}$ cup milk
$\frac{1}{4}$ teaspoon garlic powder
  salt and pepper to taste
3 cups mashed potatoes
2 tablespoons butter or margarine
  paprika

Place the beef, green beans, and corn in a 9- by 13-inch baking pan. Sauté onions and celery in 2 tablespoons of butter or margarine until barely soft. Add to the meat and vegetables. Mix together the gravy, milk, garlic powder, salt, and pepper. Pour over the vegetable-and-meat mixture. Spread a layer of mashed potatoes on top. If the potatoes are a bit thick, thin them with a little milk. Dot with butter or margarine and sprinkle with paprika. Bake in a 350° oven for 20 to 30 minutes or until potatoes are browned.

Serves 6 to 8.

Grass Valley Cornish Pasty Pie

The inspiration for this recipe—traditional Cornish pasties—are turnovers made to be packed as a workman's lunch. This version provides the same hearty flavor but puts it into a casserole form perfect for sharing with friends.

$1\frac{1}{2}$ cups leftover roast beef or lamb chunks
2 carrots, cooked and cut into chunks
2 baked potatoes, cut into chunks
1 onion, chopped
$\frac{1}{4}$ teaspoon garlic salt
$\frac{1}{4}$ teaspoon thyme
$\frac{1}{4}$ teaspoon basil
    dash of pepper
$2\frac{1}{2}$ cups leftover or canned gravy
1 prepared pastry for 9-inch pie

In a large bowl, stir together the meat, carrots, potatoes, and onion. Stir the garlic salt, thyme, basil, and pepper into the gravy. Pour gravy over meat-and-vegetable mixture and stir to coat. Place the mixture into a 9-inch round baking pan or cake pan. Place piecrust on top and seal the edges. Cut a few slits in the top to allow steam to escape. Bake in a 350° oven for 30 to 45 minutes or until crust is browned.

Serves 4 to 6.

Pasties (PASS-tees) are peppery little meat pies, brought to this country by immigrants from Cornwall, England. During the nineteenth century, Cornish miners came over to find work in the newly opened American West. Their wives continued the tradition of baking the half-moon-shaped pies filled with meat, potatoes, and onions that was the perfect portable lunch. It is still possible to find authentic examples of Cornish cookery, including pasties, in former mining towns like Mineral Point, Wisconsin, and Grass Valley, California.

··· Poultry ···

Country Fried Chicken

Though there are numerous ways to make fried chicken, first browning the pieces in hot oil and then finishing the cooking by baking keeps the coating from falling off the pieces.

1 chicken
3 cups water
$\frac{1}{2}$ cup powdered milk
2 eggs
$2\frac{1}{2}$ cups flour
1 tablespoon poultry seasoning
1 teaspoon garlic salt
$\frac{1}{2}$ teaspoon pepper
  vegetable oil for frying

Cut the chicken into serving pieces and skin it. In a bowl, stir together the water, powdered milk, and eggs, mixing well. Set aside. In a separate bowl, stir together the flour, poultry seasoning, garlic salt, and pepper.

Taking the chicken pieces one at a time, dip them first into the flour mixture, then into the liquid mixture, then back into the flour mixture. When all the pieces have been coated, heat 1 inch of oil in a frying pan. Without crowding the pieces, fry them in the oil, turning as needed, until they are golden brown. As the pieces are browned, remove them from the frying pan and place them on a cookie sheet. Bake in a 350° oven for 45 minutes.

Serves 4.

Chicken Baked in Cream

Baking chicken in cream tenderizes it until it can be cut with a fork.

1 Country Fried Chicken recipe after browning but before baking

or

6 browned chicken breasts
$2\frac{1}{2}$ cups cream

Place browned chicken in a 9- by 13-inch baking dish. Pour the cream over the chicken. Cover with aluminum foil and bake in a 325° oven for 2 hours.
Serves 4 to 6.

Creamy Tarragon-Mushroom Chicken

Elegant and delicious, this is perfect when served with a wild rice pilaf.

6 to 8 browned chicken breasts or thighs (see Country Fried Chicken)
$2\frac{1}{2}$ cups cream
2 cups fresh mushrooms, cleaned and cut in half
1 tablespoon dried tarragon

Place the browned chicken in a 9- by 13-inch baking pan. Sprinkle the mushrooms around and on top of the chicken pieces. Pour the cream over the chicken; sprinkle with tarragon. Cover with aluminum foil and bake in a 325° oven for 2 hours.
Serves 6 to 8.

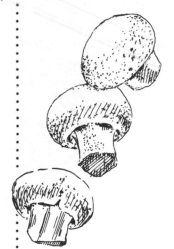

Orange-Coconut Chicken

Thinking of a South Pacific theme for your next community meal? This recipe is perfect.

1 cup uncooked brown rice
1 tablespoon dried minced onion
1 chicken, cut up and skinned
$\frac{1}{4}$ cup butter or margarine
1 tablespoon curry powder
$2\frac{1}{2}$ cups chicken broth
$\frac{1}{4}$ cup orange marmalade
1 cup flaked coconut

Sprinkle the brown rice in the bottom of a 9- by 13-inch baking dish. Place minced onion on top. Arrange the chicken on top and dot with the butter or margarine. Sprinkle on the curry powder, then pour the chicken broth on. Dot orange marmalade on top and sprinkle on flaked coconut. Cover with aluminum foil and bake in a 350° oven $1\frac{1}{2}$ hours.

Serves 4 to 6.

Wild Rice and Mushroom Chicken

This dish is not only hearty, *it's easy too.*

1 cup brown rice
1 cup wild rice
1 chicken, cut-up and skinned
1 onion, sliced
1 cup fresh mushrooms, sliced
1 can ($10\frac{3}{4}$ ounces) cream of mushroom soup, undiluted
$2\frac{1}{2}$ cups water
2 tablespoons Worcestershire sauce
$\frac{1}{4}$ teaspoon garlic salt

In the bottom of a 9- by 13-inch baking pan, place the brown rice and wild rice. Arrange the chicken on top of the rice. Place the sliced onion and mushrooms on top. In a separate bowl, stir together the mushroom soup, water, Worcestershire sauce, and garlic salt. Pour over the chicken. Cover with aluminum foil and bake in a 350° oven for $1\frac{1}{2}$ hours.

Serves 4 to 6.

Variation:

- Reduce the rices to $\frac{1}{2}$ cup each and replace with 1 cup wheat berries. These may be found in natural food stores and are delicious with rice.

Smothered Chicken

$\frac{1}{2}$ *cup crushed cracker crumbs*
$\frac{1}{4}$ *teaspoon salt*
$\frac{1}{8}$ *teaspoon pepper*
$\frac{1}{4}$ *teaspoon garlic powder*
1 large frying chicken, cut up and skinned
$\frac{1}{2}$ *cup peanut oil*
1 large onion, sliced
1 large carrot, sliced
3 ribs celery, sliced
1 cup sliced mushrooms
1 can (14$\frac{1}{2}$ ounces) clear chicken broth, undiluted

Mix together the cracker crumbs, salt, pepper, and garlic powder. Roll the chicken in the crumb mixture; brown in hot peanut oil in a large skillet. Remove the chicken from the skillet and place in a 9- by 13-inch baking pan. In the same skillet, sauté the onion, carrot, and celery slices until the onion is tender. Spoon the sautéed vegetables over the chicken and top with the mushrooms. Pour the chicken broth on top, cover with aluminum foil, and bake in a 325° oven for 1½ hours.

Serves 4 to 6.

Italian Chicken With Artichokes

Elegant and delicious, this may be served alone at a community dinner or with a platter of pasta.

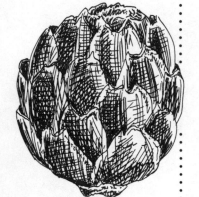

2 small jars (6 ounces each) marinated artichoke hearts
⅓ cup olive oil
1 chicken, cut up and skinned
4 tomatoes, quartered
2 cloves garlic, minced
½ pound fresh mushrooms, cleaned and halved
½ teaspoon oregano
2 teaspoons basil
  salt and pepper

Drain the oil from the artichoke hearts, pouring it into a large skillet with the olive oil. Lightly brown the chicken pieces and place them in a 9- by 13-inch baking pan. Cut the reserved artichoke hearts in half and place on top of the chicken. Add the tomatoes, garlic, mushrooms, oregano, basil, salt, and pepper. Cover with aluminum foil and bake in a 350° oven for 1½ hours.

Serves 4 to 6.

Chinese Chicken Casserole

4 cups cooked chicken or turkey, deboned and diced
1 cup cut-up fresh broccoli
1 cup diced celery
1 can (3 ounces) chow mein noodles
2 cans (10¾ ounces each) cream of mushroom soup, undiluted
2 tablespoons soy sauce
½ cup chicken broth
½ cup sliced almonds

In a large bowl, stir together the chicken, broccoli, celery, and chow mein noodles. In a separate bowl, combine the mushroom soup, soy sauce, and chicken broth, stirring until well mixed. Pour the soup mixture over the chicken mixture; stir to combine. Spoon into a greased casserole and top with almonds. Bake uncovered in a 325° oven for 40 minutes.
Serves 8.

Rock Cornish Hens With Apricot Sauce

Cornish hens work well for a community meal if you halve or quarter them before baking.

3 Rock Cornish hens, split or quartered
½ stick melted butter or margarine
2 tablespoons honey
Apricot Sauce (see recipe below)

Lay split or quartered hens in a 9- by 13-inch baking pan. Combine melted butter or margarine and honey; stir until honey is dissolved. Baste hens with honey mixture and bake uncovered in a 350°

Soy sauce is made from soy beans, flour, salt, and water. Light soy sauce is lighter in color, of a thinner consistency, and saltier than dark soy sauces. Use light soy sauce in chicken, fish, shrimp, and pork dishes. Dark soy sauces are darker and thicker because they are sweetened with molasses. Dark soy sauce may be used with beef and other red meats, for roasting and to enrich sauces.

oven for 30 to 45 minutes, basting occasionally, until nicely browned. Serve topped with Apricot Sauce.

Serves 6 to 12.

Apricot Sauce:

Though created for the Rock Cornish Hen recipe, this sauce is also delicious served over baked ham or chicken breasts.

1 can (17 ounces) peeled apricot halves with juice
¾ cup unsweetened 100% white grape juice
2 tablespoons cornstarch
¼ cup water

Place the apricot halves, juice, and white grape juice in a medium saucepan. Dissolve the cornstarch in the water, then add to the apricots. Cook, stirring gently, until the sauce thickens and clears (about 10 minutes).

Makes 2 cups.

Variation:

If desired, ¼ cup of currants or raisins may be added to the sauce when the white grape juice is added.

Chicken Enchiladas Supreme

You may assemble these ahead of time and reheat just before serving.

1½ cups cooked chicken, deboned and diced
1½ cups grated Cheddar cheese
¼ cup minced green onion
1 can (4 ounces) chopped green chiles, drained and
    seeds removed
1 package (3 ounces) cream cheese, cut into chunks
½ cup sour cream
8 flour tortillas
2 jars (8 ounces each) enchilada sauce

Optional Garnishes:
- Chopped lettuce
- Chopped tomatoes
- Chopped green onions
- Sour cream
- Chopped avocados
- Sliced black olives

In a medium bowl, mix together the chicken, Cheddar cheese, green onion, green chiles, cream cheese, and sour cream. Divide into 8 portions and place on the flour tortillas. Roll up tortillas and place in 9- by 13-inch baking dish. Cover with enchilada sauce. Bake in a 375° oven for 30 minutes or until hot and bubbly. If desired, you may sprinkle on any of the optional garnishes just before serving.

Serves 6 to 8.

Chicken Potpie

Using prepared ingredients in this recipe makes this chicken potpie very easy. It's also a great way to use leftover turkey.

Frozen pastry for a double-crust 9-inch pie
2 cups cooked chicken or turkey, deboned and cut up
$\frac{1}{4}$ cup chopped onion
2 baked potatoes, cubed
$1\frac{1}{2}$ cups frozen peas and carrots, thawed
$\frac{1}{3}$ cup cream of chicken soup, undiluted
$\frac{1}{2}$ cup milk
$\frac{1}{2}$ teaspoon poultry seasoning
1 egg, slightly beaten
1 tablespoon water

Thaw the frozen piecrusts. Place the chicken, onion, potatoes, peas, and carrots in a large bowl.

Potpie fillings are actually stews or creamed dishes inside a crust. If you wish, serve fillings over rice, noodles, toast points, or patty shells.

Toss gently to combine. In a separate bowl, stir together the chicken soup, milk, and poultry seasoning. Pour over the chicken mixture; stir gently to combine.

Line a 9-inch pie pan with pastry, then spoon in the chicken mixture. Put the other crust on top and seal. Cut slits in the top piecrust. Stir together the beaten egg and water and brush on top crust. Bake in a 325° oven 1 hour or until golden brown on top.

Serves 6.

Baked Sweet and Sour Chicken

Great for an Oriental potluck, this should be served with lots of fluffy white rice.

2 chickens, cut up and skinned
2 cups sugar
$\frac{1}{2}$ teaspoon salt
2 teaspoons instant chicken bouillon powder
1 cup ketchup
$\frac{1}{4}$ cup soy sauce
2 green peppers, cut into 1-inch pieces
$\frac{1}{4}$ cup cornstarch
$\frac{1}{2}$ cup cold water

Place the chicken in a deep bowl or casserole. In a saucepan, combine the sugar, salt, chicken bouillon, ketchup, and soy sauce. Stir over medium heat until sugar and bouillon are dissolved. Remove from heat and pour over the chicken. Marinate the chicken for 7 hours (or overnight). Remove the chicken from the marinade and place in a casserole. Add green pepper. Place the marinade in a saucepan. Mix the cornstarch and cold water together in a small bowl, then add to marinade and cook until thickened. Pour over the chicken. Cover and bake in a 350° oven for $1\frac{1}{2}$ hours.

Serves 10 to 12.

Hot Chicken Salad

Not really a salad at all, this potluck tradition is a delicious chicken casserole with lots of crunch and flavor.

4 cups cooked chicken, cut up
2 cups diced celery
1 can (8 ounces) water chestnuts, drained and chopped
2 cups cooked rice
$\frac{3}{4}$ cup grated Cheddar cheese
$\frac{1}{4}$ cup sliced green onion
$\frac{3}{4}$ cup mayonnaise
1 can (10$\frac{3}{4}$ ounces) cream of chicken soup, undiluted
1 teaspoon salt
1 tablespoon lemon juice
1$\frac{1}{2}$ cups crushed potato chips
$\frac{1}{2}$ cup sliced almonds

Mix together in a large bowl the chicken, celery, water chestnuts, rice, Cheddar cheese, and green onion. In a small bowl, stir together the mayonnaise, soup, salt, and lemon juice. Add this mixture to the chicken mixture and stir to combine. Spoon into a 9- by 13-inch casserole. Top with crushed potato chips and sliced almonds. Bake in a 375° oven for 30 minutes.
Serves 12.

A 3-pound broiler-fryer chicken will yield about 3 cups of bite-size cooked chicken for salad or casseroles. A whole chicken breast (about 1 pound) will yield about 1$\frac{1}{2}$ cups cooked cubed chicken.

Chicken Spaghetti

1 large chicken
$\frac{1}{2}$ cup butter or margarine
1 onion, chopped
$\frac{1}{2}$ cup chopped celery
1 green pepper, chopped
1 pound spaghetti
1 cup grated processed American cheese
1 cup grated Colby cheese
1 can (10$\frac{3}{4}$ ounces) cream of mushroom soup, undiluted
1 jar (2 ounces) sliced pimiento
2 cups chicken stock

Place the chicken in a large pot and cover with water. Bring to a boil and simmer until done, about 45 minutes. Cool, skin, and remove meat from the bones. Cut meat into large chunks; set aside in a large bowl.

Melt the butter or margarine in a skillet. Sauté the onion, celery, and green pepper until tender. Mix these vegetables, along with the butter or margarine they were cooked in, with the chicken. Break the spaghetti into pieces and cook according to package directions. Rinse when done.

In a casserole, layer the chicken mixture, spaghetti, and cheeses. Stir together the soup, pimiento, and chicken stock; pour over the chicken and spaghetti. Bake in a 350° oven for 1 hour.

Serves 12.

And God's sheer daylight
Pours through our shafted
sky
To proffer again
The occasion of His Grace
Where we might meet each
other.

Brother Antoninus

Creamed Chicken and Biscuits

This is a big, biscuit-topped chicken pie. Any kind of prepared biscuit dough will be tasty on it.

2 chickens, cooked, skinned, deboned, and cut into chunks
2 packages (10 ounces each) frozen peas and carrots
3 tablespoons butter or margarine
3 tablespoons flour
2 cups milk or half-and-half
1 cup chicken broth
$\frac{1}{2}$ teaspoon poultry seasoning
1 recipe Baking Powder Biscuits or 1 can refrigerated biscuits

Place chicken in 9- by 13-inch pan. Add peas and carrots; stir together. In a saucepan melt the butter or margarine. Add the flour and cook a few minutes. Add milk or half-and-half, chicken broth, and poultry seasoning. Cook, stirring constantly, until thick. Pour over chicken and vegetables. Top with biscuits. Bake in a 350° oven for about 30 to 45 minutes, until biscuits are browned and casserole is bubbling hot.
Serves 12.

Honey Butter Baked Turkey

You needn't buy expensive prebasted turkeys to have them turn out tender and succulent.

1 frozen turkey (any size)
$\frac{1}{2}$ teaspoon garlic powder
1 teaspoon poultry seasoning
1 cup chicken broth
$\frac{1}{2}$ cup butter or margarine
$\frac{1}{2}$ cup honey

Thaw the turkey according to package directions. Rinse and pat dry. Place the turkey in a roasting pan. Stir the garlic powder and poultry seasoning into the chicken broth; pour into the turkey's cavity. Place butter or margarine and honey in a small saucepan and heat until the honey dissolves. Baste the turkey with this mixture. Cover with roasting-pan lid or with aluminum foil. Bake according to package directions, basting frequently. Plan on approximately 20 minutes per pound in a 350° oven.

Yield:
A turkey will provide about half its weight in usable meat. If you have a 20-pound turkey, you will end up with about 10 pounds of edible meat. For a large community meal where there will be numerous dishes, $\frac{1}{4}$ pound of meat a person is sufficient, so a 20-pound turkey will serve 40 people. In other situations, it is good to allow $\frac{1}{3}$ to $\frac{1}{2}$ pound of turkey for each person. In this case, a 20-pound turkey will feed between 20 and 30 people.

When preparing roast turkey and chicken for large groups, consider cooking the dressing in separate casseroles rather than stuffing the poultry. This makes it much easier to bake and serve. Instead of stuffing, place chunks of onion or apple and herbs, such as thyme and sage, inside the cavity to add flavor during roasting.

Turkey Delight

This is a wonderful way to use up leftover turkey and gravy. The phyllo dough encases the leftovers and turns them into a special dish.

$\frac{1}{2}$ package ($\frac{1}{2}$ pound) phyllo dough
$1\frac{1}{2}$ cups melted butter
7 cups combined finely chopped, cooked turkey and leftover dressing
2 cups turkey gravy

Place a layer of phyllo dough in a greased 9- by 13-inch baking dish. Brush with butter and add another layer. Continue this layering until about half the phyllo dough is used up.

In a large bowl, stir together the turkey, dressing, and gravy. Spoon onto the phyllo dough in the baking dish. Add another layer of dough, brush with butter, and continue adding phyllo until all the sheets are used up. Bake in a 450° oven for 30 to 45 minutes or until crisp and brown.

Serves 6 to 8.

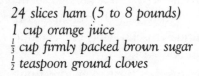

· · · Ham, Pork, and Lamb · · ·

Baked Ham

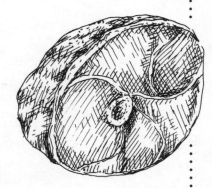

This is one of the easiest entrées for a community meal. It is cooked in serving-size portions and just needs to be reheated. To make this for a group, purchase a boneless, precooked ham. Have the butcher slice the ham into 4- to 6-ounce portions for a dinner and 2- to 3-ounce portions for a brunch. You may use this same method for baking the new turkey hams.

24 slices ham (5 to 8 pounds)
1 cup orange juice
⅓ cup firmly packed brown sugar
½ teaspoon ground cloves

Place the ham in 9- by 13-inch (or larger) baking dishes. Stir together the orange juice, brown sugar, and ground cloves; pour over the ham. Cover and bake in a 350° oven for 30 to 45 minutes or until heated through.
Serves 24.

Raisin Sauce

3 tablespoons cornstarch
¼ cup cold water
½ cup sugar
2 cups water
2 cups raisins
⅓ cup vinegar
¼ cup butter or margarine
1 teaspoon salt
¼ teaspoon pepper
½ teaspoon mace
½ teaspoon ground cloves
1 cup currant jelly

Dissolve the cornstarch in the $\frac{1}{4}$ cup of water. Place all of the remaining ingredients in a large saucepan, add the dissolved cornstarch, and bring to a boil, stirring constantly. Reduce the heat and cook, stirring constantly, until the sauce thickens slightly and clears.

Serve with Baked Ham or any kind of pork, Cornish Game Hen, or even ice cream!

Makes about 5 cups.

Down East Ham Loaf

1 pound ground ham
1 pound freshly ground raw pork
$\frac{2}{3}$ cup fresh bread crumbs
$\frac{1}{2}$ cup milk
$\frac{1}{4}$ cup chopped onion
$\frac{1}{2}$ teaspoon salt
$\frac{1}{4}$ teaspoon pepper
$\frac{1}{4}$ teaspoon dry mustard
1 egg, slightly beaten

Glaze:
$\frac{1}{2}$ cup firmly packed brown sugar
$\frac{1}{2}$ teaspoon dry mustard
2 tablespoons orange juice

Place the ground ham, ground pork, bread crumbs, milk, chopped onion, salt, pepper, mustard, and egg in a large bowl; mix well. Shape into a loaf and place into a loaf pan. Bake in a 350° oven for 1 hour.

At the end of the hour, combine the brown sugar, mustard, and orange juice. Spoon over the meat loaf, and bake for 30 minutes more.

Serves 8.

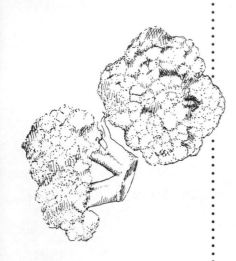

Ham and Cheese Broccoli Bake

A wonderful way to use up leftover ham.

1 package (10 ounces) frozen chopped broccoli, thawed
2 cups chopped ham pieces
3 cups cooked rice
1 can (10¾ ounces) Cheddar cheese soup, undiluted
1 cup sour cream
1 cup bread crumbs
¼ cup melted butter or margarine
  paprika

Mix together the broccoli, ham, and rice. Place in a casserole. Stir together the soup and sour cream and stir into the ham-and-rice mixture. Top with bread crumbs, spoon melted butter or margarine on top, and sprinkle with paprika. Cover and bake in a 350° oven for 35 minutes.
Serves 6 to 8.

Skillet Pork Chops and Rice

Dishes like this are always welcome at potlucks because the meat and starch are all in one dish.

6 pork chops
2 tablespoons butter or margarine
1 medium onion, chopped
½ cup chopped celery
1 cup uncooked long-grain white rice
2 cans (8 ounces each) tomato sauce
1½ cups water
¼ cup firmly packed brown sugar

$\frac{1}{2}$ teaspoon dry mustard
$\frac{1}{2}$ teaspoon salt
$\frac{1}{4}$ teaspoon pepper

Brown the pork chops in butter or margarine and place into casserole dish. In the same skillet, cook the onion and celery until barely tender, then spoon them over the pork chops. Sprinkle the rice on top.

In a separate bowl, stir together the tomato sauce, water, brown sugar, dry mustard, salt, and pepper. Pour this mixture over the pork chops. Bake in a 350° oven for 1 hour or until rice is done.

Serves 6.

Sedona Bean and Pork Burritos

You can eat this with your hands, but be sure to keep one end folded up, because they can get messy.

$\frac{2}{3}$ pound boneless pork, diced
2 cloves garlic, minced
1 cup water
2 tablespoons vegetable oil
1 can (16 ounces) pinto beans, undrained
1 medium onion, chopped
1 can (4 ounces) chopped green chiles, drained and
  seeds removed
$\frac{1}{2}$ teaspoon oregano
  dash of salt
$\frac{1}{2}$ teaspoon chili powder
8 9-inch flour tortillas

Brown the pork and garlic in the oil. Drain. Add 1 cup of water and simmer 30 minutes or until the pork is tender. Add beans, onion, chiles, and seasonings. Simmer, stirring occasionally, for 30 minutes.

Divide the filling among the tortillas and roll them up. Place in 9- by 13-inch casserole or on a cookie sheet. Just before serving, heat in a 350° oven for about 20 minutes.

Serves 8.

Pork Chops Italiano

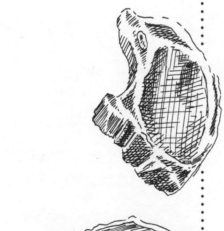

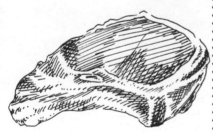

One nice thing about this recipe is that you can use any sort of pork chop or simply cut up a pork roast. This is good served with plain buttered pasta, a green salad, and French bread.

12 pork chops
2 tablespoons vegetable oil
2 cups halved fresh mushrooms
2 green peppers, cut into squares
1 onion, sliced
4 cans (8 ounces each) tomato sauce
1 clove garlic, minced
1 teaspoon basil
1 teaspoon oregano

Brown the chops a few at a time in vegetable oil and place in a 9- by 13-inch baking dish. Arrange mushrooms, green peppers, and onion around and over the meat. In a bowl, mix together the tomato sauce, garlic, basil, and oregano. Pour this over the chops. Cover with aluminum foil and bake in a 350° oven for 1 hour.

Serves 8.

Polish Sausage and Red Cabbage

Hearty and delicious. Have a little pot of Dijon-style mustard alongside the dish as a condiment.

1 large red cabbage
2 apples, peeled and diced
1 cup water
2 tablespoons lemon juice
2 tablespoons butter or margarine
2 small onions, chopped
  pinch of salt
  dash of pepper
2 tablespoons wine vinegar
2 pounds kielbasa (Polish sausage)

Grate the cabbage. Place it in a large kettle with the apples, water, and lemon juice. Bring to a boil, then simmer, covered, for about 20 minutes, stirring occasionally. Meanwhile, melt the butter or margarine in a skillet and sauté the onion until golden. Add the onion to the cabbage, along with the salt, pepper, and vinegar.

Cut the sausage into 8 pieces and place on top of the cabbage. Cook over medium heat, covered, 40 minutes. Spoon the cabbage onto a platter, then top with the sausage.

Serves 8.

Variation:

• You may put this into a casserole at the time you add the sausage. Cover and bake in a 350° oven for 45 minutes.

There is no sight on earth more appealing than the sight of a woman making dinner for someone she loves.

Thomas Wolfe

Yorkshire Hot Pot

2 tablespoons vegetable oil
1 clove garlic, minced
8 shoulder lamb chops
8 small whole onions, peeled
8 medium potatoes, halved
1 package (10 ounces) frozen green beans, thawed
  dash of ground cloves
2 teaspoons salt
  dash of pepper
1 can (10¾ ounces) cream of mushroom soup, undiluted
¾ cup water

Place the vegetable oil and garlic in a skillet and brown the chops well. Remove from the skillet and place in a casserole. Place the onions and potatoes around the chops; add the green beans. In a bowl, stir together the cloves, salt, pepper, soup, and water. Pour the soup mixture over the chops and vegetables. Cover and bake in a 350° oven for about 1 hour.
Serves 8.

Moussaka

This is a traditional Greek casserole made with sliced eggplant and lamb. It is a bit of work to make, but can be made a day ahead and reheated just before serving.

3 medium eggplants
  olive oil
2 pounds ground lamb
          or
1 pound ground lamb
1 pound ground beef
          or
2 pounds ground beef

2 onions, chopped
2 garlic cloves, chopped
  dash of cinnamon
  dash of nutmeg
$\frac{1}{2}$ teaspoon oregano
2 tablespoons chopped fresh parsley
1 can (8 ounces) tomato sauce
1 cup water
2 cups grated mozzarella cheese
4 eggs, well beaten
2 cups milk
1 cup grated Romano cheese

Slice the eggplant into $\frac{1}{4}$-inch slices and soak it in salt water for about 15 minutes. Drain and pat dry. Brush with olive oil and broil on both sides or sauté in a pan until light brown.

Sauté the ground meat, onion, and garlic until meat is browned. Drain. Add the cinnamon, nutmeg, oregano, parsley, tomato sauce, and water. Stir to combine.

In a large-size roasting pan, layer the eggplant slices, meat sauce, and grated mozzarella cheese. Stir the eggs and milk together and pour over the casserole. Top with grated Romano cheese. Bake in a 350° oven for 1 hour.

Serves 12.

Lamb and Artichokes

12 lamb steaks or chops
1 or 2 boxes (9 ounces each) frozen artichoke hearts
$\frac{1}{4}$ cup lemon juice
3 cloves garlic, minced
2 teaspoons oregano
2 cans (16 ounces each) whole tomatoes with juice,
    chopped
$\frac{1}{2}$ cup olive oil
1 teaspoon salt
$\frac{1}{2}$ teaspoon pepper

Place the lamb steaks or chops in 9- by 13-inch baking dish. Top with the artichoke hearts. In small bowl, stir together the lemon juice, garlic, oregano, tomatoes, olive oil, salt, and pepper. Pour over the chops and artichokes. Cover with aluminum foil and bake in a 350° oven for $1\frac{1}{2}$ hours.
Serves 12.

· · · Fish and Seafood · · ·

Portuguese Cod

2 pounds fillet of cod, cut into pieces
2 onions, sliced
4 potatoes, sliced
3 tomatoes, sliced
2 green peppers, sliced
$\frac{1}{2}$ teaspoon salt
    dash of pepper
1 bay leaf
1 cup chicken broth
2 tablespoons lemon juice

In a casserole, layer the cod, onions, potatoes, tomatoes, and green pepper. Sprinkle salt and pepper on top. Break bay leaf in half and tuck into the casserole. Stir together the chicken broth and lemon juice; pour over the casserole. Cover with aluminum foil and bake in a 350° oven for $1\frac{1}{2}$ hours. Remove bay leaf.

Serves 6 to 8.

Tuna Noodle Casserole

1 package (8 ounces) medium egg noodles
2 tablespoons butter or margarine
1 medium onion, chopped
1 can ($10\frac{3}{4}$ ounces) cream of mushroom soup, undiluted
1 soup can of milk
1 can ($6\frac{1}{2}$ ounces) tuna, flaked and drained
2 cups frozen peas, thawed
$\frac{1}{2}$ cup grated Cheddar cheese

Cook the noodles according to package directions and drain. In a small skillet, melt the butter or margarine and sauté the onion until it is soft. In a separate bowl, stir together the cream of mushroom soup and the milk. Combine the noodles, cooked onion, soup mixture, tuna, and peas in a casserole. Bake in a 350° oven for 30 minutes. Remove from oven, top with cheese, and bake an additional 5 minutes or until cheese is melted.

Serves 6.

Tuna, Chile, and Rice Casserole

4 cups cooked rice
1 cup cottage cheese
$\frac{1}{4}$ cup mayonnaise
$\frac{1}{2}$ cup buttermilk
2 cans (4 ounces each) chopped mild green chiles,
    drained and seeds removed
1 can ($6\frac{1}{2}$ ounces) tuna, drained and flaked
$\frac{1}{2}$ cup grated Monterey Jack cheese

Stir the rice and cottage cheese together in a medium bowl. In a separate bowl, stir together the mayonnaise and buttermilk. Add this mixture to the rice mixture. Stir in the chiles and tuna; spoon into casserole. Bake in a 350° oven for 30 minutes. Remove from oven, top with Monterey Jack cheese, and bake 5 to 10 minutes longer.
Serves 4 to 6.

Perch With Crab and Mushroom Topping

$1\frac{1}{2}$ cups fresh mushrooms, sliced
$\frac{1}{4}$ cup chopped green onion
2 tablespoons butter or margarine
1 pound perch fillets (halibut, flounder, or sole may be
    substituted)
1 can (6 ounces) crabmeat, flaked and drained
$\frac{1}{2}$ teaspoon salt
$\frac{1}{4}$ teaspoon pepper
2 tablespoons lemon juice
$1\frac{1}{2}$ cups half-and-half

Sauté the mushrooms and green onions in the butter or margarine until tender. Set aside.

Place the perch fillets in a 9- by 13-inch baking pan. Top with the crabmeat; sprinkle with the salt, pepper, and lemon juice. Pour the half-and-half on top; cover with the previously sautéed mushrooms and green onions. Cover and bake in a preheated 350° oven for 20 minutes. Uncover and bake an additional 15 minutes, basting several times during baking.

Serves 4 to 6.

Seafood Rotini

Quick and easy—a tasty seafood alternative to ground meat casseroles.

2 tablespoons butter or margarine
⅓ cup chopped green onion
1 tablespoon flour
1 can (10¾ ounces) cream of chicken soup, undiluted
½ cup milk or half-and-half
1 tablespoon Worcestershire sauce
2 tablespoons grated Parmesan cheese
1 can (3 ounces) mushroom crowns
1 can (2¼ ounces) sliced ripe olives
1 can (6½ ounces) tuna
1 cup cooked shrimp, cut into bite-size pieces
    paprika for garnish
1 package (10 ounces) rotini or other noodles, cooked

Melt the butter or margarine in a large skillet. Add green onion and cook, stirring occasionally, for about 5 minutes. Add flour and combine for a couple of minutes. Add soup, milk or half-and-half, Worcestershire sauce, and Parmesan cheese. Stir until smooth. Add mushroom crowns, olives, tuna, and shrimp. Cook over medium heat until heated through, stirring to prevent scorching.

Garnish with paprika and serve over cooked rotini.

Serves 4 to 6.

Greek Shrimp Sauté

2 boxes (9 ounces each) frozen artichoke hearts
2 tablespoons butter or margarine
2 tablespoons olive oil
1 clove garlic, minced
1½ pounds jumbo shrimp, cleaned and deveined
¼ cup fresh lemon juice
½ teaspoon oregano
3 medium fresh tomatoes, quartered .
4 ounces crumbled feta cheese

Thaw artichoke hearts and cut each in half. Set aside. In a large skillet, heat the butter or margarine with the oil. Sauté the garlic over medium heat until golden, then add the artichoke hearts and shrimp, and sauté about 10 minutes, until the shrimp is cooked. (Do not overcook.) Add lemon juice and oregano, stir gently to combine, then stir in the tomatoes and feta cheese. Cover and heat through.

Serves 6 to 8.

··· Eggs and Cheese ···

Ham and Cheese Brunch Munch

1 package (16 ounces) frozen cut broccoli, thawed
1 tablespoon butter or margarine
$\frac{1}{4}$ cup chopped green onion
$\frac{1}{4}$ cup chopped green pepper
1$\frac{1}{4}$ cups diced ham
2 tablespoons butter or margarine
12 eggs, beaten
  Cheese Sauce (see recipe below)
4 slices whole wheat bread
2 tablespoons melted butter or margarine
  paprika for garnish

Place the thawed broccoli pieces in a 9- by 13-inch pan. Melt 1 tablespoon butter or margarine in a medium skillet, add the green onion and green pepper, and sauté until pepper is barely tender. Sprinkle the sautéed green onions and peppers over the broccoli pieces. Add the diced ham.

In a medium skillet, melt 2 tablespoons butter or margarine. Add the beaten eggs and scramble them until set, but still soft. Add the eggs to the casserole, pour Cheese Sauce over everything, and stir very gently.

Cut the bread into small cubes and place on top of the cheese mixture. Pour 2 tablespoons melted butter or margarine over the bread cubes, then sprinkle paprika on top. Cover the dish and place in the refrigerator from one hour to overnight. When ready to serve, bake in a 350° oven for 45 minutes or until warmed through.

Serves 8.

Cheese Sauce:
3 tablespoons butter or margarine
3 tablespoons flour

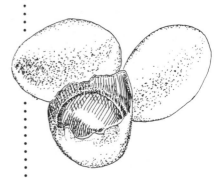

$2\frac{1}{2}$ cups reconstituted nonfat dry milk
   dash of salt and pepper
1 cup grated processed American cheese

Melt the butter or margarine in a medium skillet. Add the flour and stir in. Cook flour and butter together for a few minutes over medium heat. Add milk, stirring to blend well. Season with salt and pepper. When sauce begins to thicken, gradually add the cheese, stirring the sauce to melt the cheese. When all the cheese is melted, remove from heat.
Makes about $2\frac{1}{2}$ cups.

Mushroom and Asparagus Brunch Munch

Substitute:
• Frozen asparagus pieces for the broccoli
• Sautéed fresh mushrooms for the ham
• Swiss cheese for the American cheese

Turkey and Tomato Brunch Munch

Substitute:
• $\frac{1}{2}$ cup chopped fresh tomato for the green pepper
• Smoked turkey breast or unsmoked cooked turkey for the ham
• Broccoli can remain the same, or asparagus may be substituted
• Monterey Jack cheese for the American cheese

Zucchini and Mushroom Brunch Munch

Substitute:
• 3 cups of sliced fresh zucchini squash for the broccoli
• Mushrooms for the ham
• Monterey Jack cheese for the American cheese

Sausage Quiche

This is a bit heartier than most quiches. Use any kind of sausage you like in this: Italian, chorizo, regular breakfast sausage, hot or mild.

$\frac{1}{4}$ pound sausage, cooked and crumbled into small pieces
$\frac{1}{2}$ cup frozen cut broccoli, thawed
1 unbaked 9-inch pie shell
1 cup grated Monterey Jack cheese
$\frac{1}{4}$ cup grated Parmesan cheese
2 tablespoons chopped green onion
3 eggs
$\frac{3}{4}$ cup milk
$\frac{1}{4}$ teaspoon salt
    dash of pepper

Place the sausage and broccoli pieces in the pie shell. Stir together the Monterey Jack and Parmesan cheeses; place on top of sausage and broccoli. Sprinkle green onion on top. In a small bowl, stir together the eggs, milk, salt, and pepper, mixing well. Pour over the ingredients in pie shell. Bake in a 350° oven for 45 minutes or until browned and set. Allow to sit at least 5 to 10 minutes before cutting.
    Serves 6.

Fully thawed and/or cooked vegetables should be used in quiche so that they don't release liquid into the filling and contribute to a soggy crust.

Shrimp Quiche

Why not have a quiche buffet, where everyone brings a different kind of quiche? Add a big green salad and some rolls, and you have a wonderful meal.

2 cans ($4\frac{1}{2}$ ounces each) medium shrimp, drained
1 unbaked 9-inch pie shell
2 cups grated Swiss cheese
$\frac{1}{2}$ teaspoon tarragon
1 cup milk
1 tablespoon flour
2 eggs

Place the shrimp in the pie shell. Place the grated Swiss cheese on top and sprinkle with tarragon. Stir together the milk, flour, and eggs; pour over mixture in the pie shell. Bake in a 400° oven for 45 minutes to 1 hour, or until browned and set. Allow to stand 5 to 10 minutes before cutting.

Serves 6 to 8.

Cheese and Onion Pie

Traditional English fare, this cheese and onion pie is delicious hot or cold.

3 onions, cut in half and sliced thin
2 tablespoons butter or margarine
2 baked potatoes, peeled and sliced thin
1 unbaked 9-inch pie shell
$\frac{1}{2}$ pound grated sharp Cheddar cheese
2 eggs
1 cup milk
* salt and pepper*

Sauté the onions in butter or margarine until quite soft and browned. Layer onions and potatoes in the pie shell. In a medium bowl, stir together the cheese, eggs, milk, salt, and pepper; pour over onion and potatoes. Bake in a 350° oven for 45 to 60 minutes, or until pie is set.

Serves 6 to 8.

Deviled Eggs With Ham Sauce

This is another great brunch casserole you can assemble ahead of time and bake just before serving.

12 deviled-egg halves
2 cups diced ham
3 tablespoons butter or margarine
3 tablespoons flour
2 cups milk
$\frac{1}{4}$ teaspoon salt
  dash of pepper
  dash of liquid hot-pepper sauce
1$\frac{1}{3}$ cups bread cubes
$\frac{1}{4}$ cup melted butter or margarine
2 tablespoons chopped pimiento
1 tablespoon sliced, stuffed olives

Place the deviled eggs in one layer in a baking dish. Sprinkle the ham on top. In a skillet, melt 3 tablespoons butter or margarine, add flour, and stir for a few minutes. Add milk and cook, stirring constantly, until thick. Season with salt, pepper, and hot-pepper sauce. Pour the sauce over the eggs and ham. Top with the bread crumbs and spoon the melted butter on top. Garnish with pimiento and olives. Bake in a 350° oven for 20 to 30 minutes or until slightly browned—longer if prepared ahead and refrigerated.

Serves 6.

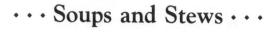

··· Soups and Stews ···

French Onion Soup

Often thought of as a sophisticated soup, French Onion Soup is actually quite simple to make. The secret to a good onion soup is to cook the onions slowly for a long time. Do not rush the process and you'll be rewarded by a richer taste.

¾ *cup butter or margarine*
¼ *cup vegetable oil*
13 large onions, thinly sliced
1 tablespoon sugar
12 cups of beef stock
   salt and pepper to taste
12 slices toasted French bread
12 slices Swiss cheese

Melt the butter or margarine in a large soup kettle. Add the vegetable oil and onions. Cook over medium heat until the onions are very soft and golden. Sprinkle on the sugar and stir into the onions, then continue cooking a few more minutes to slightly carmelize the onions. Add the broth, salt and pepper to taste, and simmer for 30 minutes.

To Serve:
   Preheat the oven to 450°. Ladle the soup into 12 soup bowls. Place a slice of toasted French bread on top of each bowl. Top the bread with a slice of cheese. Place soup bowls on cookie sheets and heat until the cheese melts, about 10 minutes. Serve immediately.
   Serves 12.

French Quarter Mushroom Soup

Creamy and delicious, this soup is good with a plain green salad tossed with a light dressing and hot French bread slices.

$\frac{1}{3}$ cup butter or margarine
2 small onions, sliced
2 pounds fresh mushrooms, cleaned and sliced
$\frac{1}{4}$ cup flour
6 cups chicken stock
4 cups half-and-half
$\frac{1}{8}$ teaspoon nutmeg
   salt and pepper to taste

Melt the butter or margarine in a large soup kettle. Cook the onions until tender, then add the mushrooms and cook over medium heat. Stir in the flour until it is absorbed by the butter or margarine. Add the chicken stock, bring to a boil, and reduce heat. Simmer for 30 minutes. Mix in the half-and-half, nutmeg, salt, and pepper. Heat through, but do not boil.
Serves 12 to 14.

Soup comes into its own, poor-man style, as a main course. One small serving of a ravishing soup is infuriating. It is like seeing the Pearly Gates swing shut in one's face after one brief glimpse of Heaven.
              Marjorie Kinnan
                   Rawlings

Curried Mushroom Soup

This is a hearty mushroom soup with a real punch to it. You can add more or less curry powder, depending upon the bravery of your taste buds.

4 tablespoons butter or margarine
2 onions, minced fine
2 to 3 cloves garlic, minced fine

3 or more teaspoons curry powder
3 cups chopped mushrooms
⅓ cup flour
¼ cup lemon juice
⅓ cup apricot jam
8 cups milk
3 cups chicken broth

Melt the butter or margarine in a large soup kettle. Add the onion, garlic, and curry powder, and sauté over low heat, stirring constantly, for 8 minutes. Add the mushrooms and cook until tender. Stir in the flour and cook 5 more minutes, then stir in the lemon juice and apricot jam, stirring until the jam liquifies. Pour in the milk and broth and heat through. Do not allow to boil.

Serves 12 to 14.

Hungarian Goulash Soup

To call this soup "hearty" is like calling Attila the Hun impolite. This is for when you are *hungry*. If you want something for a men's group winter luncheon, this would be perfect.

8 pounds beef chuck, cut into cubes
1 cup flour
1 tablespoon salt
1 teaspoon pepper
¾ cup butter or margarine
8 cups sliced onion
1 teaspoon garlic salt
2 tablespoons paprika
4 cans (8 ounces each) tomato sauce
6 cups water
6 cups beef stock
2 cups sour cream

Dust the beef cubes with the flour, salt, and pepper. Melt the butter in a large saucepan and brown the beef lightly. Add onion, garlic salt, and paprika and cook, stirring occasionally, until the onion is soft. Stir in the tomato sauce, water, and beef stock. Bring to a boil, reduce heat, and simmer for 3 hours. Just before serving, add sour cream. Serves 24.

Minestrone à la Genovese

Real minestrone is thick and delicious—not at all like that from a soup can. If you have access to fresh basil, use it generously in this soup.

1 quart water
4 potatoes, sliced
2 cans (16 ounces each) French-cut green beans undrained
3 cans (16 ounces each) stewed tomatoes
2 quarts water
3 cans (8 ounces each) tomato sauce
½ pound spaghetti, broken into 1-inch pieces
1 teaspoon salt
½ teaspoon pepper
2 teaspoons garlic powder
¼ teaspoon thyme
1 tablespoon basil
¼ cup olive oil
½ cup grated Parmesan cheese

In a large soup pot, place 1 quart of water and the potatoes. Cook for 15 minutes. Add the green beans, tomatoes (with juices), 2 additional quarts of water, tomato sauce, and spaghetti. Cook until the spaghetti is barely tender.

In a small bowl, mix together the salt, pepper, garlic powder, thyme, and basil. Add the olive oil and stir to combine. Slowly spoon this mixture into the soup, stirring constantly. Simmer 5 minutes on low heat. Just before serving, sprinkle on the Parmesan cheese.

Serves 24.

German Beef and Noodle Stew

This is almost a casserole, but since it's cooked like a stew, that is what it's called. The apple adds a bit of unexpected flavor.

3 pounds beef stew meat, cut into cubes
$\frac{1}{4}$ cup vegetable oil
3 large apples, peeled and chopped
2 large carrots, grated
2 onions, sliced
2 cloves garlic, minced
4 cups beef stock
1 bay leaf
$\frac{1}{4}$ teaspoon thyme
$\frac{1}{4}$ cup cornstarch
$\frac{1}{3}$ cup water
1 teaspoon Kitchen Bouquet
   salt and pepper to taste
12 cups cooked noodles

In a large kettle, brown the beef in vegetable oil. Add the apples, carrots, onion, and garlic. Add the beef stock, bay leaf, and thyme. Cover and cook over low heat for about 3 hours, adding liquid if necessary. At the end of that time, stir the cornstarch into the $\frac{1}{3}$ cup water and add to the stew. Cook and stir until thick. Add the Kitchen Bouquet; salt and pepper to taste. Serve over cooked noodles.

Serves 12.

A cold, crisp lettuce leaf gently dropped onto the surface of your soup or stew will absorb any elusive drops of fat or oil. Let them float until all the grease is absorbed, then carefully remove.

Fresh Cauliflower Soup

This soup is an especially good value in the summer, when cauliflower is plentiful, but if you don't have fresh cauliflower, you may use frozen. Substitute 2 large bags of frozen cauliflower for one fresh head.

1 medium cauliflower, cut into small pieces
2 onions, chopped
4 ribs celery, thinly sliced
3 cups chicken stock
4 tablespoons butter or margarine
3 tablespoons flour
1 teaspoon salt
$\frac{1}{4}$ teaspoon mace
3 cups milk
  fresh parsley for garnish

Place the cauliflower, onion, celery, and chicken stock in a saucepan. Simmer 20 minutes, or until vegetables are tender. Set aside, undrained. Melt the butter or margarine in a large soup pot; add flour, salt, and mace. Cook, stirring constantly, for 5 minutes. Pour in the milk and stir until smooth. Add cooked vegetables, along with the liquid they were cooked in, and stir over medium heat until smooth. Serve garnished with freshly chopped parsley.

Serves 6 to 8.

Soup Garnishes
· croutons
· grated cheese: Parmesan, Romano, Cheddar, Swiss
· chopped fresh herbs: dill, parsley, basil, thyme, chives
· finely chopped vegetables: cucumber, carrots, celery
· chopped green onion
· sour cream or plain yogurt
· soup crackers
· crunchy Chinese noodles

Cauliflower Cheese Soup

A very rich cauliflower soup, this tastes even better if it is made the day before or several hours before serving.

$\frac{1}{4}$ cup butter or margarine
$\frac{1}{2}$ onion, chopped
3 tablespoons flour
4 cups milk
3 cups frozen cauliflower pieces, thawed
$\frac{3}{4}$ cup grated Monterey Jack cheese
3 tablespoons grated Parmesan cheese
　　salt and pepper to taste

Melt the butter or margarine in a soup kettle and sauté the onion. Add the flour and cook a few minutes, then slowly pour in the milk, stirring constantly. Cook until the mixture begins to thicken. Add cauliflower and simmer for 10 minutes on very low heat, stirring occasionally to avoid scorching. Add cheeses, season, and stir until the cheeses dissolve.
Serves 6.

Broccoli Cheese Soup

5 tablespoons butter or margarine
2 onions, chopped
4 tablespoons flour
4 cups milk
3 cups chicken broth
4 cups cooked and chopped fresh or frozen broccoli
8 slices processed American cheese
　　salt and pepper to taste

Melt the butter or margarine in soup kettle; cook onions until soft. Add flour and blend in until the mixture is smooth. Pour in the milk and chicken broth and stir until smooth and slightly thickened. Add broccoli and cheese and stir over low to medium heat until cheese melts. Do not let soup boil. Season to taste.

Serves 12.

Split Pea Soup

With almost as many possible variations as there are for beef stew, Split Pea Soup is an American entertaining favorite. Hearty and rich, it is a soup everyone enjoys.

2 cups uncooked dried green split peas
14 cups of water
2 to 3 meaty ham hocks
1 large onion, cut into chunks
2 whole cloves garlic
2 carrots, cut into chunks
2 ribs celery, cut into chunks
2 teaspoons instant chicken bouillon powder
  salt and pepper to taste

Rinse the split peas thoroughly. Place all the ingredients in a large soup pot, bring to a boil, then reduce to simmer. Simmer, stirring occasionally, for 4 to 5 hours, or until the peas are tender. Remove the ham hocks from the soup. Cut off the meat and set the meat aside. Remove and discard the onion, garlic, carrots, and celery. Puree about half of the split peas and return to the pot. Add the reserved ham meat, adjust seasonings, and serve.

Serves 12.

Variations:
• Use yellow split peas instead of green ones.
• Use half split peas, half lentils.

Beautiful Soup, so rich and green,
Waiting in a hot tureen!
Who for such dainties
would not stoop!
Soup of the evening, beautiful Soup!
Soup of the evening, beautiful Soup!

Lewis Carroll

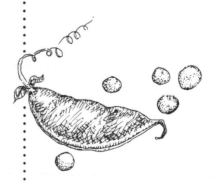

- Sauté 1 cup sliced carrots, 1 cup sliced celery, and 1 cup sliced onions until tender and add to the cooked split pea soup.
- Instead of plain water, substitute tomato sauce for some of the water. When the soup is cooked, thin with a can or two of pureed tomatoes.
- Use less water to cook the split peas and just before serving, thin with cream.
- Garnish before serving with additional chopped ham pieces or slices of sautéed sausage.

Black Bean Soup

Black beans form the basis for a number of delicious soups from South and Central America. Their delicious flavor is especially enhanced with lime and sour cream garnishes.

2½ cups uncooked dry black beans
8 cups chicken stock
2 tablespoons butter or margarine
1 onion, chopped
1 green pepper, chopped
2 tablespoons lime juice
1 teaspoon oregano
½ teaspoon cumin
1 teaspoon liquid hot-pepper sauce
1 teaspoon garlic powder
  salt to taste
  lime slices
  sour cream

Cover beans with water and soak overnight in a large soup kettle. The next day, drain off the water, add chicken stock, and cook beans until very tender (4 to 5 hours). After the beans are cooked, melt the butter or margarine in a skillet and sauté the onion and green pepper until tender.

Thicken soups, gravies, and sauces by gradually adding instant potato flakes. The flakes never lump when added directly as flour and cornstarch do, and they add to the texture.

Puree the beans, onion, and pepper in a blender or food processor until coarsely chopped, then return them to the soup kettle. Add the lime juice, oregano, cumin, hot-pepper sauce, garlic powder, and salt. Simmer 30 minutes. Adjust the seasonings. To serve, garnish with lime slices and sour cream. This soup freezes exceptionally well.

Serves 8.

All-Day Lentil Soup

1½ cups uncooked dry lentils
6 cups boiling water
1 can (16 ounces) whole tomatoes, chopped, with juice
1 can (6 ounces) tomato paste
2 large onions, sliced
6 carrots, sliced
¼ teaspoon crushed fennel seed
1 tablespoon garlic salt
1 teaspoon basil
1 tablespoon parsley
   dash of pepper

Rinse the lentils in several changes of water, then place them in a large soup kettle or a slow-cooker. Add boiling water, tomatoes (with juices), tomato paste, onion, carrots, and fennel seed. Simmer on low heat, stirring occasionally, for 8 to 10 hours. When done, season with garlic salt, basil, parsley, and pepper. Simmer for an additional 15 minutes; adjust the seasonings.

Serves 8.

Traditionally, many herbs and spices have symbolic meanings. The next time you add one of these fragrant flavors to your cooking, remember its hidden message.
allspice . . . compassion
basil . . . hatred
bay leaf . . . glory
cloves . . . dignity
coriander . . . hidden worth
marjoram . . . blushes
mint . . . virtue
parsley . . . festivity
rosemary . . . remembrance
saffron . . . beware of excess
sage . . . domestic virtue
tarragon . . . unselfish sharing
thyme . . . courage

Brunswick Stew

A traditional Southern stew that's hearty and satisfying.

$\frac{1}{3}$ cup butter or margarine
1 onion, chopped
1 chicken, cut up and skinned
6 cups chicken stock
1 package (10 ounces) frozen kernel corn, thawed
1 package (10 ounces) frozen lima beans, thawed
1 package (10 ounces) frozen cut okra, thawed
1 can (6 ounces) tomato paste
1 can (16 ounces) whole tomatoes, chopped
$\frac{1}{4}$ teaspoon cayenne pepper
  salt and pepper to taste

In a large soup pot, melt the butter or margarine and sauté the onion until tender. Cut the chicken into uniform-size pieces and brown them. Add the chicken broth, bring to a boil, then reduce to a simmer for 45 minutes. When the chicken is cooked, add the corn, lima beans, okra, tomato paste, tomatoes (with juices), cayenne pepper, salt, and pepper. Bring back to a boil, then simmer 15 minutes; adjust seasonings.
  Serves 8.

Mama's Chicken-Rice Soup

You may use either cooked chicken or <u>leftover</u> turkey in this recipe.

⅓ cup butter or margarine
1 cup finely chopped onion
1 clove garlic, finely minced
¾ cup finely chopped celery
1 carrot, finely sliced
2 tablespoons flour
12 cups chicken stock
3 cups cubed cooked chicken
2 cups cooked rice

Melt the butter or margarine in a large soup pot. Sauté the onion and garlic until tender. Add celery and carrot and cook about 10 minutes, stirring frequently. Add the flour and stir until absorbed, then pour in the chicken broth, cooked chicken, and cooked rice. Simmer for 30 minutes.
Serves 8 to 10.

Italian Wedding Soup

The Italian flavoring in the meatballs in this soup is fantastic—be sure not to use plain bread crumbs, or the flavor won't be the same.

1 pound ground chuck
1 cup Italian bread crumbs
2 eggs
13 cups chicken stock
2 onions, sliced
6 stalks celery, sliced
2 medium zucchini, sliced

Of soup and love, the first is best.
A Spanish proverb

1 package (10 ounces) frozen chopped spinach, thawed
3 cups cut-up cooked chicken
1 teaspoon garlic powder
½ teaspoon rosemary
1 tablespoon lemon juice
    salt and pepper to taste

Mix together the ground chuck, bread crumbs, and eggs. Form into 1-inch meatballs; set aside. Place chicken stock in a large soup pot. Bring to a simmer. Add the onions, celery, and zucchini. Gently add the meatballs. Simmer 20 minutes, then add the spinach, chicken, garlic powder, rosemary, lemon juice, salt, and pepper. Simmer 15 minutes until heated through; adjust the seasonings.

Serves 24.

Crab Gazpacho

The addition of crabmeat makes this traditional cold soup hearty enough to serve as a luncheon entrée on a warm summer day.

1 can (46 ounces) tomato juice
2 ripe tomatoes
1 cucumber, peeled
2 cloves garlic, finely chopped
½ green pepper, chopped
3 green onions, finely chopped
2 tablespoons parsley
1 teaspoon basil
1 teaspoon tarragon
2 tablespoons olive oil
3 tablespoons lime juice
1 can (6 ounces) crabmeat, drained and flaked
    salt, pepper, and hot-pepper sauce to taste

Using a food processor or blender, pour in part of the tomato juice and blend in batches with the

When most recipes call for herbs they mean dried herbs, which are more available. To substitute fresh herbs for dried herbs, use three times the amount called for in the recipe. The flavor of dried herbs is much more concentrated than the flavor in fresh herbs.

tomatoes, cucumber, garlic, green pepper, and green onions, until all the vegetables are just barely chopped and still chunky. Pour this mixture into a large bowl. Stir in parsley, basil, tarragon, olive oil, and lime juice. Stir in crabmeat. Season to taste with salt, pepper, and liquid hot-pepper sauce. Chill for several hours (or overnight).

Serves 10 to 12.

Clam and Mushroom Soup

Different from most clam chowders, this contains no potatoes or tomatoes.

$\frac{1}{2}$ cup butter or margarine
2 small onions, finely chopped
3 cups fresh sliced mushrooms
3 tablespoons flour
5 cups milk
3 cups half-and-half
3 cans ($6\frac{1}{2}$ ounces) minced clams with juice
    salt and pepper to taste

Melt butter or margarine in the bottom of a soup pot. Sauté the onions and mushrooms briefly, until onion pieces become clear. Add flour and cook, stirring, for 3 to 4 minutes. Add milk and half-and-half, stirring constantly, and cook until slightly thickened. Add clams and clam juice; season to taste with salt and pepper. Heat through, being careful not to boil.

Serves 12.

New England Clam Chowder

⅓ pound salt pork, finely diced
1 onion, diced
5 cups water
10 medium potatoes, peeled and cut into chunks
4 cans (6½ ounces each) minced clams with juice
4 cups milk
3 cups half-and-half
¼ cup butter
    salt and pepper to taste

In a large soup pot, fry the salt pork until it is crisp. Add onion and cook on low heat until soft and clear. Add water, potatoes, and drained liquid from the clams. Cook, covered, until the potatoes are tender, 10 to 15 minutes. Add clams, milk, half-and-half, and butter. Heat through gently, making sure you don't let it boil. Season to taste with salt and pepper.
    Serves 12.

Only the pure of heart can make a good soup.
    Ludwig van Beethoven

Boise Potato Soup

In addition to being tasty, this is one of the most inexpensive soups to make for a large group.

¼ cup butter or margarine
2 onions, chopped
3 ribs celery, finely sliced
10 potatoes, peeled and diced
6 cups of water
4 teaspoons instant chicken bouillon powder
1 cup nonfat dry milk powder
6 cups whole milk
    salt and pepper to taste

Melt the butter or margarine in a large soup pot. Add the onions, celery, potatoes, water, and chicken bouillon. Cook until the potatoes are very tender. Remove about $\frac{1}{3}$ of the potatoes and puree, then return to soup pot. Add dry powdered milk, whole milk, and salt and pepper to taste. Heat through to serve, but do not allow to boil.

Serves 12.

Variations:

There are innumerable ways you can flavor potato soup. Here are just a few ideas to get your imagination started:

- Add 1 cooked package (20 ounces) of frozen chopped broccoli
- Add 3 cups of sliced mushrooms.
- Add 2 cups of shrimp, crab, or any cooked white fish.
- Add one or two cans ($15\frac{1}{2}$ ounces each) of butter beans.
- Stir in 2 cups of grated Swiss, Cheddar, or processed American cheese.
- Add 2 cups sautéed sausage or wurst slices.
- Garnish with a pat of butter and a sprinkle of parsley.

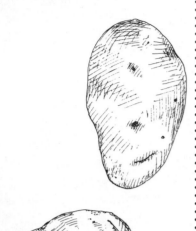

Great Plains Corn-Potato Chowder

Simple and satisfying.

12 potatoes, peeled and finely cubed
6 onions, chopped
6 cups water
8 slices bacon
2 cans (16 ounces each) whole kernel corn
2 cans (16 ounces each) creamed corn
1 quart milk
1 quart half-and-half
1 teaspoon celery salt
$\frac{1}{4}$ cup butter or margarine
  salt and pepper to taste

Place the potatoes, onions, and water in a large soup kettle. Cook until potatoes are soft. While this is cooking, sauté the bacon until crisp, drain, and crumble. Add cooked bacon, whole kernel corn, creamed corn, milk, half-and-half, celery salt, and butter or margarine to cooked potatoes. Cook over medium heat, stirring frequently, until butter or margarine is melted and soup is heated through. Do not allow to boil. Add salt and pepper to taste.

Serves 12.

Tuna Chowder

Just as hearty as some of the stews made with beef, this is an inexpensive yet satisfying main-dish soup.

⅓ cup finely diced salt pork
2 onions, diced
3 cups diced potatoes
3 cups water
2 cans (6½ ounces each) water-packed tuna, drained and flaked
3 cups milk or half-and-half
salt and pepper to taste

In a soup pot, place the salt pork and cook over low heat until crisp, then sauté onions until tender. Add potatoes and water, cook until the potatoes are tender, then add tuna, milk or half-and-half, and salt and pepper to taste. Heat through, but do not boil.

Serves 12.

Chicken Stock

Making your own homemade stock is not difficult, and the results are delicious. You can use it as a base for any soup recipe that calls for chicken stock, or you can make a light, delicious soup by simply adding a bit of pasta, rice, or a few vegetables.

When you cook chicken, save the backs, necks, and gizzards for making stock. Keep a bag in the freezer and add to it whenever you get the chance.

3 pounds chicken parts
3 quarts water
2 onions, cut into chunks
2 carrots, cut into chunks
2 ribs celery, cut into chunks

A peeled raw potato placed in a soup or stew that has been oversalted will absorb some of the salty flavor.

1 bay leaf
2 whole cloves garlic
3 peppercorns
1 teaspoon thyme

Place all ingredients into a large soup kettle. Heat to boiling, then reduce to a simmer. Skim off any scum that forms; simmer for two hours. Strain the soup. Place in refrigerator and chill until fat solidifies on the top. Remove the fat. If you want a more concentrated flavor, return to the stove and cook until reduced by one-third.

Makes about 3 quarts.

Stock will keep in the refrigerator for 3 to 4 days or in the freezer for up to 2 months.

Beef Stock

Roasting the beef bones first gives the stock a heartier flavor and nicer color. However, if you are in a hurry and are going to use the stock simply as a base for a hearty soup, you can omit roasting the bones.

5 pounds beef bones (shanks, ribs, or soup bones)
12 cups water
3 onions, cut into chunks
2 carrots, cut into chunks
3 ribs celery, cut into chunks
10 peppercorns
3 cloves garlic
2 bay leaves

Place the bones in a roasting pan and bake in a 450° oven for 45 minutes, turning occasionally. Remove bones from the oven and place them, with the remaining ingredients, in a large soup kettle. Bring to a boil, reduce to a simmer, and cook for 4 to 5 hours. Discard any scum that forms. Strain the soup and place the stock in the refrigerator until the fat solidifies. Remove the fat. If you desire a richer broth, return to the stove and cook until it is reduced by one-third.

Makes 2 to 3 quarts.

Croutons

6 slices bread
  softened butter or margarine

Very lightly butter the bread. Cut bread into $\frac{1}{2}$-inch cubes; spread on a cookie sheet. Bake in a 400° oven for 10 to 15 minutes, or until lightly browned. Turn off oven, leave door ajar, and allow the croutons to dry out for about an hour. Stir during baking and drying, and don't allow to burn.

Makes about $1\frac{1}{2}$ cups.

Variation:
For Garlic or Herb Croutons, add minced garlic or minced fresh herbs to butter before spreading it on the bread.

Vegetables and Side Dishes

· · · Vegetables · · ·

Fresh Vegetables

There is probably nothing better than fresh vegetables straight from the garden: green peas, snap beans, sweet corn, summer squash. Add a bit of butter, and, if you want, a little salt, and you have a heavenly treat.

When planning a community meal, try to feature vegetables that are in season. Or plan a harvest meal taking advantage of garden abundance. For example, the fortunate folks who live in the Midwest could celebrate with a feast of sweet corn on the cob.

For a large group, allow about $\frac{1}{2}$ cup of vegetables per serving.

Clean, trim, and cut up vegetables. A favorite method of cooking most fresh vegetables is to steam them in a little bit of water until they are very tender. Add a little butter and serve.

Another method is to cook them quickly in boiling water. Use lots of water so that it returns to boiling immediately after the vegetables are added. Cook the vegetables until tender-crisp. The best test for doneness is tasting. Drain, add butter, and serve.

And enjoy them!

Potluck Green Beans

This dish is always at potlucks and always wonderful.

2 cans (16 ounces each) green beans, drained
2 tablespoons butter or margarine
2 tablespoons flour
1 can ($10\frac{3}{4}$ ounces) cream of mushroom soup, undiluted
$\frac{1}{4}$ cup milk
1 teaspoon Worcestershire sauce — opt.
  dash of salt and pepper
$\frac{3}{4}$ cup grated Cheddar cheese
1 can (2.8 ounces) French-fried onions

Place green beans in a casserole. Melt the butter or margarine in a skillet, stir in the flour, and cook for a few minutes. Add the mushroom soup, milk, Worcestershire sauce, salt, and pepper; stir until smooth. Pour the sauce over the green beans. Stir in Cheddar cheese and top with French-fried onions. Bake in a 350° oven for 20 to 30 minutes.

Serves 8.

Sweet corn was our family's weakness. We were prepared to resist atheistic Communism, immoral Hollywood, hard liquor, gambling and dancing, smoking, fornication, but if Satan had come around with sweet corn, we at least would have listened to what he had to sell. We might not have bought it but we would've had him in and given him a cup of coffee.

Garrison Keillor

not necessary to do the marg - flour bit.

Boston Baked Beans

When we think of baked beans, this is the traditional dish it all started from.

3 pounds navy beans
6 quarts water
2 cups molasses
2 tablespoons dry mustard
2 teaspoons salt
$\frac{1}{2}$ teaspoon pepper
$\frac{1}{2}$ pound salt pork, diced
2 large onions, chopped

Never add salt to any kind of cooked beans until they are soft. If you add the salt first, it prevents the beans from absorbing the water and they will stay hard.

Rinse beans in water. Place in a very large kettle and soak overnight. In the morning bring water and beans to boiling, reduce heat and simmer about 2 hours or until tender.

Drain, reserving liquid. Add molasses, dry mustard, salt, pepper, salt pork, and onions. Stir to combine. Add enough reserved bean liquid until it covers the beans about $\frac{1}{2}$ inch. Place in a large bean pot or casserole and bake at 300° for 4 hours. Stir occasionally and add more liquid if it dries out.

Serves 24.

Easy Baked Beans

Using canned beans makes this recipe easy, and adding your own ingredients makes it delicious!

6 slices bacon, diced
1 onion, chopped
2 cans (21 ounces each) pork and beans
1 teaspoon dry mustard
1 teaspoon chili powder
  dash of garlic salt
$\frac{1}{2}$ cup ketchup
$\frac{1}{2}$ cup firmly packed brown sugar or molasses

Sauté the bacon and onion until the onion is soft. Drain. In a 1½-quart casserole stir together the bacon and onion, beans, mustard, chili powder, garlic salt, ketchup, and brown sugar or molasses. Bake uncovered in a 350° oven for about 45 minutes.

Serves 6 to 8.

Barbecued Green Beans

Lighter than barbecued baked beans, this goes well with grilled chicken.

⅓ cup chopped onion
5 slices uncooked bacon, diced
¾ cup ketchup
⅓ cup firmly packed brown sugar
½ teaspoon dried mustard
1 tablespoon Worcestershire sauce
4 cups cooked, fresh, French-cut green beans
or
2 cans (16 ounces each) French-cut green beans, drained

Place the onion and bacon in a skillet and cook until onion is soft and bacon is crisp. Add ketchup, brown sugar, dried mustard, and Worcestershire sauce. Stir to combine; simmer 2 minutes. Place beans in a casserole; top with the sauce. Bake in a 350° oven for 30 minutes.

Serves 8.

Herbed Broccoli With Brussels Sprouts and Carrots

Don't let the seemingly large amount of herbs in this recipe scare you—the strong, natural flavors of the vegetables complement the spices perfectly.

Cutting an X into the stem end of Brussels sprouts with a sharp knife will cause them to cook more quickly, evenly, and with little loss of shape.

1 pound broccoli, cut into bite-size pieces
1 pound Brussels sprouts, trimmed
1 pound carrots, sliced
$\frac{1}{2}$ cup butter or margarine
$\frac{1}{4}$ cup lemon juice
1 teaspoon salt
$\frac{1}{2}$ teaspoon pepper
1 teaspoon basil
1 teaspoon oregano
1 teaspoon marjoram

Cook the vegetables until barely tender by either steaming or boiling them. After cooking, drain well and place in a 9- by 13-inch casserole.

In a small skillet, melt the butter or margarine. Add the lemon juice and spices, cook on low heat for 5 minutes, and pour over the vegetables. Cover and bake in a 350° oven for 20 minutes.

Serves 12.

Broccoli Supreme

Dry stuffing mix is a great topper for all sorts of vegetables. If you like it in this dish, try it in others.

2 packages (10 ounces each) frozen chopped or cut
  broccoli, thawed and drained
2 cans (16 ounces each) creamed corn
2 slightly beaten eggs
2 tablespoons chopped green onion
½ teaspoon salt
  dash of pepper
2 cups herb stuffing mix
½ cup melted butter

Place the broccoli in a large bowl. In a separate bowl, stir together the creamed corn, eggs, green onion, salt, and pepper. Stir this mixture into the broccoli. In a separate bowl, toss together the stuffing mix and the butter. Reserving ½ cup of the buttered stuffing mix, stir the remainder into the broccoli mix. Spoon into a 9- by 13-inch baking dish; top with the reserved stuffing. Bake in a 350° oven for 35 to 40 minutes.

Serves 12.

Broccoli and Tomatoes

The red and green colors of this dish make it perfect for Christmastime buffets.

2 pounds fresh broccoli spears
1 pound cherry tomatoes
2 tablespoons butter or margarine
2 tablespoons flour

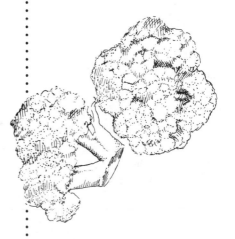

1 cup milk
½ cup salad dressing or mayonnaise
¼ cup grated Parmesan cheese

Cook broccoli in boiling water until barely tender. Drain and place in a 9- by 13-inch baking dish. Reserve a few cherry tomatoes for garnish and add the rest to the baking dish. Melt the butter or margarine in a small skillet. Add the flour and cook for a few minutes. Stir together the milk and salad dressing or mayonnaise, add to skillet, and cook, stirring constantly, until smooth. Add Parmesan cheese and cook, stirring constantly, until melted. Pour the sauce over the broccoli and tomatoes in the baking dish. Top with reserved cherry tomatoes, cut in half. Bake covered in a 350° oven for 30 minutes.
Serves 8.

Garden State Vegetable Medley

1 package (10 ounces) frozen Brussels sprouts
1 package (10 ounces) frozen broccoli flowerettes
1 package (10 ounces) frozen Chinese pea pods
1 can (8 ounces) sliced water chestnuts, drained
¼ cup butter or margarine
⅓ cup bread crumbs
1 cup sliced almonds
1 tablespoon soy sauce

Allow frozen vegetables to thaw by placing them in a colander and running warm water over them. Drain well and place in a casserole. Add water chestnuts and toss gently to combine. In a saucepan, melt the butter or margarine. Add the bread crumbs and almonds and sauté a few minutes.

Broccoli is sometimes referred to as a super-vegetable. It is low in calories and sodium, but is a good souce of vitamins A and C, calcium, potassium, and beta-carotene. Beta-carotene is thought to have cancer-inhibiting properties.

Sprinkle on soy sauce and stir in. Spoon this mixture over the vegetables. Bake covered in a 325° oven for 30 minutes.

Serves 8 to 10.

Variation:

To make the dish with fresh vegetables, you may substitute the following for the frozen vegetables:

$1\frac{1}{2}$ *cups fresh Brussels sprouts, steamed till tender*
$1\frac{1}{2}$ *cups broccoli flowerettes, steamed till tender*
1 cup Chinese pea pods, steamed till tender

Red Cabbage

A tangy, tart dish that is great with a roast or ham. It keeps well in the refrigerator.

1 medium head red cabbage, grated
2 large tart apples, peeled and grated
1 medium onion, chopped
$1\frac{1}{2}$ *cups water*
1 cup vinegar
$\frac{3}{4}$ *cup sugar*
1 piece cooked, crumbled bacon
1 bay leaf
2 whole cloves
2 whole allspice
6 peppercorns
2 tablespoons cornstarch
$\frac{1}{4}$ *cup cold water*

Place the cabbage, apples, and onion in a large kettle. In a separate bowl, stir together $1\frac{1}{2}$ cups water, vinegar, and sugar until the sugar is dissolved. Pour over the vegetables, then add the bacon. Tie the bay leaf, cloves, allspice, and peppercorns in a small cheesecloth bag and place in the kettle. Simmer for $1\frac{1}{2}$ to 2 hours. Remove the bag of spices. Mix the cornstarch with $\frac{1}{4}$ cup water and add to the cabbage. Cook, stirring gently, until the mixture thickens slightly. May be served hot or cold.

Serves 12 or more as a garnish, 6 to 8 as a vegetable.

Carrots and Walnuts

Walnuts and soy sauce spice up the carrots beautifully.

2 pounds carrots, thinly sliced
3 tablespoons butter or margarine
2 tablespoons lemon juice
1 cup coarsely chopped walnuts
1 tablespoon soy sauce

Sauté the carrots in melted butter or margarine and lemon juice until barely tender. Mix in the walnuts and soy sauce. Spoon into a casserole and bake covered in a 350° oven for 15 minutes.
Serves 8.

Scalloped Carrots With Cheese

Though similar to scalloped potatoes, the carrots are sweeter and more flavorful than potatoes.

12 carrots, thinly sliced
1 small onion, minced
$\frac{1}{2}$ cup butter or margarine
$\frac{1}{4}$ cup flour

1 teaspoon salt
$\frac{1}{4}$ teaspoon dry mustard
2 cups milk
$\frac{1}{8}$ teaspoon pepper
$\frac{1}{4}$ teaspoon celery salt
2 cups grated Cheddar cheese
3 cups fresh bread cubes
$\frac{1}{3}$ cup melted butter or margarine

Cook the carrots in boiling water or steam them until they are tender. In a saucepan, melt $\frac{1}{2}$ cup butter or margarine and sauté onion. Add the flour, salt, and dry mustard, and cook a few minutes, stirring constantly. Pour in the milk and cook, stirring until smooth. Season with pepper and celery salt; set aside.

In a 2-quart casserole, arrange a layer of cooked carrots, then a layer of cheese. Repeat until all are used up. Pour on the sauce, top with the bread cubes, and spoon on $\frac{1}{3}$ cup melted butter or margarine. Bake in a 350° oven 45 minutes.

Serves 8.

Twin Cities Celery Hot Dish

Though we usually think of celery as an ingredient in other dishes, it is a very tasty vegetable on its own and an unusual treat at a potluck.

2 tablespoons butter or margarine
5 cups sliced celery
1 jar (2 ounces) sliced pimiento
1 jar (8 ounces) sliced water chestnuts, drained
1 can (10$\frac{3}{4}$ ounces) cream of chicken soup, undiluted
$\frac{1}{4}$ teaspoon celery salt
1 cup fresh bread crumbs
$\frac{1}{4}$ cup sliced almonds

Melt butter or margarine in a skillet. Add celery and sauté gently until barely tender. Place in a casserole and add pimiento, water chestnuts, soup, and celery salt. Stir to combine. Top with bread crumbs and sliced almonds. Bake uncovered in a 350° oven for 35 minutes.

Serves 8.

Nebraska Corn Pudding

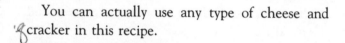

You can actually use any type of cheese and cracker in this recipe.

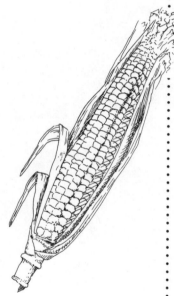

4 cups fresh or frozen corn kernels

or

2 cans (16 ounces each) whole kernel corn, undrained
2 cups milk
2 cups grated Cheddar, Monterey Jack, or American cheese
16 crushed crackers
3 eggs, slightly beaten

Stir all ingredients together and place in a casserole. Bake in a 350° oven for 45 minutes or until set.

Serves 8.

Baked Onions

A bit out of the ordinary, this makes a nice side dish with turkey or ham.

8 onions, thinly sliced
$\frac{1}{4}$ cup butter or margarine
$\frac{1}{4}$ cup flour
2 cups milk
$\frac{1}{4}$ teaspoon dry mustard
2 cups grated Cheddar or Monterey Jack cheese
    salt and pepper to taste
    paprika

Layer sliced onions in a well-buttered 7- by 11-inch casserole. In a medium saucepan, melt the butter or margarine. Blend the flour in with the butter or margarine and cook for a few minutes, stirring constantly. Pour in the milk and stir to make a smooth sauce. Add the dry mustard, then gradually stir in the cheese until it melts. Season to taste with salt and pepper. Pour cheese sauce over the onion rings and sprinkle with paprika for garnish. Bake uncovered in a 325° oven for one hour.

Serves 6 to 8.

English Pea Casserole

The celery and water chestnuts provide a tasty crunch for this casserole. This freezes well, if you want to make it a week or so in advance.

$\frac{1}{2}$ cup butter or margarine
1 cup chopped celery
1 cup chopped onion
1 can (8 ounces) water chestnuts, drained and chopped

What God gives and what we take,
'Tis a gift for Christ His sake:
Be the meal of beans and pease,
God be thanked for those and these:
Have we flesh, or have we fish,
All are fragments from his dish.

Robert Herrick

1 jar (4 ounces) sliced pimiento
2 packages (10 ounces each) frozen peas (or 3 to 4 cups cooked fresh peas)
1 can (10¾ ounces) cream of mushroom soup, undiluted

Melt butter or margarine in a skillet over medium heat. Sauté the celery and onions until the onions are barely tender. Stir in the water chestnuts and pimiento pieces.

Defrost the peas slightly by running warm water over them, then place in a casserole. Pour the other vegetables and the melted butter or margarine over the peas. Stir in the mushroom soup. Bake covered in a 350° oven for 30 minutes.

Serves 12.

Stuffed Green Peppers

One very nice thing about this dish is that the servings come in easy-to-manage containers—the green peppers.

8 green peppers
6 slices bacon
1 cup chopped onion
⅓ cup chopped green pepper
2 cans (16 ounces each) whole tomatoes, chopped, with juice
3 cups water
1 cup chili sauce
1½ cups long-grain white rice, uncooked
2 cups grated Cheddar cheese (optional)

Cut the tops off the green peppers and carefully core and seed them. Bring a big pot of water to a boil, drop in the peppers, boil for 5 minutes, and remove.

In a separate pan, sauté the bacon and remove when crisp. Sauté the onion and pepper in the bacon grease until soft. Add the tomatoes, water, chili sauce, and rice. Bring to a boil, cover, reduce heat, and cook for 30 minutes or until rice is done. When done, crumble the bacon over the rice mixture and stir it in.

Fill the peppers and place in 9- by 13-inch baking dish. Place any leftover rice around the peppers. Bake in a 350° oven for 20 to 30 minutes until heated through. If desired, you can also place grated cheese on top of the peppers.

Serves 8.

Variations:
- You may add $\frac{1}{2}$ to 1 pound of cooked ground beef to the rice mixture.
- You may pour tomato sauce over the peppers before baking them.

Potatoes With Rosemary

This dish is nice if you want to serve potatoes but don't want a heavy cream sauce with them.

3 pounds new potatoes
$\frac{1}{3}$ cup butter or margarine
$\frac{1}{2}$ teaspoon rosemary
$\frac{1}{2}$ teaspoon summer savory
1 teaspoon salt
$\frac{1}{2}$ teaspoon pepper

Scrub the potatoes, cut in half or quarter, and place in a 9- by 13-inch baking pan. Melt butter or margarine; add rosemary, savory, salt, and pepper; cook over low heat for 5 minutes. Pour seasoned

butter over potatoes; toss to coat. Cover and bake in a 350° oven for 1 hour, or until potatoes are tender. Stir to recoat with butter several times during the baking.

Serves 8.

Easy Scalloped Potatoes

Scalloped potatoes are a favorite side dish at community meals, especially when served with baked ham.

8 cups peeled and raw potatoes
1 onion, sliced and separated into rings
$\frac{1}{2}$ teaspoon salt
1 can ($10\frac{3}{4}$ ounces) cream of mushroom soup, undiluted
1 package (3 ounces) cream cheese, softened
1 cup milk
$1\frac{1}{2}$ cups grated Cheddar cheese

Layer potatoes and onion rings in a 9- by 13-inch pan. In a bowl, mix together until smooth the salt, mushroom soup, cream cheese, and milk. Pour over the potatoes; sprinkle cheese on top. Cover and bake in a 350° oven for $1\frac{1}{2}$ hours.

Serves 12.

Potatoes Primavera

6 potatoes, thinly sliced
1 large green pepper, sliced into thin strips
1 white onion, thinly sliced
$\frac{1}{4}$ cup olive oil
2 large tomatoes, sliced
$\frac{1}{4}$ teaspoon oregano
  dash of salt and pepper

In a large skillet, lightly brown the potatoes, green pepper, and onion in the olive oil. Place these vegetables in a casserole and add the tomatoes, salt, pepper, and oregano. Stir to combine. Cover and bake in a 375° oven for 30 minutes or until potatoes are cooked through.

Serves 8 to 10.

Fancy Potatoes

This is a convenient way to serve mashed potatoes, since it may be made ahead.

9 large potatoes, cooked and mashed
2 packages (8 ounces each) cream cheese, softened
1 cup melted butter or margarine
1½ cups sour cream
1½ teaspoons salt
½ teaspoon white pepper
1 cup toasted almond slivers
2 tablespoons chives or chopped green onion

Place the mashed potatoes in a large bowl. Beat the cream cheese into the potatoes, then beat in the butter or margarine, sour cream, salt, and pepper. Spoon into casserole; top with toasted almonds and chives or green onions. Bake in a 375° oven for 30 minutes.

Serves 12.

For fluffy mashed potatoes, the liquid to be added should be hot. Don't try to save time by preparing mashed potatoes in a blender—the mixture will have a gummy consistency.

Party Hash Browns

This is great to serve at a brunch with quiche and fruit.

2 tablespoons butter or margarine
1 small onion, chopped
1 green pepper, chopped
3 ribs celery, chopped
1 can (2 ounces) pimientos, chopped
2 cups grated Cheddar cheese
4 cups finely diced cooked potatoes

or

1 package (32 ounces) frozen hash browns, defrosted
1 can (10¾ ounces) cream of chicken or cream of mushroom soup, undiluted
½ cup melted butter or margarine
1 teaspoon salt
1 cup sour cream
paprika for garnish

Melt the 2 tablespoons of butter or margarine in a medium skillet. Add the onions, green pepper, and celery; sauté until onion is clear. Stir onions, green peppers, celery, pimientos, and cheese into the potatoes.

In a separate bowl, stir together the soup, ½ cup melted butter or margarine, salt, and sour cream. Stir into hash brown mixture.

Spoon into a 9- by 13-inch baking dish; sprinkle on paprika. Bake in a 350° oven for 45 to 50 minutes, or until lightly browned.

Serves 12 to 16.

Only two things in this world are too serious to be jested on—potatoes and matrimony.

An Irish proverb

Hash-Brown Heaven

4 cups finely diced cooked potatoes

or

1 package (32 ounces) frozen hash browns, thawed
1 can (10¾ ounces) cream of potato soup, undiluted
1 can (10¾ ounces) cream of celery soup, undiluted
1 cup milk
1 cup sour cream
2 teaspoons salt
½ teaspoon pepper
1½ cups grated Cheddar cheese

Place the potatoes in a 9- by 13-inch baking dish. In a separate bowl, stir together the potato soup, celery soup, milk, sour cream, salt, and pepper. Stir into hash browns. Bake in a 350° oven for 1¼ hours. Remove from oven, top with cheese, and cook until cheese melts.

Serves 12.

All-American Yams

Baked yams are a traditional Thanksgiving favorite, but the ways they are prepared vary tremendously. Below is a basic recipe with a bounty of regional variations.

6 to 8 large fresh yams
⅓ cup butter or margarine
½ cup honey or firmly packed brown sugar
¼ teaspoon salt
½ teaspoon cinnamon

Scrub the yams and bake in a 350° oven until soft, about 1 hour. Allow to cool, then peel and slice. Layer in a casserole. In a small saucepan, melt together the butter or margarine, honey or brown sugar, cinnamon, and salt. Pour over sliced yams. Bake in a 350° oven for 30 minutes.

Serves 6 to 8.

Regional Variations:
- Northeastern: Substitute maple syrup for the honey or brown sugar.
- Northwestern: Sauté 1 cup of chopped hazelnuts in 2 tablespoons of butter until golden; top yams with nuts and bake.
- Southern: Peel and slice 3 navel oranges. Layer yam slices and orange slices. Pour $\frac{1}{2}$ cup of orange juice over the casserole before baking.

Although sweet potatoes and yams belong to different botanical groups, they are interchangeable for cooking purposes—preference being a matter of individual taste.

Crunchy Topped Sweet Potatoes

6 to 8 sweet potatoes, baked, peeled, and sliced
or
3 cans (16 ounces each) sweet potatoes, drained
1 teaspoon vanilla
3 tablespoons frozen orange-juice concentrate, thawed
$1\frac{1}{4}$ cups firmly packed brown sugar
$\frac{1}{2}$ cup softened butter or margarine
1 teaspoon baking powder
3 eggs, slightly beaten
$\frac{1}{3}$ cup butter or margarine, melted and cooled
$\frac{1}{2}$ cup firmly packed brown sugar
2 cups crisp rice or corn cereal
$\frac{1}{2}$ cup finely chopped pecans

In a large bowl, beat together the sweet potatoes, vanilla, orange-juice concentrate, brown sugar, butter or margarine, baking powder, and eggs. Spoon into a casserole. Bake in a 350° oven for 20 minutes.

While baking, combine $\frac{1}{3}$ cup butter or margarine, brown sugar, cereal, and pecans. Add topping to potatoes and bake 10 minutes more.

Serves 8 to 10.

Whipped Sweet Potatoes

1 package (3 ounces) cream cheese, softened
$\frac{1}{2}$ cup sour cream
1 egg
$\frac{1}{2}$ cup firmly packed brown sugar
8 to 10 sweet potatoes, baked, peeled, and sliced
or
3 cans (16 ounces each) drained sweet potatoes
$1\frac{1}{7}$ cups miniature marshmallows
  nutmeg

Beat until smooth the cream cheese, sour cream, egg, and brown sugar. Add a few sweet potatoes at a time and beat until smooth. Spoon into a casserole. Bake in a 325° oven for 1 hour. Remove from oven, top with marshmallows, and sprinkle with nutmeg. Return to oven until marshmallows are melted, about 10 minutes.

Serves 8 to 10.

Baked Sauerkraut

4 slices uncooked bacon, diced
1 medium onion, chopped
1 cup firmly packed brown sugar
2 tablespoons cider vinegar
1 teaspoon salt
  dash of pepper
1 bag or can (16 ounces) sauerkraut, drained
1 can (16 ounces) whole tomatoes, drained and
  chopped

Fry bacon and onion until the bacon is crisp and the onion is limp. Add the brown sugar, vinegar, salt, and pepper; stir to combine. Place sauerkraut and tomatoes in a casserole and top with the bacon mixture. Stir gently to combine. Bake in a 350° oven for 30 minutes.

Serves 8.

Spinach Squares

A great vegetable for a group—bake and cut it into serving portions. Couldn't be simpler.

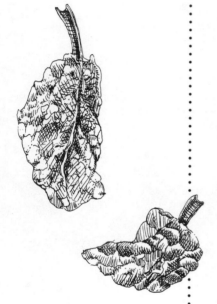

4 packages (10 ounces each) frozen chopped spinach, thawed
2 cups cooked white rice
½ cup chopped green onion
2 cups grated Swiss cheese
2 cans ((10¾ ounces each) cream of mushroom soup, undiluted
6 eggs, lightly beaten
¼ teaspoon basil
¼ teaspoon oregano
   dash of salt and pepper
¼ cup grated Parmesan cheese

Drain spinach and squeeze out as much moisture as possible. Place spinach in a large bowl and combine with the rice, green onion, and Swiss cheese. In a separate bowl, combine the mushroom soup, beaten eggs, basil, oregano, salt, and pepper. Add this mixture to the spinach mixture and stir to combine. Spoon into a well-buttered 9- by 13-inch pan; sprinkle with Parmesan cheese. Bake uncovered in a 325° oven for 35 minutes or until very lightly browned. Allow to sit 15 minutes before cutting into squares.

Serves 10 to 12.

Variations:

You may substitute other vegetables for the spinach. Chopped broccoli is especially good.

Harvest Squash Medley

Though this recipe calls for butternut squash, you may use any type of winter squash. For a surprising and tasty variation, substitute fresh pumpkin for the squash.

2 medium butternut squash
3 medium yams
3 apples
⅓ cup butter or margarine
½ cup honey
½ cup orange juice
1 teaspoon cinnamon
¼ teaspoon nutmeg
1 cup chopped walnuts

Peel and cut the squash, yams, and apples into bite-size chunks; mix together. Place in a 9- by 13-inch casserole. In a small saucepan, melt the butter or margarine. Add the honey, orange juice, cinnamon, and nutmeg. Cook, stirring constantly, until combined. Pour this mixture over the vegetables; sprinkle walnuts on top. Cover and bake in a 350° oven for 1½ hours.

Serves 6 to 8.

Creamed Zucchini and Corn

You may substitute yellow squash or any other summer squash for the zucchini in this recipe. You may also use fresh corn instead of canned. Summer or winter, this is a refreshing vegetable dish.

2 cans (16 ounces each) whole kernel corn, drained
5 cups sliced zucchini
1 can (4 ounces) sliced mushrooms, drained
$\frac{1}{2}$ cup sour cream
1 teaspoon instant chicken bouillon powder
1 teaspoon dill weed
1 tablespoon flour
$\frac{1}{2}$ teaspoon salt

Combine the corn, zucchini, and mushrooms in a casserole dish. In a separate dish, combine the sour cream, chicken bouillon powder, dill weed, flour, and salt. Stir this mixture into the vegetables. Bake in a 350° oven for 30 minutes.
Serves 12.

Silence goes hand in hand with fasting. Feasts demand sound and music. There must be singing and laughter.

Jean-Paul Aron

Zucchini Cheese Bake

Great if you have an abundance of zucchini to use up at the end of the summer.

8 zucchini, sliced
2 cans (14 ounces each) Italian tomatoes, sliced and drained
1 teaspoon basil
2 cups grated Cheddar or Swiss cheese
$1\frac{1}{4}$ cups Italian-flavored bread crumbs

Parboil zucchini for about 5 minutes; drain. Mix together the zucchini, Italian tomatoes, basil, and cheese. Spoon into a 9- by 13-inch baking dish; top with bread crumbs. Bake in a 375° oven for 20 to 30 minutes, or until bubbly

Serves 10 to 12.

··· Side Dishes ···

Apple-Chestnut Stuffing

Though the taste of this dish is quite elegant, by using a combination of prepared and fresh ingredients, you get the best of both worlds: ease in preparation and great taste.

20 fresh chestnuts
3 packages (6 ounces each) wild rice and mushroom stuffing mix
2 Granny Smith apples, chopped
2 onions, chopped
6 ribs celery, chopped

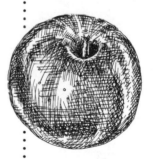

To prepare the chestnuts, cut a slit in each one and boil for 30 minutes. Allow to cool, peel with a sharp knife, and chop finely.

In a large bowl, prepare the stuffing mix according to package directions. Add apples, chestnuts, onions, and celery. Toss to combine. Place in a 9- by 13-inch baking dish, cover with aluminum foil, and bake in a 350° oven for 1 hour.

Serves 10 to 12 as a side dish.

El Paso Grits Casserole

Grits are great Southern food. They are delicious plain as a side dish at breakfast. Flavored with cheese, they make a fantastic side dish for barbecued chicken or ham.

1½ cups quick-cooking grits
6 cups water
½ cup butter or margarine
1 pound processed American cheese, chunked
3 eggs, lightly beaten
2 tablespoons seasoned salt

Boil the grits and water for 3 minutes in a large saucepan. Add the butter or margarine and cook over low to medium heat, stirring until melted. Stir in the cheese, beaten eggs and seasoned salt, pour into a 2- or 3-inch-deep casserole, and bake in a 300° oven for 45 to 60 minutes.
Serves 8 to 10.

Broccoli-Rice Quiche

Let a quiche settle at least 15 minutes before cutting it. It is important to give the custard time to firm up. It's worth the wait!

Crust:
3 cups cooked brown or white rice
¾ cup grated Cheddar cheese
2 eggs, lightly beaten
¼ teaspoon salt

Filling:
4 eggs, lightly beaten
¾ cup grated Cheddar cheese
½ cup milk
¼ teaspoon salt
¼ cup chopped green onions
2 packages (10 ounces each) frozen chopped broccoli, thawed

To make the crust, mix together the rice, Cheddar cheese, eggs, and salt. Pat this mixture into two well-greased 9-inch pie pans.

In a separate bowl, stir together the eggs, Cheddar cheese, milk, and salt. Divide the green onions and broccoli between the two pie pans. Pour the egg-and-cheese mixture over the vegetables. Bake in a 370° oven for 30 to 40 minutes or until lightly browned and set. Allow to cool 15 minutes before cutting into wedges.

Serves 12.

Variations:

You may substitute 3 cups of sliced zucchini or any other summer squash for the broccoli.

Rice and Green Chiles

A good side dish for a bland meat, because the chiles make this more exciting than plain rice or potatoes.

$1\frac{1}{2}$ cups uncooked rice
1 can (4 ounces) chopped green chiles, drained and
    seeds removed
$1\frac{1}{4}$ cups sour cream
$1\frac{3}{4}$ cups grated Monterey Jack or Cheddar cheese
1 teaspoon salt
$\frac{1}{2}$ teaspoon pepper
$\frac{1}{2}$ cup grated Monterey Jack or Cheddar cheese
2 tablespoons butter or margarine

Cook rice according to package directions; place in a large casserole. Add the green chiles, sour cream, $1\frac{3}{4}$ cups Monterey Jack or Cheddar cheese, salt, and pepper. Stir to combine. Top with $\frac{1}{2}$ cup cheese and dot with butter or margarine. Bake uncovered in a 350° oven for 30 minutes.

Serves 8.

Marg Begay
4 C. cooked rice
2 c. Sour Cream
1 c. Cottage cheese
1 onion, chopped
1/4 c. Butter
1/2 tsp. Salt & Pepper
3 cans 4 oz. green chilies, chopped
2 c. Cheddar Chee[se]
Saute Butter & onion.
add Rice, Sour Cream,
cheese. Toss
Layer half rice, chilies
+ Cheddar, Rice. top
w/ chilies + Cheddar
Bake 350°.
20-25 min

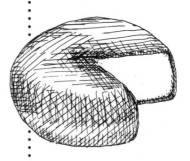

Baked Rice

$\frac{1}{3}$ cup butter or margarine
1 cup chopped celery
1 cup chopped onion
1 can ((10$\frac{3}{4}$ ounces) mushroom soup, undiluted
1 can (4 ounces) mushrooms, drained
1 cup chicken broth
$\frac{3}{4}$ cup long-grain white rice
1 teaspoon salt
1 teaspoon dried parsley
2 tablespoons butter or margarine

Melt $\frac{1}{3}$ cup butter or margarine in a skillet. Add celery and onion and sauté until soft. Place the cooked onion and celery, mushroom soup, mushrooms, chicken broth, rice, salt, and dried parsley in a casserole. Dot butter or margarine on top; cover and bake in a 350° oven for 45 minutes.
Serves 8.

Broccoli Cheese Rice

6 cups cooked rice
$\frac{1}{2}$ cup butter or margarine
1 cup chopped onion
1 cup chopped celery
1 package (10 ounces) frozen cut broccoli, thawed
1 can (10$\frac{3}{4}$ ounces) cream of mushroom soup, undiluted
1 jar (8 ounces) processed American cheese spread

Place the rice in a casserole. Melt butter or margarine in a skillet and sauté onion and celery until onion is clear. Put the onion, celery, and the butter they were cooked in into the casserole. Add the broccoli, cream of mushroom soup, and cheese spread. Stir to combine. Bake in a 350° oven for 45 minutes.
Serves 8 to 10.

Red Beans and Rice

A classic Southern side dish. If you can't find the little round red beans, you may substitute dried red kidney beans.

1 pound uncooked dried red beans
1 to 2 ham hocks
1 medium onion, cut into chunks
2 ribs celery, cut into chunks
2 bay leaves
¼ teaspoon thyme
1 dried red chili pepper
   salt and pepper to taste
3 cups cooked white rice

Rinse the beans, cover with water, and boil for 5 minutes. Take off heat and allow to soak overnight.

Drain. Add 2 quarts of water, the ham hocks, onion, celery, bay leaves, thyme, chili pepper, salt, and pepper. Bring to a boil, reduce heat, and cook until beans are tender but not mushy, about 1 hour.

Discard ham hock, onion, celery, and bay leaf. There should be some liquid remaining in the beans, but not a lot. Cook it down, if necessary. Serve over rice.

Serves 8 to 10.

Hoppin' John

This is a traditional Southern dish for New Year's Day.

1 pound uncooked bacon, cut into small pieces
1 cup finely chopped onion
1 tablespoon minced garlic
4 cups cooked rice
2 cans (16 ounces each) black-eyed peas, drained
   salt and pepper to taste

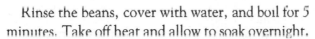

Place the bacon, onion, and garlic in a large skillet; cook until onion is crisp. Add the rice and black-eyed peas; salt and pepper to taste. Cover and heat through over low heat. This can also be put into a casserole and baked in a 325° oven for 20 to 30 minutes until heated through.

Serves 12.

Rice Pilaf

This dish is a nice change from potatoes. It is especially good with chicken or fish entrées and is a favorite side dish for vegetarian meals.

$\frac{1}{4}$ cup butter or margarine
1 small onion, chopped
2 cups uncooked long-grain white rice
$\frac{1}{2}$ cup slivered almonds
4 cups chicken stock
$\frac{1}{2}$ teaspoon salt
  dash of pepper

Melt butter in a saucepan. Add onion, rice, and almonds; sauté until onion is golden. Add chicken stock, salt, and pepper. Allow the mixture to come to a boil, then cover, reduce heat, and simmer for 30 minutes without lifting the lid.

Serves 6 to 8.

Variations:
• Add $\frac{1}{4}$ cup currants or raisins.
• Add $\frac{1}{4}$ to $\frac{1}{2}$ teaspoon curry powder or allspice.
• Use beef stock instead of chicken broth.
• Add a small can (4 ounces) of chopped mushrooms.
• Stir in a bit of fresh chopped parsley just before serving.
• Stir in 1 to 2 cups barely cooked frozen peas.

A meal, however simple, is a moment of intersection. It is at once the most basic, the most fundamental, of our life's activities, maintaining the life of our bodies; shared with others it can be an occasion of joy and communion, uniting people deeply.

Elise Boulding

Bulgur Pilaf

Bulgur is cooked cracked wheat. It has a delicious, nutty flavor. To make bulgur pilaf, follow the recipe for Rice Pilaf but substitute 2 cups of uncooked bulgur for the rice. Bulgur only needs to cook for about 20 minutes.

Kasha Pilaf

Kasha is cooked buckwheat. It has a very hearty flavor and is a favorite food in the Balkans and Russia. To make a kasha pilaf, use the Rice Pilaf recipe, substituting 2 cups of kasha for the rice. Add $\frac{1}{2}$ cup more broth and allow the pilaf to cook for about 1 hour.

Massive Macaroni and Cheese

This recipe serves 24, which makes it a natural for a community meal.

1 package (2 pounds) elbow macaroni
$\frac{3}{4}$ cup butter or margarine
$\frac{3}{4}$ cup flour
2 teaspoons salt
1 teaspoon dry mustard
2 quarts milk
2 pounds mild Cheddar cheese, grated

Cook macaroni according to package directions, drain, and set aside. Melt the butter or margarine in a large kettle. Add the flour, salt, and mustard and cook, stirring constantly, until the butter or margarine is absorbed. Pour in the milk and cook, stirring constantly, over medium heat until a smooth sauce forms. Slowly add Cheddar cheese and stir until it melts. Mix in the cooked macaroni;

When cooking pasta, adding a tablespoon of oil as the water comes to a boil not only keeps pasta from sticking together, it helps keep the water from boiling over.

spoon into 2 large buttered casseroles. Cover and heat through in a 350° oven for 30 minutes.

Serves 24.

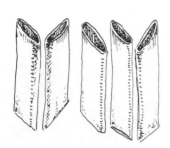

Baked Ziti

Everybody enjoys a pasta side dish, and this is very easy to make. It's also good as a vegetarian main dish.

1 package (1 pound) ziti

Sauce:
1 large onion, chopped
2 cloves garlic, finely chopped
2 tablespoons olive oil
2 cans (16 ounces each) Italian tomatoes, chopped, with juice
1 can (6 ounces) tomato paste
$\frac{1}{4}$ teaspoon salt
1 teaspoon basil
$\frac{1}{4}$ teaspoon oregano

Cheese:
1 container (15 ounces) ricotta cheese
1 package (8 ounces) mozzarella cheese, grated
2 eggs
2 tablespoons chopped fresh parsley
salt and pepper
grated Parmesan cheese

Prepare ziti according to package directions, drain, and set aside.

Sauté onion and garlic in the olive oil until soft and golden. Add the tomatoes and tomato paste and cook for 15 minutes, stirring occasionally. Add salt, basil, and oregano and simmer for 5 more minutes.

In a separate bowl, mix together the ricotta, mozzarella, eggs, parsley, salt, and pepper. Gently stir into the cooked ziti. Layer the ziti mixture and the sauce in a greased casserole; sprinkle with Parmesan cheese. Bake in a 350° oven for 30 minutes or until bubbly.

Serves 8.

Stuffed Shells

When you cook the pasta for this, be sure to undercook it. You want the shells to retain their shape, and if the shells are completely cooked, they will fall apart.

1 package (1 pound) jumbo pasta shells
2 cans (15 ounces each) tomato sauce
1 clove garlic, minced
1 teaspoon basil
½ teaspoon oregano
1 carton (15 ounces) ricotta cheese
1 package (8 ounces) mozzarella cheese, grated
½ cup grated Parmesan or Romano cheese
½ teaspoon nutmeg
2 tablespoons fresh chopped parsley
2 eggs
additional grated mozzarella or grated Parmesan (optional)

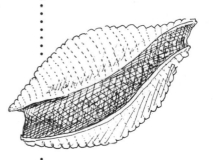

Cook pasta shells until barely tender. Drain and leave them floating in cold water.

Mix together the tomato sauce, garlic, basil, and oregano and simmer for about 5 minutes. In a separate bowl, mix together the ricotta, mozzarella, Parmesan or Romano, nutmeg, parsley, and eggs.

Pour a little of the sauce in the bottom of a greased 9- by 13-inch baking pan. Stuff the shells with the cheese mixture and set them fairly close together in the pan. Top with the remaining sauce and, if desired, sprinkle on additional cheese. Bake in a 350° oven for 30 minutes.

Serves 8.

Salads

··· Vegetable Salads ···

Country Potato Salad

Wonderful when it's warm and freshly made, the flavor improves as the salad chills.

7 medium potatoes
3 hard-boiled eggs, chopped
1 medium onion, chopped
5 ribs celery, thinly sliced
$\frac{3}{4}$ cup chopped sweet pickles
$\frac{1}{2}$ cup sweet-pickle juice
2 tablespoons vinegar

1 tablespoon sugar
1½ cups mayonnaise
2 tablespoons mustard
 salt and pepper to taste
 paprika for garnish

Boil the potatoes in their skins, rinse, and cut into cubes, leaving the skins on. Place the cubed potatoes, eggs, onion, celery, and pickles in a large bowl. Pour pickle juice over all. In a separate bowl, combine the vinegar, sugar, mayonnaise, mustard, salt, and pepper. Pour over the salad and stir to combine. Sprinkle on paprika for garnish.
Serves 12 to 15.

German Potato Salad

This may be served either hot or cold. It is especially good with broiled kielbasa.

½ cup butter or margarine
6 green onions, sliced
1 small onion, diced
⅓ cup white vinegar
⅓ cup sugar
1 teaspoon dry mustard
¼ teaspoon thyme
1 teaspoon salt
½ teaspoon pepper
5 large potatoes, cooked, peeled, and sliced

Melt the butter or margarine in a large saucepan. Sauté the onions until soft. Add the vinegar, sugar, mustard, thyme, salt, and pepper; stir until the salt and sugar are dissolved. Add the potatoes and cook over low heat for about 10 minutes, stirring occasionally.
Serves 10 to 12.

Marinated Bean Salad

Classic potluck fare and also one of the best salads to take on picnics because of its keeping ability. If you don't have the exact assortment of beans called for, feel free to substitute anything you have.

2 cans (15 ounces each) red kidney beans, drained
2 cans (16 ounces each) regular cut green beans, drained
1 can (16 ounces) garbanzo beans, drained
2 cups chopped celery
½ cup chopped green onion
1 jar (3 ounces) stuffed green olives, drained and sliced

Dressing:
⅔ cup salad oil
⅓ cup red wine vinegar
1 teaspoon salt
2 tablespoons sugar
¼ teaspoon garlic powder
¼ teaspoon pepper

Place all the beans in a salad bowl. Add celery, onion, and green olives. In a separate bowl, combine the salad oil, red wine vinegar, salt, sugar, garlic powder, and pepper. Add to beans; toss gently to combine. Cover and refrigerate until serving time.
Serves 12.

No Time to Cook?
Try these salad ideas:
· *a whole watermelon*
· *a variety of ripe melon wedges*
· *a fresh pineapple, cut into chunks and speared with decorative picks*
· *deli salads: potato, pasta, marinated beans and vegetables*
· *many markets now have salad bars, selling salad by the pound*
· *chilled applesauce, with a sprinkle of cinnamon or nutmeg*

Italian Green Bean Salad

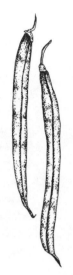

Refreshing and colorful, this salad is a perfect partner for pasta.

2 cups sliced fresh green beans
½ red onion, thinly sliced
1 can (16 ounces) sliced beets, drained
    Italian Vinaigrette Dressing

Toss together the green beans, red onion, and beets. Add dressing and allow to chill several hours (or overnight), stirring once or twice. Just before serving, retoss the salad and pour off excess dressing.
Serves 8.

Copper Pennies Carrot Salad

If at all possible, serve this salad in a clear glass bowl to show off its cheery copper color.

2 pounds fresh carrots
1 can (10¾ ounces) tomato soup, undiluted
½ cup salad oil
1 cup sugar
¾ cup cider vinegar
1 teaspoon mustard
1 teaspoon Worcestershire sauce
1 small green pepper, diced
1 medium onion, diced

Peel the carrots and cut into thin slices. Place in a saucepan and add a little bit of water. Cover and cook for about 10 minutes, until they are barely tender. Drain.

Blend together the tomato soup, salad oil, sugar, cider vinegar, mustard, and Worcestershire sauce. Layer the carrots, green pepper, and onion in a deep serving bowl. Pour on the tomato dressing. Allow to marinate 24 hours in the refrigerator before serving. Drain excess sauce and serve.

Serves 12 to 15.

Southern California Cobb Salad

This classic is great for a salad buffet. It is traditional to serve it untossed, with the various ingredients arranged across the top of the lettuce.

$\frac{1}{2}$ *large head iceberg lettuce, shredded*
2 whole chicken breasts, cooked, boned, skinned, and
    diced
2 medium tomatoes, cubed
3 hard-boiled eggs, chopped
7 slices bacon, cooked crisp and crumbled
$\frac{3}{4}$ *cup crumbled blue cheese*
2 ripe avocados, chopped
    lemon juice

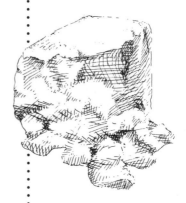

Place the lettuce in a large salad bowl. On top of the lettuce, arrange the chicken, tomatoes, eggs, bacon, and blue cheese in layers. Toss the avocados in lemon juice before adding them. Serve with a choice of dressings.

Serves 6 to 8.

Bacon and Broccoli Salad

1 head of broccoli
12 slices cooked and crumbled bacon
$\frac{1}{2}$ cup sliced green onion
$\frac{1}{2}$ cup raisins

Dressing:
2 tablespoons vinegar
$\frac{1}{2}$ cup sugar
$\frac{1}{2}$ cup mayonnaise

Wash the broccoli. Separate flowerets and cut the stalks into thin slices; place in a salad bowl. Add bacon, green onion, and raisins. In a separate bowl, stir together the vinegar, sugar, and mayonnaise. Pour the dressing over the salad and toss gently.

Serves 8 to 10.

Marinated Vegetable Medley

This is a good salad to make in the winter, when fresh lettuce may be high in price and of poor quality.

1 can (8 ounces) cut green beans
1 can ($8\frac{1}{2}$ ounces) whole kernel corn
1 can ($8\frac{1}{2}$ ounces) sweet peas
$\frac{1}{3}$ cup sliced celery
$\frac{1}{3}$ cup chopped green pepper
$\frac{1}{4}$ cup chopped green onions

Dressing:
$\frac{1}{3}$ *cup vinegar*
$\frac{1}{4}$ *cup sugar*
$\frac{1}{3}$ *cup salad oil*
$\frac{1}{2}$ *teaspoon salt*

Drain green beans, corn, and sweet peas and place in a salad bowl. Add the celery, green pepper, and green onions. In a small bowl, dissolve the sugar in the vinegar. Add the oil and salt; stir until salt is dissolved. Pour over the vegetables; stir gently to combine. Allow to marinate overnight in the refrigerator.

Serves 12.

Jicama Salad

This is a great salad to serve with Mexican food. The refreshing, light flavor of jicama is a perfect complement to some of the spicier, heavier flavors of Mexican food.

1 small jicama, peeled and cut into chunks
1 red onion, diced
3 oranges, peeled and diced

Dressing:
3 tablespoons lime juice
3 tablespoons honey
$\frac{1}{4}$ *cup salad oil*

Toss together the jicama, onion, and oranges in a medium salad bowl. In a small bowl, dissolve the honey in the lime juice, add vegetable oil, and stir to combine. Pour the dressing over the salad, toss, and serve.

Serves 8 to 10.

Jicama (HE-kah-mah), an important ingredient in Chinese and American southwestern cooking, is a grapefruit-sized vegetable with a rough orange-brown skin. The flesh is crisp and slightly sweet, similar in texture to a turnip or radish. Jicama should be peeled, then eaten raw in salads or cooked in stir fry dishes. Unused portions, well-wrapped in plastic, keep for many weeks in the refrigerator.

Sour Cream and Cucumbers

Nothing seems more refreshing than a cold cucumber salad on a hot day. Try it at your next barbecue.

To reduce the pungency of raw onion rings in tossed salads, soak them in cold water for an hour before using.

3 large cucumbers, peeled and thinly sliced
1 tablespoon salt
$\frac{2}{3}$ cup vinegar
$\frac{1}{4}$ cup sugar
3 onions, thinly sliced
1 cup sour cream
1 teaspoon dry mustard
1 teaspoon salt
2 tablespoons sugar
2 tablespoons cider vinegar

Place the sliced cucumbers in a bowl, sprinkle a tablespoon of salt over them, and let stand for 1 hour. Rinse and drain. Combine vinegar and $\frac{1}{4}$ cup sugar and pour over the cucumbers. Add sliced onions and toss gently. Allow to marinate 3 hours (or overnight).

Pour off the marinade. In a separate bowl, combine sour cream, dry mustard, the teaspoon of salt, 2 tablespoons sugar, and cider vinegar. Pour this dressing over the cucumbers and stir gently to combine. Chill well before serving.

Serves 8.

Variation:

Instead of adding the dry mustard to the dressing, add 1 teaspoon dried tarragon.

Marinated Tomato Salad

This is delicious, simple, and goes with all sorts of foods. It is especially good with heavy, hearty entrées. Be sure to let it marinate at least 5 hours before serving, to allow the flavors to blend.

6 to 8 ripe tomatoes, sliced
2 large, mild white onions, sliced
$\frac{1}{3}$ cup finely chopped fresh parsley
$\frac{2}{3}$ cup olive oil
$\frac{1}{3}$ cup red wine vinegar
$\frac{1}{2}$ teaspoon dill weed
1 teaspoon basil
  salt and pepper
  dash of garlic powder

Combine all ingredients. Chill at least 5 hours before serving, stirring every hour or so.
  Serves 8 to 10.

Tomatoes sliced verti-cally rather than hori-zontally will hold their shape and juice better.

Hot Wurst Salad

Huge and hearty, this salad is great on a chilly winter night. Served with soup and dark bread, it makes a satisfying meal.

5 pounds of thin-skinned potatoes
$1\frac{1}{4}$ pounds knockwurst
$1\frac{1}{4}$ pounds bratwurst
2 tablespoons butter or margarine
1 cup chopped onion
1 cup chopped celery
2 tablespoons flour
2 tablespoons sugar
1 teaspoon celery seed

$\frac{1}{2}$ *teaspoon dry mustard*
$\frac{1}{2}$ *teaspoon salt*
$1\frac{1}{2}$ *cups chicken broth*
$\frac{1}{3}$ *cup white wine vinegar*
$\frac{1}{3}$ *cup chopped parsley*

Boil the potatoes, then peel and slice them. Place in a large bowl. Slice the knockwurst and bratwurst. Melt butter or margarine in a large skillet, add knockwurst and bratwurst, and cook over medium heat, stirring constantly, until the sausage is lightly browned. Add the wurst to the potatoes.

Sauté the onion and celery lightly, then add to the potatoes and wurst. If there are not about 3 tablespoons of drippings left in the skillet, add butter, margarine, or oil to make about that amount. Mix the flour, sugar, celery seeds, dry mustard, and salt in with the shortening; cook, stirring constantly, for about 3 minutes. Add chicken broth and vinegar and stir until smooth and thick. Stir in parsley. Pour over the potato and wurst mixture in the salad bowl; stir gently to combine.

Serves 12 to 15.

Pasta and Grain
· · · Salads · · ·

Macaroni Salad

Whether you call it *macaroni* or *noodles* or *pasta*, it's been a favorite at community dinners for decades. No matter what you call it, just be sure you don't overcook it.

2 cups uncooked elbow macaroni
3 hard-boiled eggs, diced
$\frac{1}{2}$ cup chopped sweet pickle
1 cup chopped celery
$\frac{1}{4}$ cup chopped onion
salt and pepper to taste
$\frac{3}{4}$ cup mayonnaise
  paprika for garnish

Cook elbow macaroni according to package directions. Rinse and drain well. Place the macaroni, eggs, sweet pickle, celery, and onion in a salad bowl and stir gently to combine. Sprinkle with salt and pepper. Stir in the mayonnaise; sprinkle on the paprika for garnish.
Serves 8 to 10.

Pasta salads taste best when served chilled but not ice cold. Allow refrigerated salads to stand at room temperature for about 30 minutes before serving.

Pasta Salad Primavera

Pasta salads are a carbohydrate lover's dream come true. The Parmesan cheese makes this one especially tasty.

1 package (12 ounces) rotini
1 green pepper, seeded, diced
3 tomatoes, diced

12 small fresh mushrooms, sliced in half
5 green onions, sliced (tops included)
1½ cups frozen cut broccoli, thawed
1 can (4 ounces) ripe olives, sliced
¾ cup grated Parmesan cheese

Dressing:
1 tablespoon basil
1 teaspoon marjoram
¼ teaspoon garlic powder
¼ cup olive oil
3 tablespoons red wine vinegar
1 teaspoon black pepper
½ teaspoon salt

Cook pasta according to package directions, rinse, drain, and place in a large salad bowl. Add pepper, tomatoes, mushrooms, green onions, broccoli, and ripe olives. Sprinkle on the Parmesan cheese and toss gently.

In a small bowl, combine the basil, marjoram, garlic powder, olive oil, red wine vinegar, black pepper, and salt. Pour over the pasta salad and toss gently.

Serves 12 to 15.

Minnesota Wild Rice and Crab Salad

The Indians of Minnesota have long enjoyed wild rice. This salad carries on that tradition in a deliciously contemporary way.

4 cups cooked wild rice
2 tomatoes, diced
1½ cups thinly sliced celery
½ cup thinly sliced green onions
1 can (4 ounces) ripe olives, drained
2 cans (6 ounces each) crabmeat, drained and flaked

Wild rice is not rice at all, but a chewy, nutty, slightly smoky seed of an aquatic grass that grows wild around the lakes of Wisconsin and Minnesota. The harvesting of wild rice was for generations considered a seasonal festivity, much like a barn raising in the Midwest, the Mardi Gras of Louisiana, or the clambakes of New England. The entire family would pack up and travel to the Indian ricing camps where they would barter cloth, tobacco, and sugar for the precious grain.

Dressing:
$\frac{2}{3}$ *cup sour cream*
$\frac{1}{3}$ *cup chili sauce*
1 teaspoon lemon juice
$\frac{1}{2}$ *teaspoon prepared horseradish*
  dash of salt and pepper

Gently stir together the rice, tomatoes, celery, green onion, ripe olives, and crabmeat. In a separate bowl, combine the sour cream, chili sauce, lemon juice, and prepared horseradish. Add salt and pepper to taste.
Serves 6 to 8.

Bulgur Salad

This is also called cracked wheat or tabouleh salad. It's great for large group meals because it can be made up to 2 days ahead and tastes good at a variety of temperatures. It is also nice when you are serving a salad buffet and want variety.

2 cups uncooked bulgur or cracked wheat
4 cups boiling water
$\frac{1}{2}$ *teaspoon salt*
$\frac{1}{2}$ *cup salad oil*
$\frac{1}{2}$ *cup lemon juice (fresh, if possible)*
1 cup chopped green onions
2 cups chopped tomato
1 cup fresh chopped parsley
1 teaspoon crushed dried mint
or
1 tablespoon finely chopped fresh mint
  salt and pepper to taste

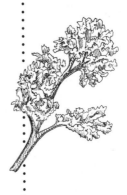

Place the bulgur in a large heat-proof salad bowl. Pour the boiling water over it, cover, and allow to sit at room temperature for one hour.

Mix together the salt, salad oil, and lemon juice; pour over the bulgar. Add the remaining ingredients and toss gently. Cover and refrigerate until serving time.

Serves 12.

Variations:

Bulgur Salad is the Middle Eastern version of our potato salad. There are innumerable variations to it.

- Add one cup cooked chick-peas or garbanzo beans to the salad.
- Omit the mint and add more parsley.
- Add one finely chopped cucumber.
- Serve with wedges of pita bread, so guests can scoop out what they want.
- Use lime juice instead of lemon juice or half of each.
- Use a really fine olive oil for the salad oil.
- Add 1 cup cooked, chilled carrots.

· · · Green Salads · · ·

Tangy Toss

Radish sprouts and mustard greens, both of which are available in many produce sections, give this salad a bit more tang than most. If radish sprouts are not available, you may use alfalfa sprouts.

$\frac{1}{2}$ pound spinach leaves
1 head leaf lettuce
4 ounces radish sprouts
4 mustard greens

½ small head of red cabbage, grated
3 bunches green onions, sliced
3 ribs celery, sliced
1 pint carton cherry tomatoes, halved
  Dijon Basil Dressing

Clean and tear into bite-size pieces the spinach, lettuce, and mustard greens. Place the radish sprouts, spinach, lettuce, cabbage, mustard greens, green onion, celery, and tomatoes into a salad bowl. Toss gently to combine. Just before serving, toss with Dijon Basil Dressing.

Serves 12 to 15.

Beet and Spinach Salad

This is a very colorful salad for a buffet.

1 pound spinach leaves
2 cups drained cooked or canned sliced beets
1 cup sliced celery
⅓ cup crumbled feta cheese
2 hard-boiled eggs, chopped
½ cup chopped walnuts
Lemon-Egg Dressing

Clean the spinach and tear it into bite-size pieces. Place the spinach, beets, celery, feta cheese, hard-boiled eggs, and walnuts into a large salad bowl. Toss gently to combine. Just before serving, pour on the Lemon-Egg Dressing and toss to combine.

Serves 8 to 10.

A bowl of fresh tender leaves from any half a hundred kinds of garden lettuces, unadorned except by the simplest possible mixture of oil, vinegar, and seasoning, is a joy to the palate.

M.F.K. Fisher

Nutty Green Salad

2 cups coarsely chopped hazelnuts
2 cups bite-size broccoli flowerets
2½ cups cooked fresh green beans
                        or
1 bag (20 ounces) frozen French-cut green beans,
*   thawed*
½ cup chopped green onion
*   Dijon Basil Dressing*

In a medium salad bowl, combine the hazelnuts, broccoli, green beans, and green onion. Toss with Dijon Basil Dressing.
Serves 10 to 12.

Spinach Carambola Salad

Carambola is an exotic fruit that cuts into star-shaped slices. Its flavor is similar to kiwi fruit or strawberries. It not only tastes delicious but looks lovely. If carambolas are not available, you may substitute either 1 cup of cantaloupe balls or 1 cup of sliced strawberries.

10 ounces fresh spinach
2 carambolas, sliced
2 kiwis, peeled and sliced
*   Orange Curry Dressing*

Clean and tear the spinach into bite-sized pieces. Place the carambolas, kiwis, and spinach in a large salad bowl. Toss gently just before serving, pour dressing over, and toss again.
Serves 8 to 10.

Carambola is called "star fruit" because of the beautiful star shapes formed when sliced into cross sections. Select firm, shiny skinned fruit and allow to ripen at room temperature. The carambola is ripe when the overall color is orange-brown and the edges are browning. It isn't necessary to remove the edges or peel the fruit before using.

Pineapple-Orange Spinach Salad

The refreshing taste of this salad makes it a perfect partner for chicken dishes.

1 fresh pineapple
2 oranges
10 ounces fresh spinach
1 cup sliced almonds
    Orange Curry Dressing

Peel, core, and cut the pineapple into bite-size pieces. Peel and cut up the oranges. Clean and tear the spinach into pieces. Place the pineapple and oranges in a bowl, top with spinach and almonds. Toss gently to combine just before serving. Add Orange Curry Dressing and toss gently again.
    Serves 8 to 10.

Layered Salad With Mayonnaise and Cheese Topping

This classic salad has many variations. If you have a favorite vegetable that isn't included, go ahead and put it in. This is especially handy to take to a potluck because it's assembled the night before, complete with the dressing.

1 medium head iceberg lettuce, shredded or chopped
1 small head cauliflower, chopped
1 small onion, chopped
2 cups frozen peas, thawed

Dressing:
1½ cups mayonnaise
1 tablespoon lemon juice
¼ cup sugar

Topping:
¼ cup sugar
1 cup grated Cheddar cheese
3 slices cooked, crumbled bacon

In a 9- by 13-inch pan, layer the vegetables in the following order: lettuce, cauliflower, onion, peas. Mix together in a separate bowl the mayonnaise, lemon juice, and ¼ cup sugar. Spread this dressing over the vegetables. Sprinkle ¼ cup sugar, cheese, and bacon on top.

Serves 15 to 20.

You can save time and have crisper greens by washing them the day before you use them. When well-drained, place them in a bowl and cover with paper towels wrung out in cold water.

Orange-Almond Salad

This salad is wonderful with chicken casseroles.

1 head leaf lettuce
2 cans (11 ounces each) mandarin orange sections, drained
½ cup thinly sliced celery
¼ cup thinly sliced green onion
½ cup sliced almonds

Dressing:
¼ cup salad oil
2 tablespoons vinegar
2 tablespoons sugar
    dash salt
⅛ teaspoon almond extract

Clean and tear the lettuce into bite-size pieces. Place the lettuce, orange sections, celery, green onion, and almonds in a bowl. In a screwtop jar, combine the salad oil, vinegar, sugar, salt, and almond extract; shake to combine well.

At serving time, pour dressing over the salad and toss gently.

Serves 6 to 8.

Salad Bars

Salad bars have become very popular the last few years and they make a wonderful addition to a community meal. Below is a list of ingredients to serve 25. Keep in mind that people tend to take more salad at a salad bar than they would eat if they were served a portion of salad and plan accordingly. Also, judge the proportions of the salad bar by how many other dishes you are serving. If the salad bar will be the main event, increase the ingredients; if there will be a large selection of entrées, decrease them.

This recipe will provide 25 people one plate of salad each.

Essential Ingredients:

- Salad greens. Use a large bowl or tub and combine the following greens:

  2 heads iceberg lettuce, chopped
  3 heads leaf lettuce, chopped
  ½ head red cabbage, finely chopped

  Other greens may also be included, such as romaine lettuce, spinach, bibb lettuce, or whatever is freshest in your market.

- The following ingredients should be chopped and placed into bowls:

  6 to 8 tomatoes, cut into wedges or slices
  2 green peppers, chopped
  1 bunch celery, chopped

Potluck Salad Bar Luncheon:
The host supplies the lettuce and dressings, and each guest brings 1 or 2 cups of vegetables or other salad ingredients. For variety, add some deli salads and relishes. With fresh bakery bread and iced tea, you have the perfect summer meal.

8 *carrots, grated*
1 *bunch green onions, thinly sliced (with tops)*
2 *cups fresh broccoli and/or cauliflower, cut into*
   bite-size pieces
2 *cucumbers, sliced*
2 *red onions, sliced and separated into rings*

• *Optional ingredients:*
   1 *to 2 cups canned garbanzo or kidney beans,*
      drained
   1 *to 2 cups chopped pickled beets or beet slices*
   3 *hard-boiled eggs, chopped*
      pitted olives (green or ripe)
      sunflower seeds
      croutons
      crisp bacon pieces

Main Dish Salad Bars may also include any or all of the following:

   cooked ham, cut into strips
   cooked chicken or turkey, cut into strips
   cottage cheese
   applesauce
   citrus fruit sections
   potato salad
   macaroni salad

Serve at least 3 choices of salad dressing, 2 to 3 cups each. Also provide lemon wedges and cruets of oil and vinegar.

Instead of bread croutons, try using coarsely crushed taco shells in your next green salad for a tasty difference.

· · · Molded Salads · · ·

Eggnog-Cranberry Salad

Red and white stripes make this a beautiful holiday salad.

1½ cups cranberry juice
1 package (3 ounces) raspberry-flavored gelatin
1 jar (14 ounces) cranberry-orange relish
1 can (8 ounces) crushed pineapple, drained
3 tablespoons orange juice
1½ cups eggnog
1 tablespoon (or envelope) unflavored gelatin
½ cup finely chopped celery

Heat the cranberry juice to boiling; stir in the raspberry gelatin until dissolved. Chill until partially set, then stir in the cranberry-orange relish. Spoon into a 12- by 7- by 2-inch pan and allow to chill until firm.

Mix together the crushed pineapple, orange juice, and eggnog. Sprinkle with the unflavored gelatin and allow it to soften for five minutes. Heat the mixture and stir until the gelatin dissolves. Chill until partially firm, then stir in the celery. Carefully spoon this mixture over the cranberry layer and chill until firm.

This can either be served out of the pan or cut into squares and served on lettuce leaves.

Serves 12.

Never add fresh pineapple, kiwi, or papaya to gelatin salads as they contain an enzyme that interferes with the jelling process. Use canned fruit or cook these first.

Spicy Aspic Salad

Refreshing and tangy, this salad is a delicious accompaniment to seafood or Mexican food. If served with seafood, top with Lemon Mayonnaise. If served with Mexican food, place a few spoonfuls of Easy Guacamole on top.

2 cups canned spicy vegetable juice
1 tablespoon (or one envelope) unflavored gelatin
$\frac{1}{4}$ cup lemon juice
1 teaspoon honey
1 rib celery, chopped
1 green onion, chopped
$\frac{1}{4}$ cup chopped green pepper
*   leaf lettuce*

Place $\frac{1}{2}$ cup of the spicy vegetable juice in a medium bowl and sprinkle the gelatin over it. Allow to sit undisturbed for 3 to 4 minutes.

Heat together the remaining spicy vegetable juice, lemon juice, and the honey, but do not allow to boil. Add this to the gelatin mixture and stir to combine. Chill until slightly firm in a 7- by 11- by 1$\frac{1}{2}$-inch pan. Stir in the celery, green onion, and green pepper.

Chill until firm and cut into squares. Serve the squares on a platter or on top of lettuce on individual plates. Top with either Lemon Mayonnaise or Easy Guacamole.

Serves 8 to 10.

Apricot Nectar Mold

2 cans (12 ounces each) apricot nectar
2 packages (3 ounces each) lemon-flavored gelatin
1 cup water
1 tablespoon lemon juice
2 cans (11 ounces each) mandarin orange sections,
    drained
1 cup seedless grapes, halved
$\frac{1}{3}$ cup chopped apple

Bring the apricot nectar to a boil. Add gelatin and stir until dissolved. Add water and lemon juice. Chill until partially set, then fold in the drained oranges, grapes, and apple. Spoon into a serving bowl or wet mold and chill until firm.

Serves 8 to 10.

Rinsing a gelatin mold in cold water and chilling before filling will help the salad unmold more easily. To unmold, hold mold in a bowl of warm hot water for a few seconds before turning out onto plate.

Cheesy Orange Mold

12 marshmallows
2 cups boiling water
1 package (6 ounces) orange-flavored gelatin
2 cups cold water
$\frac{1}{2}$ cup mayonnaise
1 cup grated Cheddar cheese
1 can (8 ounces) crushed pineapple, drained
$\frac{1}{2}$ cup finely chopped pecans

In a saucepan, melt the marshmallows in the boiling water. Add orange gelatin and stir until dissolved. Add cold water and mayonnaise; stir. Pour into a serving bowl or wet mold and chill until slightly set, then stir in the cheese, drained pineapple, and pecans. Chill until firm.

Makes 20 servings.

Sunshine Salad

This looks like its name—bright and cheery.

1 package (6 ounces) lemon-flavored gelatin
2 cups boiling water
1 cup water
1 tablespoon white vinegar
2 cans (8 ounces each) crushed pineapple,
    drained, and juice reserved
2 cups shredded carrots
½ cup chopped pecans

Dissolve the gelatin in the boiling water. Add enough water to the reserved juice to make 1 cup of liquid. Add to the dissolved gelatin along with the vinegar, crushed pineapple, carrots, and pecans. Pour into a 9- by 13-inch pan. Allow to chill until slightly set; stir to distribute the carrots, pineapple, and pecans. Chill until firm before serving. Serve on a platter or on top of lettuce leaves on individual plates.

Makes 20 servings.

Blueberry Cream Mold ✓

This is extremely rich; dieters should never touch it. *or cherry*

1 package (6 ounces) <u>black raspberry</u>-flavored gelatin
2 cups hot water
1 can (16 ounces) blueberries, undrained
1 can (20 ounces) crushed pineapple, undrained *or 8½ oz.*
½ cup chopped pecans
1 cup sour cream
1 package (8 ounces) cream cheese, softened
½ cup sugar
½ teaspoon vanilla

Dissolve the gelatin in the hot water. Add the blueberries and crushed pineapple, including their juices. Add chopped pecans. Spoon into a 9- by 13-inch pan. Allow to chill until slightly firm, then stir to distribute fruit and nuts. Chill until firm.

or walnuts

or sprinkle atop topping

In a separate bowl, combine the sour cream, cream cheese, sugar, and vanilla; whip until fluffy and creamy. Spread over chilled gelatin. Serve on a platter or on top of lettuce leaves on individual plates.

Makes 20 servings.

Cranberry-Cherry Mold

This is a tasty twist on the holiday tradition of cranberry relish. The cherries add to the bright red color and provide sweetness. To make your holiday season a bit less fattening, make this with sugar-free gelatin.

1 package (6 ounces) cherry-flavored gelatin
2 cups hot water
1 can (16 ounces) dark, sweet cherries, pitted
1 can (16 ounces) whole-berry cranberry sauce
¾ cup chopped pecans
  whipped cream (optional)
  whole pecans (optional)

Sprinkle the gelatin over the hot water and stir to dissolve. Drain the liquid from the cherries and add enough water to make 2 cups. Add this to the hot water and gelatin and stir. Chill until partially set. Add cherries, cranberry sauce, and chopped pecans. Stir in. Pour into a serving bowl or a wet mold; allow to chill until firm. If desired, just before serving, garnish with whipped cream and whole pecans.

Serves 8.

Red Hot Salad Mold

This molded salad is perfect with pork roasts or ham.

1 bag (8 ounces) Red Hots cinnamon candy
2 cups boiling water
1 package (6 ounces) cherry-flavored gelatin
2 cups applesauce

Dissolve the Red Hots in the boiling water. Add gelatin and stir to dissolve. Add applesauce. Pour into a serving bowl or wet mold. When gelatin is slightly set, stir to distribute the applesauce. Chill until firm.

Serves 15 to 20 as a garnish for meat.

Mandarin Cream Jellied Salad

The creamy cooked topping on this salad is typical of many Midwestern salads. This salad has a clear gelatin base topped with a creamy dressing.

1 package (6 ounces) orange-flavored gelatin
2 cups boiling water
2 cups miniature marshmallows
$1\frac{1}{2}$ cups cold water
1 can (11 ounces) mandarin orange sections drained with juice reserved
1 can (16 ounces) crushed pineapple, drained with juice reserved

Topping:
$\frac{1}{2}$ *cup sugar*
2 tablespoons flour
1 egg, lightly beaten
2 tablespoons butter
1 cup heavy cream
$\frac{1}{3}$ *cup grated Cheddar cheese*
$\frac{1}{4}$ *cup finely chopped walnuts*

Dissolve the gelatin in boiling water. Add the marshmallows and stir until dissolved, then add cold water. Chill until slightly firm. Fold in orange sections and crushed pineapple. Spoon into a 9- by 13-inch pan; chill until very firm.

Measure the reserved orange and pineapple juices. If necessary, add additional orange or pineapple juice to produce 2 cups liquid. In a jar with a tight fitting lid, shake $\frac{1}{2}$ cup juice with sugar and flour. Mix into remaining juice.

In a medium saucepan, add egg to the juices. Cook, stirring constantly, until the mixture thickens. Remove from heat and add butter. Cool.

Whip the heavy cream just until soft peaks form, then fold into the cooled juice mixture. Spread on top of the gelatin layer. Sprinkle Cheddar cheese and nuts on top. Serve on a platter or on top of lettuce leaves on individual plates.

Serves 24.

Lemon Dew Salad

The soda in this salad gives it a refreshing tangy taste.

1 package (6 ounces) lemon-flavored gelatin
2 cups hot water
2 cups Mountain Dew soda
1 can (8 ounces) crushed pineapple, drained
3 bananas, sliced
$\frac{1}{2}$ *cup flaked coconut*

A good make-ahead: Gelatin salads keep for several days in the refrigerator.

Dissolve the gelatin in hot water; add the soda. Pour into a serving bowl or wet mold. Allow to chill until slightly firm. Stir in the drained pineapple, bananas, and coconut. Chill until firm.

Serves 8 to 12.

Pacific Ginger Pear Mold

Very light and refreshing, this is a good salad to serve with a seafood entrée.

1 package (6 ounces) lemon-flavored gelatin
2 cups boiling water
2 cups ginger ale
2 teaspoons lemon juice
$2\frac{1}{2}$ cups diced fresh pears

Dissolve the gelatin in boiling water. Add the ginger ale and lemon juice. Allow to chill until slightly firm, then stir in the pears. Spoon into a wet mold or a 9- by 13-inch pan. Chill until firm.

Serves 12.

New York Waldorf Mold

One advantage of making a Waldorf Salad this way is that you don't have to worry about the apples turning brown.

1 package (6 ounces) cherry-flavored gelatin
2 cups boiling water
2 cups cold water
1 cup diced apples
1 cup diced celery
1 cup chopped walnuts
$\frac{1}{3}$ cup golden raisins

Sprinkle the cherry gelatin over the 2 cups of boiling water and stir until dissolved. Add the cold water; chill until slightly thickened. Stir in the apples, celery, walnuts, and raisins. Spoon into a serving bowl or a 9- by 13-inch pan. Chill until set.

Serves 12.

Raspberry-Honeydew Mold

The color of this is beautiful—deep red gelatin with jewel-like chunks of green fruit.

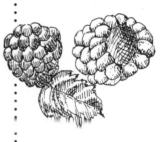

1 package (6 ounces) raspberry-flavored gelatin
2 cups boiling water
1¾ cups cold water
1 package (10 ounces) frozen raspberries, thawed and
  drained
2½ cups bite-size honeydew melon pieces

Dissolve the gelatin in the boiling water. Add cold water and raspberries; chill until slightly firm. Stir in honeydew melon, pour into a serving bowl or wet mold, and chill until firm.

Serves 12.

··· Slaws ···

Confetti Cole Slaw

This recipe gets its name from the variety of colors in the finished product. Since the dressing is clear, the vegetables don't lose a bit of their beauty.

1 small head green cabbage, shredded
½ head red cabbage, shredded
1 large carrot, grated
6 radishes, grated
1 green pepper, finely chopped

Dressing:

½ cup vegetable oil
⅓ cup white vinegar
¼ cup sugar
  dash of salt
  dash of pepper
  dash of cayenne pepper
½ teaspoon dry mustard

Place the green cabbage, red cabbage, carrot, radishes, and green pepper in a large salad bowl; toss gently to combine. In a separate bowl, combine the vegetable oil, vinegar, sugar, salt, pepper, cayenne pepper, and dry mustard. Stir or shake until the sugar is dissolved. Pour over the vegetables and toss. Chill before serving.
Serves 12 to 15.

Tangerine Cole Slaw

1 medium cabbage, shredded
2 cups tangerine pieces
1 cup seedless green grapes
$\frac{3}{4}$ cup mayonnaise
$\frac{1}{2}$ cup half-and-half

Place the cabbage, tangerine pieces, and green grapes in a salad bowl; toss gently to combine. Mix together the mayonnaise and the half-and-half; stir or beat until well combined and creamy. Pour over the salad and toss gently. Chill before serving.
Serves 8 to 10.

Granny Smith Cabbage Slaw

The tang of Granny Smith apples goes perfectly with cabbage.

$\frac{1}{2}$ medium cabbage, coarsely chopped
2 Granny Smith apples, chopped
$\frac{1}{2}$ cup golden raisins
  Creamy Slaw Dressing

Place the cabbage, apple, and raisins in a medium bowl; toss gently to combine. Pour on the dressing and toss. Chill before serving.
Serves 6 to 8.

Mixed Fruit Bowls

The great thing about fruit salads is that you don't really need a recipe at all: Almost any combination of seasonal fruits makes a delightful salad. A few tips:

- *if you choose to add a sweetener, such as sugar or honey, do so just before serving*
- *lemon juice will not only add a lovely flavor to fruit salad, it will also keep fruits like sliced apples from turning brown*
- *add finely chopped mint leaves to a fruit salad for a refreshing taste*
- *some fruits, such as melon and bananas, should be added to a fruit salad just before serving to retain their color and crispness*

Fruit platters, boats, bowls, and their like are great for any community gathering. They are colorful, require little preparation, contain few calories, and taste delicious. What more could you ask for?

Everyone is familiar with melon balls and strawberries in a scooped-out watermelon half, but if you are feeling a bit more adventurous, try some of the following ideas.

- Serve a huge bowl of fresh fruit with a variety of the following on the side: sour cream, whipped cream, a sweet fruit dressing, cottage cheese, a variety of flavored yogurts, chopped nuts, shredded coconut, and raisins. Plan on about 2 cups of fruit per person.
- Do a fruit platter containing only melons. Cut a variety of melons into easy-to-manage slices.
- Cut up cubes of cantaloupe, honeydew, and watermelon. Arrange the cubes in three sections in a glass 9- by 13-inch pan. Garnish with seedless purple grapes.
- Mint dressing: $\frac{1}{2}$ cup fresh orange juice, $\frac{1}{4}$ cup confectioner's sugar, $\frac{1}{2}$ cup fresh strawberries, 1 tablespoon fresh mint.

Combine all ingredients in a blender or food processor; puree until smooth. Use over any fresh-fruit salad.

- Combine similar colors in fruit salads.
    Green grapes, honeydew melon, kiwi fruit
    Pitted black cherries, blueberries, black grapes

Strawberries, cherries, watermelon
Oranges, cantaloupe, pineapple

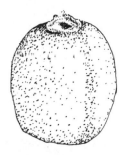

- Pomegranate seeds are a beautiful and delicious garnish sprinkled across any fruit salad. In most parts of the country, these are in season only during the winter.
- Feel free to combine canned or frozen fruits with fresh fruits. For example, canned pineapple chunks and frozen blueberries are delicious when added to almost any fruit combination.
- Sprinkle lemon juice on fruit that turns brown, such as apples and bananas.
- You can combine almost any selection of fruits ahead of time, but don't add bananas until the last minute.

Amounts Needed for a Watermelon Basket

	Serves 12	Serves 24	Serves 48
Watermelon	1 6-lb.	1 12-lb.	2 12-lb.
Strawberries	2 pts.	3 pts.	6 pts.
Pineapple	1 small	2 med.	3 med.
Canteloupe	1 med.	2 med.	3 med.
Honeydew	1 small	2 small	3 med.
Grapes	1 lb.	2 lbs.	4 lbs.

Waldorf Salad

3 green apples, coarsely chopped
3 red apples, coarsely chopped
¼ cup lemon juice
1 bunch celery (leaves removed), thinly sliced
1 cup walnuts
1 cup raisins — *use dates instead*
¾ cup mayonnaise or salad dressing

Place the apples in a salad bowl. Pour on the lemon juice and toss to coat the apples. Add the celery, walnuts, and raisins. Toss the salad gently with mayonnaise or salad dressing.
Serves 8 to 10.

Variations:
• You may add 1 or 2 teaspoons of curry powder to the mayonnaise for a tangier salad.
• 2 cups of cooked cut-up chicken may be added to make a delicious chicken salad.

Garnish salads or apple pies with cheese curls. Use a vegetable parer to shave thin strips of Cheddar cheese, roll each strip around your finger, secure with a toothpick, if necessary, and chill.

Fresh Cranberry Salad

This is so tasty you needn't save it for the holidays.

2 cups ground or chopped fresh cranberries
¾ cup sugar
3 cups miniature marshmallows
½ cup seedless grapes
2 apples, diced
½ cup chopped walnuts or pecans
1 cup heavy cream, whipped

Combine the cranberries and sugar; chill overnight. The next day, add marshmallows, grapes, apples, and nuts. Stir gently to combine. Fold in whipped cream and chill until serving time.

Serves 10 to 12.

Cranberry Relish

This recipe makes a large amount—enough for a big community dinner of about 50 to 75 people. If you aren't cooking for a large crowd, it is a great recipe to make up and store in jars with tight-fitting lids. It will keep up to 2 weeks and makes a great gift.

3 navel oranges
1 pound sugar
1 cup water
2 cups raisins
3 pounds cranberries
2 cups chopped walnuts
$\frac{1}{2}$ teaspoon cinnamon
$\frac{1}{8}$ teaspoon salt
$\frac{1}{2}$ teaspoon vanilla

Grind the oranges, rind and all, in a food grinder or processor. Set aside.

Place the sugar and water in a large saucepan; heat until the sugar is dissolved, then bring to a boil and cook for 5 minutes, stirring constantly. Add the ground oranges, raisins, and cranberries. Simmer for about 20 minutes, stirring often. Add the walnuts, cinnamon, salt, and vanilla, and simmer for 10 more minutes, stirring often.

Makes about $2\frac{1}{2}$ quarts.

Cranberries are truly native Americans, growing wild throughout most of the country long before the arrival of European settlers. This tiny berry was prized first by the Indians and then by the Pilgrims and other New England settlers. Cranberries freeze well, so the next time you find them in the produce section, buy several bags . . . one to eat and two to freeze. Then start enjoying the wonderful taste all year round.

Frozen Fruit Salad

This salad is convenient because it may be made several days ahead and kept in the freezer until serving time.

1 package (3 ounces) cream cheese, softened
$\frac{1}{2}$ cup mayonnaise
$1\frac{1}{2}$ cups miniature marshmallows
1 can (17 ounces) fruit cocktail, drained
1 can (11 ounces) mandarin orange sections, drained
$\frac{1}{2}$ pint heavy cream, whipped just until soft peaks form

Beat the cream cheese and mayonnaise until soft and fluffy. Gently stir in the marshmallows, fruit cocktail, and mandarin oranges. Fold in the whipped cream.

Pour into a fancy mold or ice cube trays; freeze until firm. Cut into slices, place on lettuce leaves, and serve.

Serves 6 to 8.

Ambrosia Salad

2 oranges
2 apples
3 bananas
2 cups green grapes
1 can ($8\frac{1}{2}$ ounces) pineapple tidbits, drained
2 tablespoons lemon juice
1 cup heavy cream
2 tablespoons confectioners' sugar
1 teaspoon vanilla
$\frac{1}{4}$ cup flaked coconut

Peel and cut the oranges into chunks. Peel, core, and dice the apples. Peel and slice the bananas. Place all the fruit in a large bowl. Sprinkle lemon

Vanilla Sugar
Cut open a vanilla bean and bury in two cups of sugar. Store in a tightly covered glass jar for several weeks until the sugar is flavored. Perfect for sweetening whipped cream, fresh fruits, or meringues.

juice on top and toss gently to coat. Whip heavy
cream with sugar and vanilla until soft peaks form.
Fold into fruit. Sprinkle flaked coconut on top.
   Serves 8.

Five-Cup Salad

You just can't have a proper potluck without at
least one serving of this great salad. In addition, it
is convenient because it can be made a day ahead.

1 can (8 ounces) pineapple tidbits, drained
1 can (10 ounces) mandarin orange sections, drained
1 cup flaked coconut
1 cup miniature marshmallows
1 cup sour cream

Mix all ingredients. Allow to chill several hours
or overnight.
   Serves 6.

can add grapes and pecans

· · · Fluff Salads · · ·

Watergate Salad

1 package (3 ounces) pistachio-flavored instant pudding
1 carton (8 ounces) frozen nondairy whipped topping,
   thawed
1 can (20 ounces) crushed pineapple, drained
1 cup miniature marshmallows, colored if possible
1 cup chopped maraschino cherries
1 cup chopped pecans

In a medium bowl, stir the pudding mix into the
whipped topping. Allow to sit a minute to dissolve

*1 - 12g coolwhip
1 - 6g pistachie
2 c. cottage cheese*

*I used mandrin
oranges. cr. pineapple
+ nuts - Went
over good
didn't use marshmellaus*

Also:
cool whip
cottage cheese
peach or apricot jello
cantalope cubed

the pudding. Stir in the crushed pineapple, marshmallows, cherries, and pecans. Chill and serve.
  Serves 6 to 8.

Orange Stuff

1 carton (12 ounces) frozen nondairy whipped topping,
  thawed
1 package (6 ounces) orange-flavored gelatin
1 pint cottage cheese
1 can (15 ounces) mandarin orange sections, drained
1 can (20 ounces) crushed pineapple, drained

In a medium bowl, stir together the whipped
topping and the dry orange gelatin mix. Add
cottage cheese, mandarin oranges, and crushed
pineapple. Chill at least for 1 hour before serving.
  Makes 8 to 12 servings.

Fast Fruit Fluff

1 carton (12 ounces) frozen nondairy whipped topping,
  thawed
1 package (3 ounces) raspberry-flavored gelatin
1 pint cottage cheese
1 cup chopped walnuts or pecans
1 can (17 ounces) fruit cocktail, drained opt.

In a medium bowl, stir together the whipped
topping and the dry raspberry gelatin mix. Stir in
cottage cheese, walnuts, and fruit cocktail. Chill
for at least 1 hour before serving.
  Makes 8 to 12 servings.

Try adding
rasp berries

Salad Dressings
· · · and Toppings · · ·

Dijon Basil Dressing

$\frac{2}{3}$ cup olive oil
$\frac{1}{3}$ cup white wine vinegar
2 tablespoons Dijon-style mustard
2 tablespoons basil
1 tablespoon oregano
1 tablespoon sugar
  dash of salt and pepper

Combine all ingredients in a jar with a snug-fitting lid. Shake well until blended.
Makes about $1\frac{1}{4}$ cups.

Lemon-Egg Dressing

$\frac{1}{2}$ cup olive oil
$\frac{1}{4}$ cup fresh lemon juice
1 raw egg yolk
$\frac{1}{2}$ teaspoon oregano
  dash of salt and pepper

Puree all ingredients in a blender or food processor until creamy.
Makes about $\frac{3}{4}$ cup.

Lettuce, like conversation, requires a good deal of oil, to avoid friction and keep the company smooth.
Charles Dudley Warner

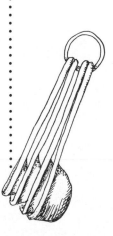

Italian Vinaigrette Dressing

This dressing is perfect for chilled vegetable salads as well as for tossed salads. It holds its own flavor well, even with strong salad greens such as romaine or endive.

$1\frac{1}{4}$ cups olive oil
$\frac{3}{4}$ cup lemon juice
$\frac{1}{3}$ cup honey
1 teaspoon Italian seasoning
$\frac{1}{2}$ teaspoon basil
$\frac{1}{4}$ teaspoon garlic
   dash of salt and pepper

Combine olive oil and lemon juice. Add honey and stir until honey is dissolved. Add remaining seasonings and mix well.

Makes about $2\frac{1}{2}$ cups.

According to a Spanish proverb, four persons are wanted to make a good salad: a spendthrift for oil, a miser for vinegar, a counselor for salt, and a madman to stir it all up.
Abraham Hayward

Lemon Mayonnaise

Created for aspic, this dressing also works well for simple fruit salads.

$\frac{1}{2}$ cup mayonnaise
1 teaspoon fresh lemon juice
1 teaspoon grated lemon peel

Combine all ingredients well. Allow to chill at least one hour before serving for lemon flavor to permeate mayonnaise.

Makes about $\frac{1}{2}$ cup.

Orange Curry Dressing

The tiny touch of curry powder is just enough to tantalize without overwhelming.

3 tablespoons sugar
⅓ cup white wine vinegar
½ cup olive oil
2 tablespoons grated orange peel
½ teaspoon curry powder

Add sugar to the white wine vinegar and stir until dissolved. Add olive oil, orange peel, and curry powder. Combine well, either by stirring or in a blender.
Makes about ¾ cup.

Creamy Russian Dressing

1 cup mayonnaise
⅓ cup chili sauce
⅓ cup pickle relish
2 teaspoons lemon juice
2 teaspoons sugar
dash of salt and pepper

Combine all ingredients and mix well.
Makes about 1½ cups.

Creamy Cucumber Dill Dressing

1 cup mayonnaise
$\frac{1}{2}$ cup peeled and finely chopped cucumber
2 tablespoons finely chopped green onion
2 tablespoons milk
1 tablespoon lemon juice
$\frac{1}{4}$ teaspoon dill weed
   dash of salt

Combine all ingredients and mix well.
Makes about $1\frac{1}{2}$ cups.

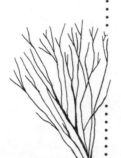

To allow full development of the flavor of herbs in salad dressings, add them to the vinegar or lemon juice and let stand for a few minutes before adding the oil.

French Dressing

$\frac{1}{4}$ cup vinegar
$\frac{1}{2}$ cup oil
$\frac{1}{3}$ cup ketchup
$\frac{1}{2}$ cup sugar
1 teaspoon salt
1 teaspoon paprika
1 teaspoon celery seed
$\frac{1}{4}$ teaspoon garlic powder
$\frac{1}{2}$ teaspoon dry mustard
   dash of pepper

Combine all ingredients and mix well.
Makes about 2 cups.

Blue Cheese Dressing

If you've never tasted homemade blue cheese dressing, you won't believe how good it is.

$\frac{1}{2}$ cup crumbled blue cheese
2 cups mayonnaise
$\frac{1}{4}$ cup milk
    dash of salt and pepper
    dash of garlic powder

Combine all ingredients and mix well.
Makes about $2\frac{1}{2}$ cups.

Creamy Slaw Dressing

3 tablespoons sugar
1 tablespoon white vinegar
$\frac{1}{2}$ cup heavy cream

Dissolve the sugar in the vinegar. Add the cream; stir to combine.
Makes about $\frac{3}{4}$ cup.

Cherry Cream Topping for Fresh Fruit

If you want to make a large bowl of fresh fruit or berries extra special, make up some of this topping.

1 package (3 ounces) cream cheese, softened
2 tablespoons mayonnaise
2 tablespoons half-and-half
2 tablespoons maraschino cherry juice
1 container (8 ounces) frozen nondairy whipped topping, thawed
1 to 2 tablespoons finely chopped maraschino cherries
    drop of red food coloring (optional)

In a small bowl, beat together the cream cheese, mayonnaise, half-and-half, and maraschino cherry juice. Stir in whipped topping and the finely chopped maraschino cherries. Add food coloring if desired.

Makes about 2 cups.

Breads

· · · Quick Breads · · ·

Banana Bread

A favorite American quick bread, delicious plain or spread with cream cheese. It freezes very well.

$\frac{1}{2}$ cup shortening
$\frac{1}{2}$ cup granulated sugar
$\frac{1}{2}$ cup light brown sugar, firmly packed
2 eggs
3 medium ripe bananas, well mashed
1 tablespoon buttermilk
2 cups flour

$\frac{1}{2}$ teaspoon salt
1 teaspoon baking soda
1 cup coarsely chopped walnuts

Cream together the shortening and sugars. Add eggs, bananas, and buttermilk; mix well. In a separate bowl, combine the flour, salt and baking soda, then stir into banana mixture. Stir in the nuts. Spoon into a greased and floured 5- by 9-inch loaf pan. Bake in a preheated 350° oven for 60 minutes or until a toothpick inserted into the center of the loaf comes out clean. Remove from the pan and cool on a rack.

Makes one loaf.

Don't throw away ripe bananas. Mash, freeze, and save them for making banana bread or muffins.

Brethren's Cheese Bread

A wonderfully hearty combination of cheese, onions, and dill.

$2\frac{1}{4}$ cups flour
1 tablespoon baking powder
$\frac{1}{2}$ teaspoon salt
2 tablespoons sugar
$\frac{3}{4}$ cup milk
$\frac{1}{4}$ cup melted butter or margarine
1 egg, lightly beaten
1 cup grated sharp Cheddar cheese
2 tablespoons finely chopped onion
$1\frac{1}{2}$ tablespoons dried dill weed

In a large bowl, stir together the flour, baking powder, salt, and sugar. In a separate bowl, combine the milk, melted butter or margarine, and beaten egg. Stir this into the flour mixture. Add cheese, onion, and dill weed; mix well. Spoon into a greased 5- by 9-inch loaf pan. Bake in a preheated 350° oven for 40 to 50 minutes or until a toothpick inserted in the loaf comes out clean. Remove from the pan and cool on a rack.

Makes one loaf.

Poppy Seed Bread

Sweet and moist, perfect for a tea party.

2 cups flour
$\frac{1}{4}$ teaspoon salt
2 teaspoons baking powder
1 cup sugar
2 eggs
1 cup evaporated milk
1 cup vegetable oil
1 teaspoon vanilla
$\frac{1}{4}$ cup poppy seeds

In a medium bowl, stir together the flour, salt, baking powder, and sugar. In a separate bowl, combine the eggs, evaporated milk, vegetable oil, and vanilla; mix well. Pour into the flour mixture and mix on low speed to combine. Stir in poppy seeds. Pour into a greased 5- by 9-inch loaf pan. Bake in a preheated 350° oven for 60 minutes or until a toothpick inserted in the center of the loaf comes out clean. Remove from pan and cool on a rack.

Makes one loaf.

No Time to Cook?
Stop by your bakery
for . . .
· special bakery breads:
  shepherd's loaf, sour-
  dough, oatmeal, pum-
  pernickel. The fresher
  the better!
· bagels, always a favor-
  ite
· muffins, a great addi-
  tion to any brunch or
  luncheon
· croissants

Strawberry Breakfast Bread

1 package (16 ounces) frozen unsweetened strawberries
3 cups flour
$\frac{1}{2}$ cup sugar
1 teaspoon baking soda
1 teaspoon ground coriander
1 teaspoon salt
$1\frac{1}{4}$ cup melted butter or margarine
4 eggs, lightly beaten
1 cup chopped pecans

Thaw and puree the frozen strawberries. Set aside.

In a medium bowl, stir together the flour, sugar, baking soda, coriander, and salt. In a separate bowl, stir together the melted butter, eggs, and pureed strawberries. Stir the two mixtures together until all of the dry ingredients are moist. Stir in pecans. Spoon into two greased 5- by 9-inch loaf pans. Bake in a preheated 350° oven for 45 to 60 minutes or until a toothpick inserted in the center comes out clean. Remove from pans and cool on a rack before slicing.

Makes 2 loaves.

Brown Sugar Bread

This is an old farm recipe that couldn't be better or easier.

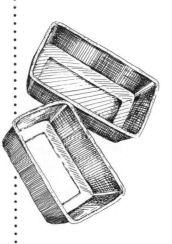

¾ cup granulated sugar
½ cup firmly packed brown sugar
3 tablespoons butter or margarine, softened
1 egg
¾ cup milk
2 cups flour
2 teaspoons baking powder
½ teaspoon salt
1 tablespoon butter or margarine
  cinnamon
  brown sugar

In a medium bowl, stir together the sugars, then beat in the softened butter. Add egg and beat. Mix in the milk.

In a separate bowl, stir together the flour, baking powder, and salt. Combine the two mixtures, stirring to form a stiff batter. Spoon into greased 5-by 9-inch loaf pan. Dot on butter. Sprinkle with cinnamon and brown sugar. Bake in a preheated 350° oven for 50 to 60 minutes or until a toothpick inserted in the center comes out clean. Remove from pan and cool on a rack.

Makes 1 loaf.

Boston Brown Bread

The perfect accompaniment to Baked Beans, the traditional Sunday supper in New England.

1 cup cornmeal
1 cup whole wheat flour
1 cup rye flour
2 teaspoons baking soda
1 teaspoon salt
2 cups buttermilk
¾ cup molasses
1 cup dark raisins

Stir together the cornmeal, flours, baking soda, and salt. Mix together the buttermilk and molasses until the molasses dissolves into the buttermilk. Add to the flour mixture and mix well. Stir in the raisins.

Spoon the batter into three well-greased 1-pound coffee cans. Cover tightly with foil. Place in a steamer (if you don't have a steamer, a deep canning kettle or other pot will work) on the top of the stove. Add boiling water one third the way up the cans. Cover the kettle, bring water to a boil, then reduce to a simmer. Steam cans over moderate heat for 2 to 3 hours, replacing the water if necessary. Remove from water and take off foil immediately. Let cool 10 minutes and remove from cans. Cool on a rack.

Makes 3 loaves.

How to cut Boston Brown Bread:

There's even a traditional way to cut this bread. While the bread is still hot, draw a string around it, crossing the ends across the top of the bread, then pull the ends of the string in opposite directions until the string slices the bread.

Cheesy Corn Bread

The very best bread to serve with baked beans—
as far as a Western tummy is concerned.

1½ cups yellow cornmeal
¾ cup flour
⅓ cup sugar
½ teaspoon salt
2 teaspoons baking powder
¼ cup vegetable oil
1 egg
½ cup milk
1 cup grated Cheddar cheese

Stir together the cornmeal, flour, sugar, salt, and
baking powder. In a separate bowl, blend the
vegetable oil, egg, and milk. Add to dry mixture,
mixing well. Stir in cheese. Pour into a well-
greased 9- by 9-inch baking pan. Bake in a preheated 375° oven for 45 minutes or until nicely
browned.

Serves 6 to 8.

*Instead of butter, try
cream cheese spreads
with your favorite
breads. Soften the cream
cheese and mix with any
of the following:*

- *minced chutney*
- *marmalade*
- *raspberry preserves*
- *deviled ham*
- *crumbled blue cheese*
- *chopped pimiento*
- *drained, crushed pine-
  apple*
- *prepared white horse-
  radish*
- *minced stuffed olives*
- *crumbled cooked bacon*
- *vegetables: grated carrots, chopped celery,
  green pepper, chives*

Date-Nut Loaf

Try serving this with soft cream cheese and pineapple spread.

*2 cups chopped, pitted dates
1 cup chopped walnuts
2 teaspoons baking soda
2 cups boiling water
$\frac{1}{4}$ cup butter or margarine, softened
2 cups sugar
2 eggs
1 teaspoon vanilla
$2\frac{2}{3}$ cups flour
$\frac{1}{2}$ teaspoon salt*

Place the dates, walnuts, and baking soda in a mixing bowl. Pour boiling water over them and allow to sit for 30 minutes. Cream the butter or margarine and sugar. Add eggs and vanilla; mix well. Blend the butter mixture into the date mixture and mix well.

Mix together the flour and salt then stir into the date mixture. Spoon the batter into two greased 5- by 9-inch bread pans. Bake in a preheated 325° oven for about 50 minutes or until a toothpick inserted into the center comes out clean. Remove from pans and cool on a rack.

Makes 2 loaves.

Hearty Apricot Bread

An exotic combination of apricots, walnuts, and bananas.

1 cup boiling water
1½ cups chopped dried apricots
¼ cup butter or margarine, softened
1 cup sugar
2 ripe bananas, mashed
2 eggs
3 cups whole wheat flour
3 teaspoons baking powder
½ teaspoon salt
1 cup chopped walnuts

Pour boiling water over the apricots; allow to sit 10 minutes. In a separate bowl, beat together the butter or margarine and the sugar. Mix in the bananas and eggs. Add the apricot mixture and stir to combine well. Stir together the flour, baking powder, and salt, and then add to the batter and stir to combine. Mix in the walnuts. Spoon mixture into two greased and floured 5- by 9-inch bread pans. Bake in a preheated 350° oven for 45 to 60 minutes or until a toothpick inserted into a loaf comes out clean. Remove from pans and cool on a rack.

Makes 2 loaves.

Cranberry Tea Bread

¾ cup butter or margarine, softened
1 cup granulated sugar
½ cup firmly packed brown sugar
4 eggs
3 cups flour
2 teaspoons baking powder
1 teaspoon baking soda

½ teaspoon salt
1 teaspoon grated orange rind
1 can (16 ounces) whole-berry cranberry sauce
1 cup chopped walnuts

Cream together the butter or margarine and the sugars. Add the eggs one at a time, mixing well after each addition. In a separate bowl, stir together the flour, baking powder, baking soda, salt, and grated orange rind. Add to the egg batter and mix well. Stir in the cranberry sauce and walnuts. Spoon batter into two greased and floured 5- by 9-inch bread pans. Bake in a preheated 350° oven for 50 to 60 minutes or until a toothpick inserted into a loaf comes out clean. Remove from pans and cool on a rack.

Makes 2 loaves.

Pumpkin Date Bread

Rich and warm, a great bread to serve with cider on a fall afternoon.

½ cup butter or margarine, softened
1¼ cups sugar
2 eggs
1 cup cooked or canned pumpkin, pureed
2 cups flour
2 teaspoons baking powder
½ teaspoon salt
1½ teaspoons pumpkin pie spice
1 teaspoon cinnamon
½ teaspoon ginger
⅛ teaspoon cloves
⅔ cup chopped walnuts
⅔ cup chopped dates

Cream together the butter or margarine and sugar. Add the eggs and pumpkin; blend until well combined. In a separate bowl, stir together the flour, baking powder, salt, and spices. Add to the pumpkin mixture and mix well. Stir in the walnuts and dates. Spoon into two well-greased and floured 5- by 9-inch loaf pans. Bake in a preheated 350° oven for one hour or until a toothpick inserted into the bread comes out clean. Remove from pan and cool on a rack.

Makes 2 loaves.

Irish Soda Bread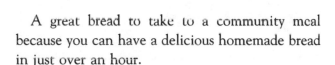

A great bread to take to a community meal because you can have a delicious homemade bread in just over an hour.

3 cups flour
$\frac{1}{4}$ cup sugar
1 tablespoon baking powder
$\frac{1}{2}$ teaspoon salt
$\frac{1}{2}$ teaspoon baking soda
1 cup raisins
$\frac{1}{2}$ cup chopped walnuts
$1\frac{1}{2}$ cups buttermilk
1 beaten egg (optional)

Mix together the flour, sugar, baking powder, salt, and baking soda. Stir in the raisins and walnuts. Add buttermilk and stir to form a soft dough. Turn out of bowl onto a well-floured surface. Knead just a few turns until smooth. Shape into a round loaf and place on a greased cookie sheet. Cut two to three slashes $\frac{1}{4}$-inch deep across the top. If desired, brush with beaten egg. Bake in a preheated 350° oven for 40 to 45 minutes.

Makes 1 loaf.

Variations:
- Currants may be substituted for the raisins.
- Walnuts may be omitted.
- A wonderfully aromatic Irish Soda Bread with herbs can be made by adding $\frac{1}{4}$ teaspoon marjoram, $\frac{1}{4}$ teaspoon oregano, $\frac{1}{2}$ teaspoon basil, and a pinch of thyme. Add the herbs to the flour mixture.

· · · Coffee Cakes · · ·

Georgia Peach-Pecan Coffee Cake

Two of Georgia's treasures combine to make this delicious coffee cake. What a wonderful treat to welcome house guests with in the morning.

$\frac{1}{2}$ cup butter or margarine, softened
1 cup firmly packed brown sugar
$\frac{1}{2}$ cup granulated sugar
1 egg
1 teaspoon vanilla
1 tablespoon lemon juice
1 cup milk
2 cups flour
1 teaspoon baking soda
$\frac{1}{2}$ teaspoon salt
$1\frac{1}{2}$ cups peeled and diced fresh peaches

Topping:
$\frac{3}{4}$ cup chopped pecans
$\frac{1}{4}$ cup granulated sugar
$\frac{1}{4}$ cup firmly packed brown sugar
$\frac{1}{2}$ teaspoon cinnamon
$\frac{1}{2}$ teaspoon ground coriander

The warmer the coffee cake when drizzling frosting or glaze on top, the more the glaze will run off the top. If a decided design is wanted, be sure the cake is cool.

Cream the butter or margarine and sugars. Beat in the egg and vanilla until light in color. Stir the lemon juice into the milk and add to egg mixture.

In a separate bowl, stir together the flour, baking soda, and salt. Stir into the batter and beat at low speed until mixture is just combined. Gently stir in the peaches. Pour into a greased 9- by 13-inch baking pan.

In a small bowl, combine the pecans, sugars, cinnamon, and coriander. Sprinkle this mixture over the batter. Bake in a preheated 350° oven for approximately 40 to 45 minutes or until a toothpick inserted in the center comes out clean.

Serves 12.

Overnight Coffee Cake

This is an especially convenient coffee cake for an early brunch because you can assemble it the night before, put it in the refrigerator, and bake it in the morning.

2 cups flour
1 cup granulated sugar
$\frac{1}{2}$ cup firmly packed brown sugar
$\frac{1}{2}$ teaspoon cinnamon
$\frac{1}{2}$ teaspoon grated lemon rind
$\frac{1}{2}$ teaspoon salt
1 teaspoon baking soda
$\frac{2}{3}$ cup butter or margarine
1 cup buttermilk
2 beaten eggs

Topping:
$\frac{1}{2}$ cup firmly packed brown sugar
$\frac{1}{2}$ cup nuts, finely chopped
$\frac{1}{2}$ teaspoon cinnamon
$\frac{1}{2}$ teaspoon nutmeg

Stir together the flour, sugars, cinnamon, grated lemon rind, salt, and baking soda. With a pastry blender or two knives, cut in the butter or margarine. Add buttermilk and eggs; mix well. Set aside.

For the topping, in a separate bowl, stir together the brown sugar, nuts, cinnamon, and nutmeg.

Pour half of the batter into a 9- by 13-inch greased and floured baking pan. Sprinkle on half of the topping. Pour on the remainder of the batter and sprinkle with the remaining topping. Refrigerate the coffee cake for up to 24 hours before baking in a preheated 350° oven for 30 to 40 minutes or bake immediately in a 350° oven for 20 to 30 minutes.

Serves 24.

Sour Cream Coffee Cake

This is a very rich coffee cake with a delicate almond flavor.

1 cup butter or margarine, softened
1¼ cups sugar
2 eggs
1 cup sour cream
1 teaspoon almond extract
2 cups flour
1 teaspoon baking powder
½ teaspoon baking soda

Topping:
½ cup finely chopped almonds
2 tablespoons granulated sugar
1 tablespoon brown sugar
½ teaspoon cinnamon

Cream together the butter and sugar; beat in the eggs. Add sour cream and almond extract; beat until well combined.

Sour cream coffee cakes are good choices for community meals since they are moist and keep well.

In a separate bowl, stir together the flour, baking powder, and baking soda. Add to other mixture and stir until well combined. Pour batter into a greased and floured 9- by 13-inch baking pan.

In a separate bowl, stir together the almonds, sugars, and cinnamons. Place the nut mixture on top of the batter by spoonfuls. Swirl into the cake with a knife, being careful not to stir in too well. Bake in a 350° oven for 45 minutes or until lightly browned.

Serves 24.

Fruit Basket Upset Coffee Cake

This is a great recipe because you can make it with any fruit that happens to be in season.

2 cups flour
1 cup sugar
2 teaspoons baking powder
1 teaspoon salt
1 teaspoon grated lemon rind
$\frac{1}{2}$ cup butter or margarine
2 eggs
1 cup milk
1 teaspoon vanilla or almond extract
$3\frac{1}{2}$ cups prepared fruit, such as blueberries, apricots, cherries, nectarines, peaches, plums, or apples

Topping:
$\frac{1}{3}$ cup firmly packed brown sugar
$\frac{1}{4}$ cup flour
1 teaspoon cinnamon
2 tablespoons butter or margarine, softened

Prepare the fruit by peeling, pitting, and slicing into bite-size pieces, as necessary. Set aside.

In a large bowl, stir together the flour, sugar, baking powder, salt, and grated lemon rind. Cut in the butter or margarine with a pastry blender or two knives until the mixture resembles coarse cornmeal.

In a separate bowl, stir together the eggs, milk, and vanilla or almond extract. Add to the flour mixture and stir until just barely combined. Spoon batter into a well-greased 7- by 11-inch baking pan.

Arrange the fruit on top of the batter and press it in lightly.

In a small bowl, combine the brown sugar, flour, and cinnamon. Work in the butter or margarine. Sprinkle this mixture on top of the fruit. Bake in a 350° oven 50 minutes to 1 hour or until a toothpick inserted in the center comes out clean.

Serves 12.

Graham Streusel Coffee Cake

Streusel makes a good topping for fruit pies—a nice change from the traditional double-crust pie.

Especially quick and easy to make because you use a prepared cake mix as one of the ingredients.

Streusel topping:
2 cups graham cracker crumbs
¾ cup chopped nuts
½ cup melted butter or margarine
¾ cup firmly packed brown sugar
½ teaspoon cinnamon
½ teaspoon nutmeg

Coffee cake:
1 box yellow cake mix
¼ cup vegetable oil
3 eggs
1 cup water

Glaze:
1 cup confectioners' sugar
1 tablespoon melted butter or margarine
1 teaspoon vanilla
1 to 2 teaspoons milk

In a small bowl, combine the graham cracker crumbs, chopped nuts, butter or margarine, brown sugar, cinnamon, and nutmeg. Set mixture aside.

In a separate bowl, combine the cake mix, oil, eggs, and water. Beat for 3 minutes. Spoon half of the batter into a greased and floured 9- by 13-inch baking pan. Sprinkle on half of the streusel topping. Add the remainder of the cake batter and the rest of the topping. Bake in a preheated 350° oven for 40 to 50 minutes or until a toothpick inserted into the cake comes out clean.

While cake is baking, make the glaze by combining the confectioners' sugar, melted butter or margarine, vanilla, and just enough milk to make a smooth glaze. Spread glaze on cake while cake is still warm.

Serves 24.

Quick Cherry Coffee Cake

1 cup sugar
$\frac{1}{2}$ cup butter or margarine, softened
1 egg
$\frac{3}{4}$ cup milk
2 cups flour
2 teaspoons baking powder
$\frac{1}{4}$ teaspoon salt
1 can (21 ounces) cherry pie filling or other flavor of your choice

Topping:
1 cup flour
1 cup sugar
$\frac{1}{2}$ cup butter or margarine

Glaze:
1 cup confectioners' sugar
1 tablespoon melted butter or margarine
1 teaspoon vanilla
1 to 2 tablespoons milk

Blend the sugar and butter or margarine together; beat in the egg. Add milk and stir.

In a separate bowl, stir together the flour, baking powder, and salt. Add to the batter and combine. Spread in a 7- by 11-inch greased baking pan. Top with cherry pie filling.

To make the topping: Combine flour, sugar, and butter or margarine with a pastry blender or two knives until it resembles coarse crumbs. Sprinkle on top of the cherries. Bake in a preheated 350° oven for 30 to 35 minutes.

While cake is baking, make glaze by combining the confectioners' sugar, melted butter or margarine, vanilla, and just enough milk to make a smooth but not runny glaze. Spread the glaze on the still-warm cake.

Serves 12 to 16.

Cocoa-Swirl Coffee Cake

The chocolate flavor in this coffee cake isn't overwhelming. It makes a delightfully different addition to a selection of coffee cakes at a tea or brunch.

$\frac{1}{2}$ cup vegetable shortening
$\frac{1}{2}$ cup butter or margarine, softened
2 cups granulated sugar
$\frac{1}{2}$ teaspoon imitation butter flavoring
1 teaspoon vanilla
3 eggs
$3\frac{1}{2}$ cups sifted flour
1 tablespoon baking powder
$\frac{1}{2}$ teaspoon salt
1 can (12 ounces) evaporated milk

Cocoa mixture:
$\frac{1}{3}$ cup sugar
1 tablespoon cocoa
2 teaspoons cinnamon

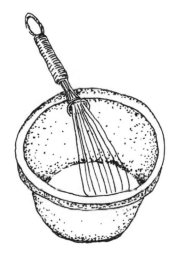

Cream the shortening, butter or margarine, and sugar until light and fluffy. Beat in the butter flavoring and vanilla. Add the eggs one at a time.

In a separate bowl, stir together the flour, baking powder, and salt. Add this flour mixture to the batter alternately with the evaporated milk.

In a separate bowl, stir together the sugar, cocoa, and cinnamon.

Grease two 4- by 8-inch bread pans. Divide one half of the batter between the two pans. Divide half of the cocoa mixture between the two pans. Add the remaining batter to each pan and sprinkle the rest of the cocoa mixture on top. Marbleize the batter by running a knife through the batter several times.

Bake in a preheated 325° oven for 1 hour or until a toothpick inserted into the coffee cake comes out clean.

Makes 2 loaves.

German Apple Kuchen

3 cups peeled, sliced Granny Smith apples
⅓ cup firmly packed brown sugar
1 cup confectioners' sugar
1¾ cups flour
1 cup margarine, softened (do not use butter)
2 cups sour cream
2 eggs
¼ cup sugar

Place apples in a bowl; sprinkle the brown sugar over them. Toss very gently to combine, then set aside.

In a separate bowl, stir together the confectioners' sugar and flour. Beat in the margarine. Pat this crust mixture into a greased 9- by 13-inch baking pan. Arrange the apples on top.

Beat together the sour cream, eggs, and sugar; pour over the fruit. Bake in a preheated 375° oven for 45 minutes.

Serves 12.

Variations:
You can make a variety of kuchen by substituting 3 cups of any of the fruits below for the apples:

• blueberries
• sliced apricots
• sliced peaches
• sliced plums
• cranberries
• gooseberries

· · · **Batter Breads** · · ·

Herb-Onion Bread

This is a good wintertime bread, toasted, buttered, and served with a hearty stew.

$3\frac{1}{4}$ cups flour
2 packages active dry yeast
2 tablespoons sugar
1 teaspoon salt
$\frac{1}{4}$ teaspoon ground sage
$\frac{1}{2}$ teaspoon rosemary leaves
$\frac{1}{4}$ teaspoon thyme leaves
$\frac{1}{4}$ teaspoon basil leaves
$\frac{1}{8}$ teaspoon oregano leaves
1 cup chopped onion
$\frac{1}{3}$ cup butter or margarine
1 egg
$1\frac{1}{4}$ cups water

Place the flour, yeast, sugar, salt, sage, rosemary leaves, thyme leaves, basil leaves, and oregano in a large bowl. Stir to combine. Sauté the onion in the butter or margarine until soft. Add to flour mixture. Stir egg into water and then add to flour mixture and beat until batter is smooth. Spoon into two greased 5- by 9-inch bread pans. Bake in a 375° oven for 35 to 40 minutes or until browned.

Makes 2 medium loaves.

The term batter bread is used to refer to breads that contain yeast but do not require kneading.

Sally Lunn

One of the oldest and most traditional of batter breads. Depending upon which story you prefer, the name comes either from the name of a lady from Bath, England, who first sold the bread or from *solet-lune*, a French phrase meaning "sun and moon" that refers to the bread's golden top and white base.

4 cups flour
1 package active dry yeast
1 cup milk
$\frac{3}{4}$ cup butter or margarine
$\frac{1}{4}$ cup sugar
$1\frac{1}{2}$ teaspoons salt
4 eggs

In a large bowl, stir together $2\frac{1}{2}$ cups of flour and the yeast; set aside. Place the milk, butter or margarine, sugar, and salt in a medium saucepan. Heat slowly, stirring constantly until the butter is melted and the sugar and salt dissolved. Be very careful not to let the milk boil. Remove from heat and cool to lukewarm. When cool, add to flour and beat for two minutes or until smooth. Add the eggs one at a time, beating after each addition. Add one more cup of flour and beat, then add enough of the remaining flour to make a stiff dough.

Cover and let rise in a warm, draft-free place until light and bubbly, about 45 minutes to one hour. When risen, stir down. Spoon into a well-greased, 10-inch tube pan. Cover and let rise until doubled, about 45 minutes. Bake in a preheated 375° oven for 40 to 45 minutes or until top is golden brown. Remove from pan immediately, and cool on a rack.

Makes 1 loaf.

Dill Bread

Dill makes a wonderfully flavorful bread to serve with cauliflower and broccoli soups.

$3\frac{1}{4}$ cups flour
2 packages active dry yeast
3 tablespoons sugar
1 tablespoon dried minced onion
2 tablespoons dill seed
1 teaspoon salt
1 cup plain yogurt
$\frac{1}{2}$ cup water
2 tablespoons vegetable oil
1 egg

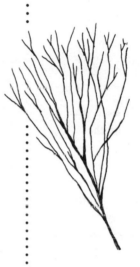

In a large bowl, stir together the flour, yeast, sugar, dried onion, dill seed, and salt. In a separate bowl, mix the yogurt, water, oil, and egg until smooth. Stir into flour mixture and mix well. Spoon into a greased $1\frac{1}{2}$- to 2-quart casserole or two 5- by 9-inch bread pans. Cover and let rise in a warm place until double in bulk, about 1 hour. Bake in a preheated 375° oven for 35 to 40 minutes or until golden brown. Remove from pans and cool on a rack. Makes 1 large loaf or 2 medium loaves.

Saffron is widely used in cooking throughout the Middle East, Italy, France, Spain, and India as well as Sweden, England, and Portugal. True saffron is unusually fragrant and has a pleasantly spicy and pungent taste.

Some ideas for using saffron:

- *add a pinch of crushed saffron to mashed potatoes*
- *dissolve $\frac{1}{8}$ teaspoon saffron in $\frac{1}{4}$ cup chicken broth and add to cooking liquid when cooking rice*
- *add a pinch of saffron to your pound cake recipe for subtle flavor and golden color*

· · · Yeast Breads · · ·

Challah

Traditional Jewish braided bread that's wonderful any time, for any occasion.

1 package active dry yeast
$\frac{1}{2}$ cup warm water
$\frac{3}{4}$ cup milk
$\frac{1}{4}$ cup butter or margarine
2 tablespoons sugar
2 teaspoons salt
2 eggs
$\frac{1}{8}$ teaspoon saffron threads, crushed (optional)
4 to 5 cups flour
1 egg
1 tablespoon poppy seeds

Stir yeast into water and allow to soften about 10 minutes. Meanwhile, heat milk and butter together over low heat and stir until the butter dissolves. Remove from heat, pour into a large bowl, and add sugar and salt. Stir until sugar and salt dissolve; allow to cool until lukewarm. Stir in eggs, saffron, and dissolved yeast.

Begin adding the flour, one cup at a time, while stirring. Continue adding flour until a stiff dough forms. Turn out of the bowl onto a floured board and knead 8 to 10 minutes. Place in a greased bowl, cover, and allow to rise in a warm place until double in bulk, about 1 hour. Punch down and divide into thirds.

Roll out each piece to about 18 inches. Braid dough and tuck ends under. Place on greased baking sheet and let rise until double, about 30 minutes. Beat egg with a bit of water and brush on dough. Sprinkle on poppy seeds and bake in a preheated 375° oven for 45 to 50 minutes or until browned.

Makes 1 loaf.

Swedish Rye Bread

This bread is dense and heavy because rye flour does not have the gluten content of wheat flour, so it does not rise as much.

2 packages active dry yeast
$\frac{1}{4}$ cup lukewarm water
$\frac{1}{3}$ cup molasses
$\frac{1}{2}$ cup firmly packed brown sugar
1 tablespoon butter or margarine
$1\frac{1}{7}$ cups boiling water
$1\frac{1}{2}$ teaspoons caraway seed
$1\frac{1}{2}$ teaspoons anise seed
1 tablespoon salt
$3\frac{1}{2}$ cups sifted white flour
2 cups rye flour
2 tablespoons cornmeal

Stir yeast into warm water and set aside for about 10 minutes. Place the molasses, brown sugar, and butter or margarine in a large bowl, and pour the boiling water over them. Stir until sugar is dissolved and butter is melted. Allow to cool until lukewarm.

In a blender or using a mortar and pestle, grind the caraway seed, anise seed, and salt until coarse. Blend into the liquid mixture, then stir in the yeast mixture.

In a separate bowl, stir together the rye and white flours. Add to liquid mixture a cup at a time, stirring until a stiff dough is formed.

If you want to create a shiny brown crust, brush yeast bread or coffeecake with an egg wash: one whole egg or one egg yolk beaten with one teaspoon milk; or one egg white beaten with one teaspoon water.

Turn out of the bowl onto a floured board and knead for about 10 minutes. Return to a clean greased bowl and cover. Let rise in a warm place until doubled in bulk, about $1\frac{1}{2}$ hours. Punch down and shape into two round loaves. Sprinkle corn-meal on a greased baking sheet and place loaves on top. Cover and allow to rise until doubled, about 45 minutes to 1 hour. Cut a slash across the top of each loaf. Bake in a preheated 375° oven for 30 minutes. Remove from pans and allow to cool on rack.

Makes 2 loaves.

Swedish Coffee Braid

The ground cardamom in this recipe gives this sweet bread its distinctive taste.

$\frac{1}{4}$ cup lukewarm water
$\frac{1}{4}$ teaspoon sugar
1 package active dry yeast
1 cup milk
1 cup sugar
$\frac{1}{2}$ cup butter or margarine, softened
1 teaspoon salt
1 teaspoon cardamom
1 egg, slightly beaten
3 to 4 cups flour
  beaten egg white

In a small bowl, dissolve the sugar in the warm water. Add the yeast and allow to dissolve for 5 minutes. Heat the milk, but do not allow to boil. Place sugar, butter or margarine, and salt in a large bowl. Pour the hot milk over them, stirring to melt the butter or margarine and dissolve the sugar and salt. Allow to cool to lukewarm. Add yeast mixture and stir in. Add cardamom and egg and stir in. Gradually add flour until a stiff dough is formed.

Smell of bread. Homely words.
The light faded
In the snow's whirling ashes.

Dag Hammarskjold

Turn out of bowl onto a floured board and knead for about 5 minutes. Return to a clean greased bowl. Cover and let rise in a warm place until double, 45 to 60 minutes. Punch down and divide into 6 pieces. Roll each piece into a rope about 15 inches long. On a greased cookie sheet, braid three pieces to form a braided loaf; repeat for the second loaf. Tuck ends under, cover, and allow to rise until double, about 45 minutes. Brush with beaten egg white. Bake in a preheated 375° oven for 20 to 25 minutes or until golden brown.

Makes 2 medium loaves.

Homemade Oat Bread

This rich and creamy bread makes delicious toast.

1 cup regular or quick-cooking rolled oats
2 cups boiling water
2 packages active dry yeast
⅓ cup lukewarm water
2½ teaspoons salt
½ cup molasses or honey
2 tablespoons butter or margarine, softened
6 cups flour

In a large bowl, place the oats and pour boiling water over them. Allow to stand 30 minutes. In a separate bowl, sprinkle yeast over the ⅓ cup warm water and let stand 5 minutes. Add salt, honey or molasses, butter or margarine, and yeast mixture to oat mixture and stir until butter melts. Stir in 4 cups flour, 2 cups at a time. Turn dough out of bowl onto a floured board and knead in the final 2 cups of flour.

Place dough in a clean oiled bowl, cover, and allow to rise in a warm place about 2 hours. Punch down and divide in two. Place in greased 5- by 9-inch bread pans, cover, and let rise 1 hour. Cut a slash across the top of each loaf and bake in a preheated 325° oven for 50 minutes or until golden brown on top. Remove from pans and allow to cool on rack.

Makes 2 loaves.

When planning to freeze yeast breads, bake only to a light golden brown to prevent separation of crust from loaf.

Holiday Greek Bread

This is a very rich, sweet bread—a treasured recipe from a Greek friend.

$1\frac{1}{2}$ cups lukewarm milk
2 packages active dry yeast
$\frac{1}{2}$ teaspoon salt
$1\frac{1}{2}$ cups sugar
5 eggs, lightly beaten
1 teaspoon vanilla
1 cup melted butter or margarine
8 or more cups flour
1 egg, lightly beaten
1 tablespoon sesame seeds

Heat milk, but do not allow to boil. Cool to lukewarm. Sprinkle yeast over the top and allow to sit for 5 minutes. Add salt and sugar, stirring until dissolved. Add beaten eggs, vanilla, and butter or margarine; mix well. Add enough flour to form a stiff dough. Turn out of the bowl onto a floured board.

The dough will be sticky when you begin to knead it, but continue to add flour as you knead, until the dough is smooth. Knead for about 10 minutes. Place in a large greased bowl and allow to rise in a warm place until double in bulk, about 1 hour. Punch down. Divide into three parts. Roll each part into a rope about 15 inches long. Place on a greased cookie sheet, braid the three parts together, and tuck under each end. Cover and allow to rise until double in bulk. Brush with beaten egg and sprinkle on sesame seeds. Bake in preheated 350° oven for 35 to 50 minutes or until lightly browned.

Makes 1 large loaf

Banana Yeast Bread

$\frac{1}{4}$ teaspoon sugar
$\frac{1}{4}$ cup lukewarm water
1 package active dry yeast
$\frac{1}{2}$ cup reconstituted nonfat dry milk
1 teaspoon vanilla
$\frac{1}{2}$ teaspoon nutmeg
1 teaspoon salt
$\frac{1}{2}$ cup sugar
$\frac{1}{2}$ cup melted butter or margarine
2 to 3 ripe bananas, mashed (enough to make 1 cup)
2 eggs
5 to 6 cups flour (use one-half white, one-half whole wheat)

In a small bowl, combine the $\frac{1}{4}$ teaspoon sugar and the warm water; sprinkle yeast over this and set aside for about 10 minutes. In a large bowl, combine the milk, vanilla, nutmeg, salt, and sugar. Stir until salt and sugar are dissolved. Add butter or margarine, bananas, and eggs; mix well. Add yeast mixture and stir in. Gradually stir in flour until a dough stiff enough to knead is formed.

Turn dough out of bowl, onto a floured board. Knead about 10 minutes. Return dough to a clean, greased bowl. Allow to rise until double in bulk, about 1 hour. Punch down and shape into two loaves. Place into two greased 5- by 9-inch pans. Allow to rise until double, about 45 minutes. Cut a slash across the top of each loaf and place in a preheated 350° oven. Bake for 45 minutes or until browned and hollow sounding when tapped. Remove from pans and allow to cool on rack.

Makes 2 loaves.

Banana Raisin Bread:

Follow recipe for Banana Yeast Bread, but when ready to shape the loaves for their final rising, pat each piece out into a 9- by 12-inch rectangle. Sprinkle $\frac{3}{4}$ cup raisins on each piece of dough. Roll up jelly-roll fashion, place in greased loaf pans, and proceed with the recipe.

Note: Banana Yeast Bread and Banana Raisin Bread both make fantastic French toast.

Walnut Bread

Hearty and delicious, this bread is especially nice to serve at a salad luncheon.

pinch of sugar
$\frac{1}{2}$ *cup lukewarm water*
1 package active dry yeast
$\frac{1}{2}$ *cup melted butter or margarine*
1$\frac{1}{4}$ cups water
$\frac{1}{4}$ *cup nonfat dry milk*
$\frac{1}{2}$ *teaspoon vanilla*
$\frac{1}{4}$ *cup honey*
1 tablespoon salt
1$\frac{1}{2}$ cups chopped walnuts
$\frac{1}{2}$ *cup chopped onion*
2 cups white flour
3 to 4 cups whole wheat flour

For a soft bread crust, brush melted butter or margarine over the top when you first take it out of the oven.

Dissolve sugar in the warm water; add yeast and allow to sit about 5 minutes. During this time, stir together butter, water, nonfat dry milk, vanilla, honey, and salt. Stir in walnuts and onions. Add yeast mixture. Add white flour and then enough whole wheat flour to form a stiff dough.

Turn out of bowl onto a floured board and knead for about 5 minutes. Place in a greased bowl, set in a warm place, and allow to rise until double in bulk, about 1½ hours. Punch down, turn out of bowl, and shape into two round loaves. Place on greased cookie sheets. Allow to rise until double, about 45 minutes to 1 hour. Cut 2 or 3 slashes across the top of the bread. Bake in a preheated 350° oven for about 45 minutes. Remove from pans and allow to cool on racks.

Makes 2 loaves.

Kentucky Wheat Bread

The perfect partner for a rich winter stew.

½ cup lukewarm water
1 teaspoon sugar
1 package active dry yeast
1½ cups hot water
½ cup honey
2 cups scalded and cooled milk
⅓ cup melted butter or margarine
1½ teaspoons salt
12 cups whole wheat flour

Mix warm water and sugar together in a small bowl; sprinkle yeast over the top and allow to sit until bubbly. In a separate bowl, stir together the hot water, honey, milk, melted butter or margarine, and salt, stirring until honey and salt are dissolved. Allow liquid to cool until lukewarm and then stir in yeast mixture. Add whole wheat flour one cup at a time, stirring until a soft dough forms. Turn dough out onto a well-floured board and knead until smooth and elastic, about 10 minutes. Return dough to a clean, greased mixing bowl. Cover and let rise in a warm place until double in bulk, about 1 to 1½ hours. Punch down and turn out of the bowl. Shape into three loaves and place into three greased 5- by 9-inch bread pans. Allow to rise until double in bulk, about 45 minutes. Cut a slash across the top of each loaf and bake in a preheated 350° oven for 50 minutes or until loaf sounds hollow when tapped on top. Remove from pan and allow to cool on a wire rack.

Makes 3 loaves.

Powdermilk Biscuits. Heavens! They're tasty and expeditious. Made from the whole wheat that gives shy persons the strength to get up and do what needs to be done.

Garrison Keillor

Biscuits, Rolls, · · · and Muffins · · ·

Baking Powder Biscuits

The beauty of biscuits is that they are quick and easy—and they taste heavenly!

2 cups flour
1 teaspoon salt
1 tablespoon baking powder
¼ cup shortening
¾ cup milk

Stir together the flour, salt, and baking powder. Cut in the shortening with two knives or a pastry blender until the mixture resembles coarse corn-meal. Add milk all at once, stirring just until combined. Turn dough out of bowl and knead until dough is not sticky. Roll dough out with a lightly floured rolling pin until $\frac{1}{2}$-inch thick. Cut with a round biscuit cutter. Arrange on an ungreased cookie sheet, touching, if you want them to have soft edges, or about an inch apart if you prefer them crisp. Bake in preheated 450° oven for 12 to 15 minutes or until lightly browned on top.

Makes 24 small or 12 large biscuits.

Variations:

Add 1 to 2 tablespoons of any of the following ingredients to the flour mixture.

- Finely chopped fresh parsley or chives
- Crisp, cooked bacon
- Grated Cheddar cheese
- Sautéed onion

Drop biscuts:

Increase milk to 1 cup to make a softer dough. Drop by spoonfuls onto a lightly greased cookie sheet.

Makes 12 large or 24 small biscuits.

All-Purpose Rolls

True to its name, this recipe makes a variety of rolls from simple dinner rolls to fancy sticky buns. The basic recipe will make enough for two generous batches, and it's easily doubled for feeding multitudes.

Basic Recipe:
1 package active dry yeast
$\frac{1}{4}$ cup lukewarm water

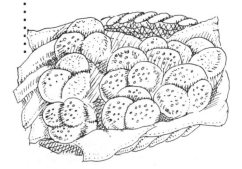

$\frac{1}{4}$ teaspoon sugar
2 cups milk
$\frac{1}{2}$ cup shortening
1 tablespoon salt
$\frac{1}{2}$ cup sugar
1 egg
1 cup mashed potatoes (prepared instant mashed pota-
    toes may be used)
6 to 7 cups flour

Mix yeast with water and $\frac{1}{4}$ teaspoon sugar; set aside for about 10 minutes.

Place milk, shortening, salt, and sugar in a saucepan and heat (do not boil), stirring until shortening melts. Remove from heat, pour into a large mixing bowl, and cool until lukewarm.

Stir in egg, mashed potatoes, and yeast mixture. Add flour one cup at a time and stir until a stiff dough forms. Turn out of bowl onto a well-floured board and knead about 10 minutes. Return to a clean, oiled bowl. Cover and allow to rise in a warm place until double in bulk, about 1 hour. Punch down. Shape, using one of the variations in the following directions. Allow to rise until double, about 30 minutes. Bake in a preheated 350° oven 20 to 30 minutes until light brown.

Makes 24 large rolls.

Variations:

Each variation uses $\frac{1}{2}$ of the Basic Recipe.

• *Dinner Rolls:*

Divide dough into 12 pieces. Shape into balls. Place in a greased 9- by 13-inch baking pan or space apart and flatten slightly on a larger cookie sheet. (In the baking pan, they will come out with softer sides because the sides will touch as they bake.) This dough may be shaped in any number of ways—into sandwich buns, finger

For biscuits and rolls with soft sides, place them in a baking pan with the sides barely touching. After they bake, they will pull apart easily.

rolls, knots, or whatever. Allow to rise in a warm place until double in bulk. Bake as directed in Basic Recipe.

• *Cinnamon Rolls:*

Roll out dough on a floured bread board to form a 10- by 15-inch rectangle. Mix together and sprinkle on top: 1 teaspoon cinnamon, $\frac{1}{2}$ cup brown sugar, $\frac{1}{2}$ cup granulated sugar. If desired, top with $\frac{1}{2}$ cup or more chopped nuts or raisins or both. Starting with the long side, roll up like a jelly roll. Cut into 12 rolls and lay on their sides in a 9- by 13-inch baking pan. Allow to rise in a warm place until double in bulk. Bake as directed in Basic Recipe.

• *Sticky Buns:*

Make Cinnamon Rolls. Prepare baking pan: Combine 2 tablespoons butter, 2 tablespoons corn syrup, and 1 cup brown sugar in a saucepan and heat just until combined. Pour syrup mixture into 9- by 13-inch pan. Sprinkle 1 cup chopped pecans or walnuts over the syrup mixture. Place cinnamon rolls in the baking pan. Allow to rise in a warm place until double in bulk. Bake as directed in Basic Recipe. Immediately after removing from oven, invert the pan of rolls onto a large serving platter, allowing the syrup to drip down over the rolls. It is necessary to get them out of the pan right away so the brown sugar glaze doesn't harden in the pan.

• *Orange Rolls:*

Roll out dough to a 10- by 15-inch rectangle. Mix together $\frac{1}{2}$ cup sugar, $\frac{1}{3}$ cup softened butter or margarine, 2 teaspoons grated orange peel; spread over the dough. Roll up and cut into 12 rolls. Place in baking pan. Allow to rise in a warm place until double in bulk. Bake as directed in Basic Recipe.

To reheat rolls or bread, put them in a paper bag, sprinkle a little water on top of the bag, and place in a 325° oven for 10 minutes.

• *Pineapple Rolls:*

Prepare filling: In a small saucepan, place 1 small can (8 ounces) crushed pineapple (with juice) and $\frac{1}{4}$ cup sugar. Mix together 2 tablespoons water and 1 tablespoon cornstarch; add to pineapple mixture. Cook over medium heat, stirring constantly, until mixture thickens and clears. Remove from heat and stir in 1 tablespoon butter. Allow to cool until lukewarm.

Roll out dough to form a 10- by 5-inch rectangle. Spread filling over dough. Starting with long edge, roll up like a jelly roll and cut into 12 rolls. Place in a greased 9- by 13-inch baking pan. Allow to rise in a warm place until double in bulk. Bake as directed in Basic Recipe.

Orange Scones

No tea is complete without scones, especially this orange and raisin variation.

Don't discard lemon and orange rinds. Grate them and store in freezer until needed as flavorings.

$2\frac{1}{2}$ *cups flour*
1 teaspoon salt
$\frac{1}{2}$ *cup sugar*
2 teaspoons baking powder
1 teaspoon baking soda
1 teaspoon grated orange rind
1 teaspoon grated lemon rind
$\frac{1}{3}$ *cup butter or margarine*
1 egg
1 teaspoon water
$\frac{3}{4}$ *cup sour cream*
3 tablespoons orange juice
$\frac{1}{2}$ *cup raisins or currants*

Stir together the flour, salt, sugar, baking powder, baking soda, orange rind, and lemon rind. Using a pastry blender or two knives, cut in the butter or margarine. In a separate bowl, beat together the egg, water, sour cream, and orange juice; stir in raisins or currants. Combine the two mixtures until well blended.

Turn batter out of bowl onto a floured surface and knead a few times. Divide dough into 24 balls; place on greased cookie sheets. Bake in a preheated 425° oven for 12 to 15 minutes or until golden brown.

Makes 24.

Hot Cross Buns

These traditional Easter breads are perfect after an Easter sunrise service.

$\frac{1}{4}$ teaspoon sugar
$\frac{1}{2}$ cup lukewarm water
1 package active dry yeast
1 cup reconstituted nonfat dry milk
$\frac{1}{4}$ cup sugar
$\frac{1}{3}$ cup melted butter or margarine
1 egg, lightly beaten
1 teaspoon cinnamon
1 teaspoon salt
$\frac{1}{4}$ teaspoon cloves
$\frac{1}{4}$ teaspoon nutmeg
$\frac{3}{4}$ cup currants
2 tablespoons grated lemon rind
3 to 4 cups flour
1 egg yolk
1 tablespoon water
   Sugar Glaze Frosting (recipe follows)

In a small bowl, dissolve the $\frac{1}{4}$ teaspoon sugar in the water. Sprinkle yeast on top and allow to sit about 5 minutes. In a large bowl, stir together the milk, sugar, melted butter or margarine, egg, cinnamon, salt, cloves, nutmeg, currants, and grated lemon rind. Stir in the yeast mixture. Add flour and stir until a soft dough forms.

The Hot Cross Bun is the most famous, and probably the oldest of the many English buns. Unlike today, when it is to be found throughout Lent, the Hot Cross Bun was originally eaten only on Good Friday.

Hot Cross Buns, and other forms of Good Friday bread, were considered blessed, and were believed to provide powerful protection against disease and danger.

Evelyn Birge Vitz

Turn out of bowl onto a floured surface and knead until smooth and elastic, about 8 minutes. Cover and let rise in a warm place until double in bulk, about 45 minutes. Punch dough down and turn out of bowl. Divide dough into thirds, then divide each of these into 6 pieces. Shape into 18 smooth balls. Place on a greased cookie sheet with the sides barely touching. Cover and allow to rise until double, about 30 minutes. Stir together egg yolk and water; brush on top of the buns. Bake in a preheated 375° oven for 10 to 12 minutes or until golden brown. Remove from oven and form a cross on top of each bun with Sugar Glaze Frosting.

Makes 18 buns.

Sugar Glaze Frosting:
1 cup confectioners' sugar
½ teaspoon vanilla
3 to 4 tablespoons water

Place sugar in a small bowl and add vanilla and water, stirring into a smooth, thick frosting.

Makes about ⅓ cup.

Angel Biscuits

These biscuits are an all-purpose bread, wonderful with any meal.

5 cups flour
¼ cup sugar
1 teaspoon salt
1 teaspoon baking powder
1 teaspoon baking soda
1 package active dry yeast
2 cups buttermilk
¼ cup water
¾ cup shortening

In a large bowl, mix 1½ cups of the flour with the sugar, salt, baking powder, baking soda, and dry yeast. In a saucepan, heat the buttermilk, water, and shortening gently over low heat, stirring constantly until the shortening melts. Cool 5 minutes, then gradually add to dry ingredients and beat with an electric mixer for 2 minutes at medium speed. Add 1 cup flour and beat at high speed for 2 minutes. Stir in enough additional flour to make a soft dough.

Turn out onto a floured board and knead 5 minutes. Roll dough about ½-inch thick and cut into rounds with a 2-inch cookie cutter, or whatever size is desired, from 1½ to 4 inches across. Place rounds on ungreased cookie sheets. Cover and allow to rise in a warm place about 1 hour. Bake in a preheated 375° oven for 15 to 20 minutes or until lightly browned.

Makes 3 to 5 dozen biscuits.

Six Weeks Bran Muffins

These muffins get their name from the fact that the batter can be stored in the refrigerator for up to six weeks. Then, when you want fresh muffins, just take out some batter and bake.

7 cups bran flakes
3 cups sugar
5 cups flour (whole wheat, white, or half of each)
5 teaspoons baking soda
2 teaspoons salt
4 eggs, lightly beaten
1 cup vegetable oil
1 quart buttermilk
  raisins, chopped apples, nuts, or dates (optional)

In a large bowl, stir together the bran flakes, sugar, flour, baking soda, and salt. In a separate bowl, blend the eggs, oil, and buttermilk. Add the liquid mixture to the bran mixture and stir to combine. Store batter, covered, in the refrigerator.

To bake: Add raisins, chopped apples, nuts, or dates if desired. Spoon batter into greased muffin tins, filling each cup two-thirds full. Bake in a preheated 400° oven for 15 to 20 minutes.

Makes about 1 gallon of batter, enough for 4 dozen muffins.

Sunshine Muffins

The orange and coconut flavors make these muffins a cheerful accompaniment to brunches or salad lunches.

2 beaten eggs
$\frac{1}{2}$ cup reconstituted nonfat dry milk
$\frac{1}{3}$ cup melted butter or margarine
$\frac{1}{4}$ cup frozen orange juice concentrate, thawed
1 tablespoon grated orange rind
$1\frac{2}{3}$ cups flour
3 tablespoons sugar
$2\frac{1}{2}$ teaspoons baking powder
$\frac{1}{2}$ teaspoon salt
$\frac{2}{3}$ cup flaked coconut

In a medium bowl, beat together the eggs, milk, melted butter or margarine, and orange juice concentrate. In a separate bowl, stir together the orange rind, flour, sugar, baking powder, salt, and coconut. Stir the two mixtures together just until dry ingredients are moistened. Do not beat the batter, or the muffins will be tough. Spoon into greased muffin tins, filling each cup about two-

For a crunchy-soft top on sweet breads or muffins, brush with melted butter immediately after removing from the oven, then sprinkle lightly with granulated sugar.

thirds full. Bake in a 375° oven for 15 to 20 minutes or until lightly browned.

Makes 12 muffins.

Apple-Cinnamon Puffs

These aren't true muffins, since they contain yeast and must rise before baking, but are they ever good!

2 cups flour
1 package active dry yeast
3 tablespoons sugar
$\frac{1}{2}$ teaspoon salt
$\frac{3}{4}$ cup warm water
$\frac{1}{4}$ cup vegetable oil
1 egg
1 cup chopped apples
$\frac{1}{2}$ cup chopped walnuts
$\frac{1}{3}$ cup melted butter or margarine
$\frac{1}{4}$ cup sugar mixed with 1 teaspoon cinnamon

In a medium bowl, stir together the flour, yeast, sugar, and salt. In a small bowl, stir together the water, oil, and egg. Add to the flour mixture and mix until well blended. Stir in the apples and walnuts. Cover and let rise in a warm place until double in bulk or about 45 minutes. Stir down and spoon batter into 12 greased muffin cups. Cover and let rise until double, about 45 minutes to one hour. Bake in a preheated 375° oven for 15 to 20 minutes or until browned. Remove from muffin cups. When just cool enough to handle, dip tops of warm rolls into melted butter or margarine and then into cinnamon sugar.

Makes 12 puffs.

To avoid tunnels and large holes in muffins, don't beat or overmix the batter. The batter should look lumpy.

· · · Special Butters · · ·

Orange Butter

$\frac{1}{2}$ cup butter or margarine, softened
$\frac{1}{3}$ cup orange marmalade
$\frac{1}{2}$ teaspoon grated orange rind
1 teaspoon confectioners' sugar

Beat all ingredients together until fluffy.
Makes about $\frac{1}{2}$ cup.

Strawberry Butter

$\frac{1}{2}$ cup butter or margarine, softened
$\frac{1}{3}$ cup strawberry jam
1 teaspoon confectioners' sugar

Beat all ingredients together until fluffy.
Makes about $\frac{1}{2}$ cup.

Sunshine Butter

$\frac{1}{2}$ cup butter or margarine, softened
2 tablespoons honey
1 tablespoon grated orange rind
1 tablespoon finely flaked coconut

Beat all ingredients together until fluffy.
Makes about $\frac{1}{2}$ cup.

Almond Butter

$\frac{1}{2}$ cup butter or margarine, softened
2 tablespoons honey
$\frac{1}{4}$ cup finely ground almonds
$\frac{1}{4}$ teaspoon almond extract

Beat all ingredients together until fluffy.
Makes about $\frac{3}{4}$ cup.

Spicy Honey Butter

$\frac{1}{2}$ cup butter or margarine, softened
2 tablespoons honey
$\frac{1}{4}$ teaspoon ground coriander
$\frac{1}{4}$ teaspoon ground nutmeg

Beat all ingredients together until fluffy.
Makes about $\frac{1}{2}$ cup.

Raspberry Butter

$\frac{1}{2}$ cup butter or margarine, softened
$\frac{1}{3}$ cup raspberry jam
1 teaspoon confectioners' sugar

Beat all ingredients together until fluffy.
Makes about $\frac{1}{2}$ cup.

Herb Butters
In addition to making sweet butters for breads, butters flavored with herbs are delicious over potatoes, vegetables, fish, and even sautéed chicken breasts.

Basil-Parsley Butter

Serve with pasta, chicken, tomatoes, zucchini, shellfish, or corn.

$\frac{1}{2}$ cup butter or margarine, softened
$\frac{1}{2}$ teaspoon crushed basil
1 teaspoon chopped parsley

Dress up plain or flavored butters by piping softened butter through a pastry bag with a large rosette tip. Refrigerate until firm.

Beat ingredients together until smooth.
Makes about $\frac{1}{2}$ cup.

Dill-Chive Butter

Serve with baked potatoes, corn, white fish, chicken, salmon, or peas.

$\frac{1}{2}$ cup butter or margarine, softened
$\frac{1}{4}$ teaspoon dill weed
1 teaspoon chives
   dash of garlic powder

Beat all ingredients together until smooth.
Makes about $\frac{1}{2}$ cup.

Desserts

· · · Cakes · · ·

Oatmeal Cake

The topping makes this cake special:

$\frac{1}{2}$ cup butter or margarine, cut in pieces
1 cup quick-cooking rolled oats
$1\frac{1}{4}$ cups boiling water
1 cup granulated sugar
1 cup firmly packed brown sugar
2 eggs
$1\frac{1}{3}$ cups flour
$\frac{1}{2}$ teaspoon salt

1 teaspoon baking soda
$\frac{1}{2}$ teaspoon nutmeg
1 teaspoon cinnamon
  Broiled Cake Topping

Place the butter or margarine and the quick-cooking oats in a medium bowl. Pour boiling water over them, and stir until the butter or margarine is melted. Allow to sit 15 minutes.

In a separate bowl, combine the sugars and eggs; beat well. In a small bowl, stir together the flour, salt, baking soda, nutmeg, and cinnamon. Mix the oatmeal mixture into the sugar mixture, then add the flour mixture. Stir together until well blended. Pour into a 9-inch-square baking pan. Bake in a preheated 350° oven for 45 to 60 minutes or until a toothpick inserted in the center comes out clean. Top with Broiled Cake Topping.

Serves 9 to 12.

Pound Cake

A wonderful classic that is especially good because it keeps so well. Traditionally, the cake got its name because a pound of each main ingredient was used in the recipe, but the version below is much easier to make. In addition, it is made in a bundt cake pan instead of loaf pans, which makes it much prettier for a community meal or potluck. If you want a true New England Pound Cake, add $\frac{1}{2}$ teaspoon mace to the recipe.

$\frac{2}{3}$ cup butter or margarine, softened
$1\frac{1}{4}$ cups sugar
5 eggs
$\frac{1}{4}$ cup milk
1 tablespoon lemon juice
1 teaspoon grated lemon rind

No Time to Cook?
Dessert doesn't need to
be difficult . . .
· *pound cake with ice*
  cream or berries
· *baskets filled with*
  sweet, ripe
  strawberries
· *a local bakery favorite:*
  brownies, eclairs,
  cream puffs, pastries
· *chocolate: no one can*
  resist a selection of
  miniature candy bars,
  M & Ms, or candy
  kisses
· *a carton of your favor-*
  ite ice cream, topped
  with a special dessert
  sauce
· *a selection of fruits*
  and cheeses

1 teaspoon vanilla
2½ cups flour
1 teaspoon baking powder
½ teaspoon salt
  confectioners' sugar

Beat together the butter or margarine and sugar. Add eggs one at a time and beat well. Beat in the milk, lemon juice, lemon rind, and vanilla.

In a separate bowl, mix the flour, baking powder, and salt; gradually beat into the batter. Grease and flour an 8-cup bundt cake pan. Spoon in the batter and bake in a preheated 350° oven for 45 to 60 minutes or until a toothpick inserted in the cake comes out clean. Cool 10 minutes on a wire rack, then remove from pan. Dust with confectioners' sugar.

Serves 12.

Seed Cake

This is an old traditional cake. To make it, use the Pound Cake recipe above. Omit the lemon juice, but keep the lemon rind, and add:

2 teaspoons caraway seed
⅓ cup very finely cut citron

Chocolate Pound Cake

Pound cake is wonderful; chocolate is wonderful. Combine the two and you have a fantastic dessert. To really overdo it, top this cake with raspberry sauce and whipped cream.

1 cup butter or margarine
$\frac{1}{2}$ cup shortening
$2\frac{1}{2}$ cups sugar
2 eggs
$1\frac{1}{4}$ cups milk
2 teaspoons vanilla
3 cups flour
$\frac{1}{2}$ teaspoon baking powder
$\frac{1}{2}$ teaspoon salt
$\frac{1}{2}$ cup cocoa

In a medium bowl, cream together the butter or margarine and shortening, add sugar, and mix well. Beat in the eggs one at a time; mix in the milk and vanilla.

In a separate bowl, stir together the flour, baking powder, salt, and cocoa. Add gradually to the sugar mixture, stirring in well. Pour batter into a greased and floured 10-inch tube pan. Bake in a preheated 350° oven for 1 hour and 10 minutes or until a toothpick inserted in the center comes out clean. Dust with confectioners' sugar or frost with Chocolate Glaze.

Serves 12 to 16.

Carrot Cake

2 cups sugar
1¼ cups vegetable oil
4 large eggs
3 cups flour
1 tablespoon cinnamon
1 teaspoon coriander
1 teaspoon baking soda
2 teaspoons baking powder
3 cups grated carrots
½ cup chopped walnuts
  Cream Cheese Frosting
1 cup chopped black walnuts (optional)

Beat together the sugar and oil in a large bowl. Add the eggs and beat until well combined.

In a separate bowl, stir together the flour, cinnamon, coriander, baking soda, and baking powder. Add this mixture to the batter and stir to combine. Stir in the carrots and walnuts. Spoon into a greased and floured 9- by 13-inch baking pan. Bake in a preheated 350° oven for 35 to 45 minutes until a toothpick inserted in the center comes out clean. Cool in pan and frost with Cream Cheese Frosting. If desired, top with chopped black walnuts.

Serves 24.

German Chocolate Cake

Making this in a large pan instead of as a layer cake makes it easy to serve at a community meal. Needless to say, it's always a great hit.

1 cup butter or margarine
1 bar (4 ounces) sweet baking chocolate
1¾ cups sugar
4 eggs

1 teaspoon vanilla
1 cup sour cream
$\frac{1}{2}$ cup milk
$2\frac{1}{4}$ cups flour
$1\frac{1}{2}$ teaspoons baking soda
1 teaspoon salt
  German Chocolate Cake Frosting

Dust greased baking pans with unsweetened cocoa instead of flour to give outside of chocolate cakes a rich, dark chocolate color.

Heat the butter or margarine in a small saucepan until barely melted. Break chocolate bar into bits and add, stirring until the chocolate melts. Allow to cool slightly.

In a medium bowl, add the sugar to the melted butter and chocolate. Beat in the eggs and vanilla. Add the sour cream and milk and beat until smooth.

In a separate bowl, stir together the flour, baking soda, and salt. Add to the batter and beat until combined. Pour batter into a greased and floured 9-by 13-inch baking pan. Bake in a preheated 350° oven for 45 minutes or until a toothpick inserted in the center comes out clean. Allow to cool in the pan and frost with German Chocolate Cake Frosting.

Serves 24.

Cocoa Sheet Cake

$\frac{1}{2}$ cup butter or margarine, softened
$1\frac{1}{2}$ cups sugar
2 eggs
$1\frac{1}{2}$ cups buttermilk
1 teaspoon vanilla
$1\frac{2}{3}$ cups flour
$\frac{2}{3}$ cup cocoa
$1\frac{1}{2}$ teaspoons baking soda
$\frac{1}{2}$ teaspoon salt
  Chocolate Cream Icing
1 cup chopped walnuts

Beat together the butter or margarine and sugar in a large bowl. Add eggs and beat again. Beat in the buttermilk and vanilla.

In a separate bowl, stir together the flour, cocoa, baking soda, and salt. Add the flour mixture to the batter and beat until well combined. Pour into a well-greased 15½- by 10½- by 1-inch jelly-roll pan. Spread evenly in the pan. Bake in a preheated 350° oven for 20 to 25 minutes or until a toothpick inserted in the center comes out clean. Remove from oven and cool in pan. Frost with Chocolate Cream Icing and sprinkle chopped walnuts on top. Serves 24.

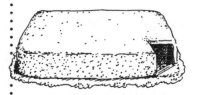

Self-Frosted Date Cake

Quite rich and delicious, this cake is great to take to a picnic or other casual community meal because the cake forms a frosting-like topping that is easier to handle and travels better than regular frosting.

1 cup chopped dates
1 teaspoon baking soda
1½ cups boiling water
1¼ cups granulated sugar
½ cup butter or margarine, softened
2 eggs
2 cups flour
¾ teaspoon baking soda
¾ teaspoon salt
1 cup (6 ounces) semisweet chocolate chips
½ cup firmly packed brown sugar
½ cup chopped nuts

Place dates and baking soda in a small bowl and pour the boiling water over them. Allow mixture to cool. In a medium bowl, cream together the granulated sugar and butter or margarine. Add the eggs and beat well. Stir in the cooled date mixture.

In a separate bowl, stir together the flour, baking soda, and salt. Add this to the batter and stir until well combined. Pour into a well-greased 9- by 13-inch baking pan. Sprinkle the chocolate chips, brown sugar, and chopped nuts on top. Bake in a preheated 350° oven for 40 to 45 minutes.

Serves 24.

Pineapple Upside-Down Cake

This is delicious at any temperature, but served just out of the oven and topped with whipped cream, it's a special treat!

2 tablespoons melted butter or margarine
½ cup firmly packed brown sugar
4 to 6 drained pineapple slices
4 to 6 maraschino cherries
⅓ cup butter or margarine
1 cup granulated sugar
1 teaspoon vanilla
⅔ cup milk
1½ cups flour
2 teaspoons baking powder
½ teaspoon salt

or 11×7 pan

In a 9-inch-square baking pan, place the 2 tablespoons of melted butter. Add the brown sugar. Cut the pineapple slices in half and arrange on top of the sugar with the cherries. Set aside.

In a bowl, combine ⅓ cup butter or margarine and granulated sugar, mixing well. Add vanilla and milk and beat in.

Pineapples are a traditional symbol of hospitality in America. Native to South America, pineapples were introduced to Hawaii, some say, by a Spanish adventurer in 1790. Now Hawaii is the largest single producer of pineapple in the world.

In a separate bowl, stir together the flour, baking powder, and salt. Add to the batter and beat to combine well. Pour the batter carefully over pineapple and cherries. Bake in a preheated 350° oven for 40 to 50 minutes or until a toothpick inserted in the center comes out clean. Take out of oven and immediately invert onto a serving platter.

Serves 9.

Rhubarb Cake

One of the first products from the spring garden, rhubarb makes delicious cakes, muffins, pies, and sauces. If you don't grow your own, it's available fresh in many grocery stores and is also available frozen. Use the frozen in the same amounts as the fresh, but measure after it is thawed and drained.

$\frac{1}{2}$ cup vegetable oil
2 cups sugar
1 egg
1 cup buttermilk
1 teaspoon vanilla
2 cups flour
1 teaspoon baking soda
1 teaspoon cinnamon
$1\frac{1}{2}$ cups finely chopped rhubarb
Broiled Cake Topping

Beat the oil and sugar in a large bowl. Add the egg and beat again. Beat in the buttermilk and vanilla.

In a separate bowl, stir together the flour, baking soda, and cinnamon. Add to the liquid mixture and beat until well blended. Stir in the rhubarb. Pour into a greased and floured 9- by 13-inch baking pan. Bake in a preheated 350° oven for 60 minutes or until a toothpick inserted in the center comes out clean. Frost with Broiled Cake Topping.

Serves 16 to 24.

Covering a cake with a hot water-confectioners' sugar glaze will eliminate crumbs and make the cake easier to frost.

Johnny Appleseed Cake

$\frac{1}{2}$ cup butter or margarine
$1\frac{3}{4}$ cups applesauce
2 cups flour
$\frac{1}{2}$ cup granulated sugar
$\frac{1}{2}$ cup firmly packed brown sugar
1 teaspoon salt
1 teaspoon baking soda
1 teaspoon cinnamon
$\frac{1}{2}$ teaspoon nutmeg
$\frac{1}{4}$ teaspoon cloves
1 cup raisins
1 cup chopped nuts

Combine butter or margarine with applesauce in a saucepan; stir over medium heat until the butter or margarine is melted.

In a medium bowl, stir together the flour, granulated sugar, brown sugar, salt, baking soda, cinnamon, nutmeg, and cloves. Pour the applesauce mixture over this; beat until well blended. Stir in raisins and nuts. Spoon into a greased and floured 9-inch-square baking pan. Bake in a preheated 350° oven for 30 to 35 minutes or until a toothpick inserted in the center comes out clean. This may be eaten plain, topped with whipped cream or ice cream, or topped with Broiled Cake Topping.

Serves 9 to 12.

If your raisins or currants are hard from sitting on the shelf too long, don't despair. Pour boiling water over them and allow them to sit for about 10 minutes before you use them. This restores their moisture, making them plump and juicy. If you use dried-out raisins in baked goods, they will often absorb so much moisture from the batter that the end result can be somewhat dry.

Angel Chiffon Cake

What a delight for special occasions!

2 cups flour
1 cup sugar
3 teaspoons baking powder

$\frac{1}{2}$ teaspoon salt
$\frac{1}{3}$ cup vegetable oil
2 egg yolks
$\frac{7}{8}$ cup water
$1\frac{3}{4}$ cups egg whites (approximately 14 to 18)
$\frac{1}{7}$ teaspoon cream of tartar
$\frac{1}{2}$ cup sugar
1 teaspoon vanilla

Sift the flour, sugar, baking powder, and salt into a large bowl. In a separate bowl, stir together the oil, egg yolks, and water. Combine with the flour mixture. Beat the egg whites until foamy in a separate bowl; add cream of tartar. Continuing to beat, add the sugar and vanilla a little at a time. Beat until very stiff, then fold into the batter. Spoon into an *ungreased* 10-inch tube pan. Bake in a preheated 325° oven for 40 minutes. Then raise heat to 350° for the final 10 minutes. Turn the pan upside down and cool for 1 hour. Take out of pan and frost with either Whipped Cream and strawberries or Seven Minute Icing.

Apple-Raisin Cake

Moist and delicious, this cake needs no frosting. Serve it topped with either whipped cream or ice cream.

2 cups sugar
$1\frac{1}{4}$ cups vegetable oil
2 eggs
1 teaspoon vanilla
3 cups flour
1 teaspoon baking soda
1 teaspoon cinnamon
$\frac{1}{2}$ teaspoon salt
3 cups chopped apples
1 cup golden raisins
1 cup chopped walnuts or pecans

In a large bowl, beat together the sugar and the oil. Add eggs and vanilla and beat until well combined.

In a separate bowl, stir together the flour, baking soda, cinnamon, and salt. Beat into the egg mixture. Add apples, raisins, and nuts. The batter will be very thick. Spoon into a greased and floured 9- by 13-inch baking pan. Bake in a preheated 350° oven for 45 minutes or until a toothpick inserted in the center comes out clean.

Serves 16 to 24.

Gingerbread

You can bake this in a large loaf pan or two small ones and serve it as a dessert bread or bake it in a cake pan and serve with either whipped cream or vanilla ice cream on top.

1 cup sugar
$\frac{1}{2}$ cup butter or margarine, softened
1 egg
$\frac{1}{2}$ cup molasses
1 cup boiling water
$2\frac{1}{2}$ cups flour
$1\frac{1}{2}$ teaspoons baking soda
1 teaspoon cinnamon
1 teaspoon ginger
1 teaspoon grated orange rind
$\frac{1}{2}$ teaspoon salt

In a medium bowl, cream together the sugar and butter or margarine. Beat in the egg. Add molasses and boiling water and stir until the molasses is dissolved.

In a separate bowl, stir together the flour, baking soda, cinnamon, ginger, orange rind, and salt. Combine the two mixtures until well blended; pour

Coarse-grained cake is usually caused by insufficient creaming of shortening and sugar. But extreme overbeating of cake batter can cause tunneling.

into a greased 9-inch-square baking pan. Bake in a preheated 350° oven for 1 hour or until a toothpick inserted in the center comes out clean.

Serves 12 to 16.

Blackberry Jam Cake

A great favorite on the frontier and a personal favorite of President Andrew Jackson. Often the cake was made in 2 to 4 layers with jam and frosting in between. Though wonderful, a high layer cake is difficult to transport and serve at a community meal. The version below, made in a sheet-cake pan, loses none of its delicious flavor and is certainly easier to carry and serve.

1 cup sugar
$\frac{1}{2}$ cup butter or margarine, softened
3 eggs
$\frac{2}{3}$ cup buttermilk
2 cups flour
1 teaspoon cinnamon
1 teaspoon baking soda
$\frac{1}{2}$ teaspoon allspice
$\frac{1}{2}$ teaspoon nutmeg
$\frac{1}{2}$ cup chopped walnuts
$\frac{3}{4}$ cup blackberry jam

Frosting:
2 tablespoons butter or margarine
$\frac{1}{2}$ cup firmly packed brown sugar
3 tablespoons milk
$1\frac{1}{2}$ to 2 cups confectioners' sugar

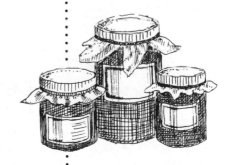

Beat together the sugar and butter or margarine. Add eggs one at a time and beat in. Beat in the buttermilk.

In a separate bowl, stir together the flour, cinnamon, baking soda, allspice, and nutmeg. Combine with the egg mixture; stir in the nuts and jam. Spoon into a well-greased and floured 10- by 15- by 2-inch sheet-cake pan. Bake in a preheated 350° oven for about 40 minutes or until top springs back when touched lightly.

To prepare frosting: Melt butter or margarine and brown sugar over moderate heat. Cook, stirring constantly, until mixture bubbles. Stir in the milk and blend well. Remove from heat and pour into a large bowl. Beat in the confectioners' sugar one cup at a time, until smooth. Frost when cake has cooled.

Serves 24.

Buttermilk Spice Cake

Topped with Brown Sugar and Butter Icing, this cake is perfect for dessert after a meal of fried chicken.

1 cup butter or margarine, softened
2 cups sugar
2 eggs
2 cups buttermilk
3 cups flour
2 teaspoons baking soda
$\frac{1}{2}$ teaspoon salt
1 teaspoon allspice
1 teaspoon cinnamon
1 cup raisins
1 cup chopped walnuts

Beat together the butter or margarine and sugar. Add the eggs and buttermilk; beat in.

In a separate bowl, stir together the flour, baking soda, salt, allspice, and cinnamon. Stir into the

Cinnamon, one of the oldest spices in recorded history, comes from the bark of the cinnamon tree, which grows in China and southeast Asia. The fragrance of cinnamon is probably one of the fondest memories of childhood for many of us. Cinnamon toast, creamy rice pudding, cinnamon rolls, apple pie—the scent of comfort and hospitality.

egg-and-milk mixture; add raisins and walnuts. Pour into a greased and floured 9- by 13-inch baking pan. Bake in a preheated 350° oven approximately 45 minutes or until a toothpick inserted into the center comes out clean. When cool, frost with Brown Sugar and Butter Icing.

Serves 12 to 16.

Hazelnut Cocoa Cake

This cake is so rich and tasty that it is baked in a jelly-roll pan. Thicker slices would be too much to eat.

$\frac{1}{2}$ cup butter or margarine, softened
1 cup sugar
1 package (8 ounces) cream cheese, softened
4 eggs
1 teaspoon vanilla
$1\frac{3}{4}$ cups flour
$\frac{1}{4}$ cup cocoa
$\frac{1}{2}$ teaspoon salt
1 cup chopped hazelnuts
  Chocolate Cream Icing
  chopped hazelnuts for garnish

Cream together the butter or margarine and sugar. Beat in the cream cheese. Add the eggs one at a time and beat in; add vanilla.

In a separate bowl, stir together the flour, cocoa, and salt. Combine with butter mixture. Add the hazelnuts. Spread in a well-greased and floured 15- by 10- by 2- inch baking pan. Bake in a 350° oven approximately 20 minutes or until the center feels firm when pressed. Remove from oven and cool in pan. Frost with Chocolate Cream Icing and garnish with additional chopped hazelnuts.

Serves 24.

Hazelnuts (or filberts, as they are sometimes called) have long been considered by European bakers as a superior nut for desserts. They are quite perishable: buy them from a good market and store them well-wrapped in the freezer. To remove the tough skins, spread the nuts on a cookie sheet, roast in a 350° oven for 10 to 15 minutes. Cool slightly, then rub between your hands or in a towel and the skins will flake off.

Scripture Cake

A very famous old cake that contains only ingredients mentioned in the Bible. Theoretically, if you know your Bible well, you'll discover the ingredients by looking up the verses. Just in case, the ingredients are given just after each reference.

¾ cup Genesis 18:8 (butter)
1½ cups Jeremiah 6:20 (sugar)
5 Jeremiah 17:11 (eggs)
½ cup Judges 4:19 (milk)
3 cups Leviticus 6:15 (flour)
2 teaspoons Amos 4:5 (baking powder)
1 teaspoon 2 Kings 2:20 (salt)
1 teaspoon Exodus 30:23 (cinnamon)
¼ teaspoon each 2 Chronicles 9:9 (nutmeg and allspice)
¾ cup chopped Genesis 43:11 (almonds)
¾ cup 2 Samuel 16:1 (oil)
¾ cup chopped Jeremiah 24:5 (figs or dates)

Glaze:
1½ cups Jeremiah 6:20 (sugar)
½ cup Genesis 24:45 (water)
¼ cup Genesis 18:8 (butter)

Cream together the Genesis 18:8 and the Jeremiah 6:20. Add Jeremiah 17:11 one by one and beat in. Add Judges 4:19 and beat in.

In a separate bowl, stir together the Leviticus 6:15, Amos 4:5, 2 Kings 2:20, Exodus 30:23, and 2 Chronicles 9:9. Add to other mixture until just combined. Stir in Genesis 43:11, 2 Samuel 16:1, and Jeremiah 24:5.

Spoon into a bundt cake pan that has been greased and floured. Bake in a preheated 325° oven for about 60 minutes or until golden brown. Allow to cool a few minutes in the pan and then turn out onto a cake plate. Allow to cool completely.

In a saucepan or heavy skillet, place the Jeremiah 6:20. Heat until it melts, stirring constantly. Keep cooking until it turns golden, then add Genesis 24:45. Cook until smooth; remove from heat. Add Genesis 18:8 and stir until combined. Spoon over cooled cake.

Serves 12.

Cupcakes

Don't forget these wonderful vestiges of childhood! And they are perfect for community meals: easy to make, easy to transport, and easy to serve.

Just about any white, butter, or chocolate cake recipe will make good cupcakes. A recipe for one layer cake will yield about 24 cupcakes. Line muffin tins with paper cupcake liners and fill each cup about halfway. Cupcakes take less time to bake than layers, about 15 to 20 minutes in a preheated 350° oven.

To frost cupcakes, you will need about the same amount of frosting needed to frost an 8- or 9-inch layer cake. Decorate with colored sugars, flaked coconut, candy kisses, etc.

· · · Frostings · · ·

Chocolate Glaze

¼ *cup butter or margarine, softened*
2 *squares baking chocolate, melted*
1 *pound confectioners' sugar*
1 *teaspoon vanilla*
  cream or milk

Beat together the butter or margarine and chocolate. Stir in some of the confectioners' sugar and vanilla. Add the remainder of the sugar and enough milk to produce the spreading consistency you desire.

Makes $1\frac{1}{2}$ cups.

Chocolate Cream Icing

This frosting is lighter than Cream Cheese Frosting. It will frost the top of a 9- by 13-inch cake generously.

6 tablespoons butter or margarine, softened
$\frac{1}{4}$ cup unsweetened cocoa
$\frac{1}{4}$ cup milk
1 teaspoon vanilla
$2\frac{1}{4}$ cups confectioners' sugar

In a medium bowl, beat the butter and cocoa together. Blend in the milk and vanilla. Add the confectioners' sugar, using enough to produce a good spreading consistency.

Makes 1 cup.

German Chocolate Cake Frosting

Traditional for German chocolate cake, this also turns a plain white cake or sponge cake into something extraordinary.

$\frac{1}{2}$ cup granulated sugar
$\frac{1}{4}$ cup firmly packed brown sugar
1 cup evaporated milk
$\frac{1}{2}$ cup butter or margarine, cut into pieces

Keep powdered-sugar icings moist by adding a pinch of baking powder. It prevents hardening and cracking.

3 beaten egg yolks
1 teaspoon vanilla
1 cup chopped pecans
1⅓ cups flaked coconut

In a medium saucepan, stir together the sugars, evaporated milk, butter, and egg yolks. Cook over medium heat, stirring constantly, until thick. Remove from heat and stir in the vanilla, pecans, and coconut.
Makes 2¼ cups.

Cream Cheese Frosting

This recipe is enough to frost a 9- by 13-inch cake. You can halve the recipe for a 9-inch-square cake.

2 packages (3 ounces each) cream cheese, softened
½ cup butter or margarine, softened
2 teaspoons vanilla
2 cups confectioners' sugar

Beat together the cream cheese and butter or margarine until fluffy; add vanilla. Gradually add confectioners' sugar until you get the consistency you need.
Makes 1½ cups.

Variations:
You may flavor this frosting just about any way you can imagine. Here are just a few ideas.
- Chocolate: Replace ¾ cup of the confectioners' sugar with hot-cocoa mix.
- Chocolate mint: Add ¼ teaspoon mint extract to the Chocolate variation

For a quick and elegant decoration on a cake, place a paper doily on top of the cake, then sift with cocoa (for a cake with white topping) or confectioners' sugar (for a cake with chocolate icing). Carefully remove the doily.

- Banana: Beat in one mashed banana.
- Orange: Replace vanilla with 1 teaspoon orange extract and 1 teaspoon grated dried orange rind.
- Piña Colada: Replace vanilla with 1 teaspoon imitation pineapple extract; add $\frac{1}{2}$ cup finely flaked coconut.

Seven-Minute Icing

Also sometimes called Boiled Icing.

2 egg whites
5 tablespoons water
$1\frac{1}{2}$ cups sugar
$\frac{1}{4}$ teaspoon cream of tartar
$1\frac{1}{2}$ teaspoons light corn syrup
1 teaspoon vanilla

Place egg whites, water, sugar, cream of tartar, and corn syrup in the top of a double-boiler. Beat with an electric beater until combined. Place over boiling water, and cook, beating constantly, for 7 minutes. Remove from heat, add vanilla, and beat a few more minutes until it reaches a good spreading consistency.
Makes $1\frac{1}{2}$ cups.

Broiled Cake Topping

This can be used over any spice cake.

$\frac{1}{2}$ cup firmly packed brown sugar
$\frac{1}{2}$ cup butter or margarine
1 cup flaked coconut
$\frac{1}{4}$ cup milk
1 teaspoon vanilla
1 cup chopped walnuts or pecans (optional)

Combine all ingredients with a fork, stirring until crumbly. Sprinkle over a 9- by 9-inch cake. Place under broiler for 5 minutes or until hot and bubbly.

Frosts one 9-inch-square cake.

Brown Sugar and Butter Icing

¼ cup butter or margarine
½ cup firmly packed brown sugar
2 tablespoons milk
¾ cup to 1 cup confectioners' sugar

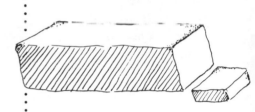

Melt butter or margarine in a medium saucepan. When melted, add brown sugar and boil slowly for another two minutes. Add milk and boil for one additional minute. Remove from heat and add confectioners' sugar until the icing reaches spreading consistency.

Makes ¾ cup.

Whipped Cream

Whether or not whipped cream is sweetened depends on how sweet the dessert is and the personal tastes of the community.

To top a pie or cake:
  2 cups heavy cream
  2 to 3 tablespoons confectioners' sugar (optional)
  ½ to 1 teaspoon vanilla (optional)

Makes 3½ to 4 cups.

For garnish:
> *1 cup heavy cream*
> *1 to 2 tablespoons confectioners' sugar (optional)*
> *$\frac{1}{4}$ to $\frac{1}{2}$ teaspoon vanilla (optional)*

Makes $1\frac{1}{2}$ to 2 cups (6 to 8 servings as garnish)

With a whisk or an electric beater, whip the cream until very soft peaks form. Incorporate as much air as possible, as this is what gives the cream its volume. Watch carefully; the cream can quickly turn to butter if beaten too long. The sugar and vanilla may be added any time after you have begun whipping. Whipped cream may be prepared several hours in advance and stored in the refrigerator. Place it in a strainer set over a bowl so that any accumulated liquid will drain off.

Heavy cream whips better if cream is cold and the bowl and beaters have been chilled.

· · · Pies · · ·

Water Whip Pastry

This is a novel way of making piecrust, but it works!

$\frac{3}{4}$ cup shortening
$\frac{1}{4}$ cup boiling water
1 tablespoon milk
2 cups flour
1 teaspoon salt

Put shortening in medium bowl. Pour boiling water and milk on top. Beat until smooth, with the consistency of whipped cream. Stir together the flour and salt. Add to the shortening and, using cross strokes with two knives, cut in the flour. Stir quickly until everything is blended. Chill for at least 30 minutes. Roll out and use as desired.

Makes enough for two 9-inch piecrusts.

Chocolate Pastry:

Use Water Whip Pastry recipe, but use butter-flavored shortening instead of plain and substitute $\frac{1}{2}$ cup cocoa for $\frac{1}{2}$ cup of the flour. This pastry will be very soft. It should be refrigerated for at least 30 minutes before rolling out.

Nutty Pastry:

Use Water Whip Pastry recipe, but substitute $\frac{1}{2}$ cup finely ground nuts for $\frac{1}{2}$ cup of flour. Add a dash of cinnamon and nutmeg to the dough.

Traditional Pastry

2 cups flour
1 teaspoon salt
$\frac{2}{3}$ cup shortening
$\frac{1}{4}$ cup water

Stir together the flour and salt. Using two knives or a pastry blender, cut the shortening into the flour mixture until it is in pea-size pieces. Gradually add the water, bit by bit, stirring in gently until the dough holds together. Do not overstir or overwork the dough, or the crust will be tough. For easier handling, chill in the refrigerator 15 to 30 minutes before rolling out.

Makes enough pastry for 1 two-crust pie or 2 one-crust pies.

Piecrust will stick to a work surface and rolling pin if you don't work quickly enough because the shortening begins to melt. To avoid this, be sure to use ice-cold liquids when mixing dough.

Crumb Piecrusts

You can use this recipe for any kind of crumb piecrust: graham cracker, chocolate, vanilla wafer, gingersnap . . . even zwieback! The varieties are endless. You may substitute ground nuts (almonds, pecans, or walnuts) for part of the crumbs. One-half teaspoon of cinnamon, nutmeg, or coriander may also be added, if desired.

$1\frac{1}{2}$ cups finely ground crumbs
$\frac{1}{3}$ cup melted butter or margarine
$\frac{1}{4}$ cup white or brown sugar

Mix all the ingredients together and blend well. Grease an 8- or 9-inch pie pan and pat in the crumb mixture. Bake in a preheated 325° oven for 7 to 10 minutes to firm the crust. Chill before filling.
Makes one 8- or 9-inch crust.

All-American Apple Pie

1 cup granulated sugar
$\frac{1}{4}$ cup firmly packed brown sugar
2 tablespoons flour
$\frac{1}{2}$ teaspoon cinnamon
$\frac{1}{4}$ teaspoon nutmeg
$\frac{1}{4}$ teaspoon salt
5 cups peeled, cored, and thinly sliced apples
2 teaspoons lemon juice
2 tablespoons butter, cut into bits
    Pastry for a double-crust, 9-inch pie
2 tablespoons milk
    sprinkle of sugar
    sprinkle of cinnamon

In a small bowl, stir together the sugars, flour, cinnamon, nutmeg, and salt.

Good Apples for Pies
Golden Delicious
Granny Smith
Jonathan
McIntosh
Newtown Pippin
Northern Spy
Rome Beauty

In a large bowl, toss the apples with the lemon juice. Add the sugar mixture to the apples and toss together. Gently stir in the butter bits. Place the apples in a 9-inch pie pan lined with pastry, letting the apples mound a little in the center. Moisten rim of crust with water and add the top crust. Press pastry edges together and flute to seal. Make several cuts in the top of the crust to allow steam to escape. Brush with milk and sprinkle on some cinnamon and sugar. Bake in a preheated 400° oven for 50 to 60 minutes or until golden brown.

Serves 6 to 8.

English Apple Pie

This is an apple custard without a crust, but it holds its shape well when cooled and cut into wedges.

$\frac{3}{4}$ cup sugar
2 eggs, lightly beaten
1 teaspoon vanilla
$\frac{1}{2}$ cup flour
$1\frac{1}{2}$ teaspoons baking powder
$\frac{1}{2}$ teaspoon salt
1 cup peeled, cored, and diced apples
$\frac{1}{2}$ cup chopped walnuts or pecans
1 pint vanilla ice cream

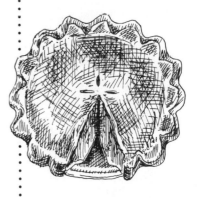

Grease a 9-inch pie plate well. In a medium bowl, beat together the sugar, eggs, and vanilla. In a small bowl, stir together the flour, baking powder, and salt. Add to the egg mixture and blend well. Stir in apples and nuts. Pour into the pie pan. Bake in a preheated 350° oven for 35 to 40 minutes. Cool. Cut into wedges and serve with ice cream.

Serves 6.

Crumb-Topped Apple Pie

Instead of using a crust, the crumb topping seals in the flavor of this pie.

6 cups peeled, cored, and sliced tart apples
$\frac{2}{3}$ cup granulated sugar
$\frac{1}{2}$ teaspoon cinnamon
$\frac{1}{2}$ teaspoon nutmeg
2 tablespoons flour
$\frac{1}{3}$ cup milk
$\frac{1}{2}$ cup butter or margarine
$1\frac{1}{2}$ cups firmly packed brown sugar
1 cup flour
1 unbaked 9-inch pie shell

Place apples in a large bowl.

In a separate bowl, stir together the granulated sugar, cinnamon, nutmeg, and flour. Add this mixture to the apples and toss to coat. Spoon into pie shell and pat down. Pour milk over the apples. Combine the butter, brown sugar, and flour. Using a pastry blender or a fork, work this together to make a crumb mixture. Pat crumb mixture over the apples. Bake in a preheated 350° oven for 45 to 60 minutes or until browned.

Serves 6 to 8.

Deep-Dish Apple Pie:

Use the recipe for Crumb-Topped Apple Pie, but place apple mixture in a greased 9-inch-square baking pan without a crust. Top with the crumb mixture and bake in a preheated 350° oven for 30 to 45 minutes. Serve with ice cream or whipped cream.

Serves 9.

Allow a pie to cool at room temperature for about an hour after baking. The pie will still be warm, yet will hold its shape when sliced.

French Apple Pie

A custard apple pie with a meringue topping.

1 large apple, peeled, cored, and thinly sliced
1 unbaked 9-inch pie shell
1 tablespoon melted butter
1 cup half-and-half
2 eggs, lightly beaten
$\frac{1}{2}$ teaspoon vanilla

Topping:
3 egg whites
$\frac{1}{8}$ teaspoon cream of tartar
$\frac{1}{4}$ cup sugar

Place the sliced apple in the pie shell. Combine the melted butter, half-and-half, eggs, and vanilla in a medium bowl. Beat a couple of minutes on low speed until well combined. Pour over the apples and bake in a preheated 350° oven for 30 minutes.

Just before the pie is done, beat the egg whites until foamy. Add cream of tartar. Gradually beat in the sugar until firm, but not dry. When the pie is done, remove from the oven and cover with the meringue. Make certain that the meringue touches the inner edge of the piecrust, so that it will not shrink when toasted. Turn the heat up to 400°, return the pie to the oven, and bake 8 minutes more.

Serves 6 to 8.

Leftover egg whites freeze well. One method is to freeze individually in a plastic ice-cube tray. When frozen, unmold, wrap in freezer paper, and label for future use.

Cherry Pie

Apple pie may be the all-American favorite, but this is a close second.

2 cans (16 ounces each) pitted tart cherries, drained (juice reserved)
$\frac{1}{2}$ cup reserved cherry juice
$\frac{3}{4}$ cup sugar
$1\frac{1}{2}$ tablespoons quick-cooking tapioca
$\frac{1}{4}$ teaspoon almond extract
  Pastry for a double crust, 9-inch pie
2 tablespoons milk
  sprinkle of sugar

In a medium bowl, stir together the cherries, cherry juice, sugar, tapioca, and almond extract. Allow to sit for 15 minutes, then spoon the cherry mixture into a 9-inch pie pan lined with pastry. Put second crust on top, seal edges, and cut slits in top. Brush top with milk, and sprinkle on sugar. Bake in a preheated 350° oven for 50 to 55 minutes or until lightly browned.
Serves 6 to 8.

Fresh Strawberry Pie

This is the kind of pie that is sold for ridiculous prices during the spring. It is actually very easy to make and a wonderful treat.

5 cups fresh strawberries
$\frac{3}{4}$ cup water
2 tablespoons cornstarch
$\frac{1}{2}$ cup sugar
$\frac{1}{4}$ teaspoon salt
1 baked 9-inch pie shell
  Whipped Cream for garnish

Clean the strawberries, crush one cup (reserving 4 cups), and place in a medium saucepan. Add water and bring to a boil. Simmer for 5 minutes, remove from heat, and strain, returning the strawberry water to the saucepan. Combine the cornstarch, sugar, and salt; add to the strawberry water. Bring to a boil and cook, stirring constantly, until the mixture thickens and clears. Cool.

Place the remaining 4 cups of strawberries in the pie shell. Pour the glaze over the berries; cool several hours. Top the pie with Whipped Cream before serving.

Serves 6 to 8.

Strawberry Cream Pie

When strawberries are plentiful and at a good price, you can't find enough great ways to prepare them.

1 package (8 ounces) cream cheese, softened
$\frac{1}{4}$ cup granulated sugar
$\frac{1}{2}$ teaspoon vanilla
$1\frac{1}{2}$ cups sliced strawberries
1 cup heavy whipping cream
$\frac{1}{4}$ cup confectioners' sugar
1 baked 9-inch Crumb Piecrust made with graham crackers
   additional strawberries for garnish

Beat together the cream cheese, granulated sugar, and vanilla. Mash the strawberry slices slightly; stir into the cream cheese mixture.

In a separate bowl, beat together the whipping cream and confectioner's sugar, until soft peaks form. Fold into the cream cheese-and-strawberry mixture. Spoon into pie shell; chill several hours or overnight. Before serving, garnish with additional strawberries.

Serves 8 to 10.

Blueberry Pie

This pie is a special treat when made with fresh blueberries. Canned fillings don't even come close in flavor.

6 cups cleaned blueberries
1 cup sugar
4 tablespoons cornstarch
½ teaspoon coriander
  dash of salt
Pastry for a double-crust, 9-inch pie
2 tablespoons butter
1 egg, lightly beaten

Place the blueberries in a medium bowl. In a separate bowl, stir together the sugar, cornstarch, coriander, and salt. Sprinkle this over the blueberries and allow to sit for 15 minutes.

Spoon the berries into a 9-inch pie pan lined with pastry. Cut the butter into bits and dot on top of the berries. Add the top crust, seal the edges, and cut a few slits on top. Brush the crust with beaten egg and place in a preheated 400° oven for 40 to 50 minutes.

Serves 6 to 8.

Variations:
You may substitute the following for the blueberries:
• blackberries
• raspberries
• gooseberries
• any combination of the above

When baking fruit pies, place a cookie sheet or piece of foil on the rack below the pie to catch the overflow.

Peach Pie

You may substitute apricots or nectarines in this recipe. To prepare the fruit, plunge it into boiling water for 1 to 2 minutes. Remove from water, and plunge it into cold water. If the fruit is ripe, the skins should slip right off. If it isn't, you have a rather messy peeling job on your hands, but you tried.

6 cups peeled and sliced peaches
2 teaspoons lemon juice
1 teaspoon coriander
$\frac{1}{2}$ teaspoon almond extract
1 cup sugar
3 tablespoons quick-cooking tapioca
    dash of salt
    Pastry for a double crust, 9-inch pie
2 tablespoons milk
    sprinkle of sugar

Place the fruit in a large bowl; sprinkle with lemon juice. Mix together the coriander, almond extract, sugar, tapioca, and salt. Stir into the fruit. Allow to sit 15 minutes.

Spoon the fruit into a 9-inch pie pan lined with pastry. Add the top crust and seal edges. Cut a few slices in the top of the pie. Brush pie crust with milk; sprinkle on sugar and an additional bit of coriander. Bake in a preheated 400° oven for 40 to 50 minutes.

Serves 6 to 8.

Maple Pumpkin Pie

Pumpkin pies are an essential part of Thanksgiving and Christmas meals, but the same old thing can become boring. Add some maple syrup and place the filling in a nutty crust and you have a deliciously updated tradition.

1 can (16 ounces) solid-pack pumpkin
¾ cup maple syrup
¼ cup firmly packed brown sugar
1 teaspoon brandy extract
½ teaspoon vanilla
½ teaspoon mace
½ teaspoon ground ginger
½ teaspoon salt
2 eggs
½ cup half-and-half
1 Nutty Pastry
  Whipped Cream for garnish
  chopped walnuts or pecans for garnish

In a medium bowl, beat together the pumpkin, maple syrup, and brown sugar. Stir in brandy extract, vanilla, mace, ground ginger, and salt. Beat in eggs and half-and-half. Line a 9-inch deep-dish pie pan with Nutty Pastry. Fill with pumpkin mix and bake in a preheated 350° oven for 45 to 60 minutes or until firmly set. At serving time, garnish with Whipped Cream and chopped walnuts or pecans.

Serves 6 to 8.

Sweet Potato Pie

A Southern favorite, this is tasty with any fall or winter meal.

2 cups cooked, mashed sweet potatoes
1 cup firmly packed brown sugar
$\frac{1}{4}$ cup granulated sugar
$\frac{1}{2}$ cup butter or margarine, softened
2 eggs
$\frac{1}{4}$ teaspoon ginger
$\frac{1}{4}$ teaspoon cinnamon
$\frac{1}{4}$ teaspoon nutmeg
$\frac{1}{2}$ teaspoon salt
1 teaspoon vanilla
$\frac{1}{2}$ cup evaporated milk
1 unbaked 10-inch piecrust
    Whipped Cream for topping
    pecan halves for garnish (optional)

Beat the sweet potatoes, sugars, and butter or margarine until well combined. Add eggs, ginger, cinnamon, nutmeg, salt, and vanilla; beat again. Mix in the milk until light and fluffy. Pour into piecrust. Bake in a preheated 350° oven for 50 to 60 minutes until set. Allow to cool. At serving time, spoon on Whipped Cream and garnish with pecan halves.

Serves 8 to 10.

Pecan Pie

One of the easiest pies to make and a perfect ending to a fried chicken dinner.

1 cup chopped pecans
1 unbaked 9-inch pie shell
$\frac{3}{4}$ cup sugar
3 eggs
1 cup light or dark corn syrup
2 tablespoons melted butter or margarine

To keep sweet potatoes from turning dark before cooking, place them in salted water (5 teaspoons salt to 1 quart water) immediately after paring.

Arrange chopped pecans in the piecrust. Beat together the sugar and eggs. Add corn syrup and melted butter or margarine; beat again. Pour over pecans and bake in a preheated 325° oven for 45 to 60 minutes or until set and browned.

Serves 8.

Pumpkin Pecan Pie

Nothing is more fun to serve for holiday parties than a traditional food with a bit of a twist to it. This pumpkin pie with pecans fits that description perfectly.

$\frac{1}{3}$ cup granulated sugar
$\frac{1}{3}$ cup firmly packed brown sugar
$\frac{1}{2}$ teaspoon coriander
$\frac{1}{2}$ teaspoon cinnamon
$\frac{1}{2}$ teaspoon ginger
$\frac{1}{2}$ teaspoon mace
$\frac{1}{2}$ teaspoon salt
2 eggs
$\frac{1}{2}$ cup half-and-half
$\frac{1}{2}$ cup milk
1 can (16 ounces) solid-pack pumpkin
$\frac{1}{2}$ cup chopped pecans
1 unbaked 9-inch pie shell

Stir together the sugars, coriander, cinnamon, ginger, mace, and salt. Mix in the eggs. Add the half-and-half, milk, and pumpkin; beat until smooth. Place pecans in the bottom of the pie shell and pour the mixture over them. Bake in a preheated 350° oven 45 to 60 minutes or until set. If desired, serve with whipped cream.

Serves 6 to 8.

When buying pecans in the shell, choose nuts that are clean and free of cracks and flaws; the kernel should not rattle in the shell. Shelled pecans should be crisp, meaty and plump. Pecans have a very high fat content, and unless they are stored properly, they will become rancid and bitter. Pecans should be stored in cold temperatures; shelled nutmeats stored in the freezer will last as long as two years. At the very least, keep them refrigerated. Thaw the nuts before using them.

Impossible Coconut Custard Pie

This pie has been around forever. What makes it "impossible" is that it comes out with a crust—when you didn't put one there.

4 eggs
2 cups milk
¾ cup sugar
½ cup flour
¼ cup melted butter or margarine
   dash of salt
1 teaspoon vanilla
1 cup flaked coconut

Grease a 9-inch pie plate. Place all the ingredients in a blender or a food processor and blend for 12 seconds. Pour into greased pie plate. Bake in a preheated 350° oven for 55 minutes or until set and golden brown on top.
Serves 8.

Buttermilk Custard Pie

This is so easy and seems so plain, but it is a wonderful old-fashioned pie—creamy, rich, and delicious.

½ cup butter or margarine, softened
1½ cups sugar
¼ cup flour
3 eggs
⅔ cup buttermilk
2 teaspoons vanilla
1 unbaked 9-inch pie shell

Cream together the butter or margarine and sugar. Beat in the flour. Add the eggs one at a time and beat in. Mix in the buttermilk and vanilla. Pour filling into pie shell and bake in a preheated 350° oven for 45 to 60 minutes or until golden brown on top and set.

Serves 4 to 6.

Easy Peanut Butter Pie

One of the richest pies around. Making it with a chocolate crust makes it taste like a big peanut butter cup.

1 package (8 ounces) cream cheese, softened
1 cup peanut butter
1 cup confectioners' sugar
1 teaspoon vanilla
½ cup milk
1 carton (8 ounces) frozen, nondairy whipped topping, thawed
1 Crumb Piecrust made with chocolate wafers (Page 304)
  in a 9-inch pie pan
½ cup semisweet chocolate chips

In a medium bowl, cream together the cream cheese, peanut butter, and confectioners' sugar. Add the vanilla and milk; beat until well blended. Stir in the whipped topping. Spoon into pie shell and top with chocolate chips. Refrigerate at least 3 hours before serving.

Serves 8 to 10.

Peanut Butter Cream Pie:

Prepare Easy Peanut Butter Pie and put into a plain baked pie shell. Do not top with chocolate chips, but just before serving, top with Whipped Cream.

To remove pie with graham cracker or cookie crust with the crust intact, dip the pan in warm water for a few minutes.

Raisin Cream Pie

1 cup raisins
2 tablespoons boiling water
$\frac{1}{2}$ cup sugar
3 tablespoons cornstarch
   pinch of salt
2 cups milk
2 egg yolks, beaten
1 teaspoon vanilla
1 baked 9-inch pie shell
   Whipped Cream for topping

Place the raisins in a small bowl with the boiling water. Let stand 5 minutes.

In a medium saucepan, stir together the sugar, cornstarch, and salt. Mix in $\frac{1}{2}$ cup of the milk; add and mix the beaten egg yolks. Pour in the rest of the milk and beat until smooth. Add the raisins. Cook over medium heat, stirring constantly, until the mixture comes to a boil. Boil for one minute, then add vanilla. Pour the mixture into a baked pie shell; chill thoroughly. Just before serving, spoon the Whipped Cream over the pie.

Serves 8.

White Christmas Pie

This is a very old recipe. The pie looks like a snowdrift and melts in your mouth.

$\frac{1}{4}$ cup cold water
1 package unflavored gelatin
4 tablespoons flour
$\frac{1}{2}$ cup sugar
1$\frac{1}{2}$ cups milk
$\frac{1}{2}$ teaspoon salt
1 cup finely flaked coconut
1 teaspoon vanilla

Raisins—little bundles of sweetness that add a special succulence to many dishes:

- *add to poultry stuffings, especially those made with fruit*
- *in rice pilaf, remove rice from heat and stir in about $\frac{1}{4}$ cup for every one cup of cooked rice*
- *great in chicken salads, fruit salads, and with cottage cheese*
- *mix with cream cheese, marmalade, and chopped nuts for a wonderful spread for bagels or fresh breads*

3 egg whites
½ cup sugar
1 baked 9-inch pie shell
   Whipped Cream for topping
   flaked coconut for garnish

Place the water in a cup, sprinkle gelatin over it, and allow to soften. Stir the flour, sugar, milk, and salt in a medium saucepan. Cook over medium heat, stirring constantly, until mixture begins to thicken. Add the softened gelatin; stir until dissolved. Add coconut and vanilla. Allow mixture to cool until it begins to thicken.

In a separate bowl, beat the egg whites until almost stiff, gradually add sugar, and beat until firm (not dry) peaks form. Fold beaten whites into the gelatin mixture. Spoon into baked pie shell. Chill until firm. Just before serving, top with Whipped Cream and sprinkle with flaked coconut for garnish.
Serves 8.

Eggs will separate more easily when cold, but the whites whip better at room temperature.

Chocolate Mint Pie

This pie is a chocoholic's dream come true.

½ cup butter, softened (don't substitute margarine)
2 eggs
1 cup confectioners' sugar
1½ squares semisweet baking chocolate, melted
¼ teaspoon peppermint extract
1 baked 9-inch pie shell
or
1 Crumb Piecrust made from chocolate wafers
   in a 9-inch pan
   Whipped Cream for garnish
   Chocolate shavings

Cream together the butter and eggs; beat in the confectioners' sugar. Add the melted chocolate and peppermint flavoring, and beat until fluffy. Spoon into pie shell. Allow to chill. Just before serving, place spoonfuls of Whipped Cream around the edge of the pie and sprinkle on chocolate shavings.

Serves 8 to 10.

Pecan Chocolate Chip Pie

Imagine a rich, dark chocolate truffle filled with pecans. That's what this pie tastes like. And if the filling itself isn't rich enough, the pie is encased in chocolate pastry. Rich and elegant, a tiny slice makes a marvelous dessert.

1 cup sugar
⅓ cup butter, softened
2 eggs
1 teaspoon vanilla
½ teaspoon brandy extract
⅓ cup flour
1 cup chopped pecans
1½ cups semisweet chocolate chips
1 unbaked 9-inch Chocolate Pastry pie shell
  Whipped Cream for garnish

Beat the sugar and butter until creamy. Add the eggs; beat again until smooth. Mix in the vanilla and brandy extracts. Beat in the flour; add pecans and chocolate chips. Spoon mixture into an unbaked chocolate crust. Bake in a preheated 350° oven about 40 minutes or until filling is set. At serving time, cut into small pieces and garnish with sweetened Whipped Cream.

Serves 8 to 10.

··· **Special Desserts** ···

Apple Crisp

This is so easy to make. It's delicious by itself and even better when served with ice cream or whipped cream on top.

$\frac{1}{4}$ cup quick-cooking tapioca
6 cups peeled, cored, and sliced apples
$\frac{1}{4}$ teaspoon cardamom
1 teaspoon cinnamon
$\frac{1}{4}$ teaspoon nutmeg
$\frac{1}{2}$ cup firmly packed brown sugar
$\frac{1}{2}$ cup milk
1 cup granulated sugar
$\frac{1}{2}$ cup butter or margarine, cut in pieces
$\frac{3}{4}$ cup flour

Sprinkle the tapioca on the bottom of a 9- by 13-inch baking dish. Place the apples on top. Combine the cardamom, cinnamon, nutmeg, and brown sugar; sprinkle over the apples. Pour the milk on top. Place the granulated sugar, butter or margarine, and flour in a small bowl. Using a pastry blender or a fork, cut in the butter or margarine to form a crumb mixture. Sprinkle over the apples and bake in a 375° oven for 45 minutes.
Serves 12 to 16.

Strawberry-Topped Flan

Flan is a traditional Mexican custard. It isn't necessary to serve with strawberries, but they add a tasty touch.

3 cups halved strawberries
2¼ cups sugar
⅓ cup water
8 eggs
2 teaspoons vanilla
2 cans (12 ounces each) evaporated milk

Place the strawberries in a small bowl. Top with
¼ cup of the sugar and allow to sit in the refrigerator
at least an hour.

In a stainless steel saucepan, combine 1½ cups
sugar and ⅓ cup water. Stir to combine over medium
heat; bring to a boil. Boil for 4 minutes or until the
sugar is golden brown. Pour the melted sugar into a
4- by 9-inch loaf pan, coating the bottom.

Beat together ½ cup of sugar and the eggs. Add
the vanilla and evaporated milk; beat until well
combined. Pour this mixture over the sugar coating
in the loaf pan.

Carefully place the loaf pan into a larger pan
containing hot water. Bake in a preheated 350°
oven for about an hour or until a knife inserted in
the middle comes out clean. Remove from oven
and chill well before serving.

To serve, turn flan out of the pan, cut into slices,
and serve with a spoonful of strawberries on top.
Serves 8 to 10.

Baklava

1 pound butter
1 pound phyllo pastry
2 pounds almonds, finely ground
1 pound walnuts, finely chopped
1 cup sugar
1 teaspoon grated lemon rind
2 teaspoons cinnamon

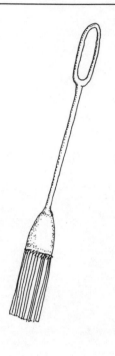

1 teaspoon allspice
   whole cloves for garnish

Syrup:

2 cups light clover honey
2 cups water
2 cups sugar
2 cinnamon sticks
1 teaspoon grated orange rind
1 teaspoon vanilla
$\frac{1}{2}$ teaspoon lemon extract

Melt the butter and keep it warm. Unwrap the phyllo leaves, lay them out, and cover them with a damp towel. In a medium bowl, stir together the almonds, walnuts, sugar, grated lemon rind, cinnamon, and allspice.

Butter a 9- by 13-inch baking pan. Lay a sheet of phyllo in the bottom; brush with melted butter. Cover with another sheet; brush with butter. Repeat this layering until you have used twelve sheets.

Spread one thin layer of nuts on top. Add a sheet of phyllo dough, brush with butter. Add another layer of nuts, then a sheet of phyllo dough brushed with butter. Repeat this layering until all the nuts are used up.

Cover with the remaining sheets of phyllo dough, brushing each sheet with butter. If you run out of butter, melt some more.

When all the sheets are used up, cut the top phyllo sheets into triangles by cutting diagonally across the pan. Make the triangles about 2 inches across in size. Insert a clove in the center of each triangle and bake the Baklava in a preheated 350° oven for $1\frac{1}{2}$ hours or until lightly browned.

While baking, make the syrup by combining the honey, water, sugar, cinnamon sticks, orange rind, vanilla, and lemon extract in a large saucepan.

Bring to a boil, reduce heat, and allow to simmer for 10 minutes. Strain syrup and allow to cool.

When the Baklava is browned, remove it from the oven and pour the cooled syrup over it, allowing it to penetrate all the layers. Cool Baklava several hours before serving.

Serves 24 or more.

Fruit Shortcake

6 cups strawberries or other fruit
1½ cups sugar (or to taste)
½ teaspoon almond extract
12 large Shortcakes (see below)
  whipped cream for garnish

One of the secrets of a good shortcake is to marinate the fruit in sugar and almond flavoring for 2 to 4 hours before serving. Place the sliced strawberries or other fruit in a bowl, then sprinkle the sugar and almond flavoring over them. To serve, split the shortcakes; spoon fruit and juice over the bottom halves. Replace the tops, and spoon more fruit over the top halves. Add whipped cream and, if desired, garnish with whole fruits.

Shortcake:
Use the recipe for Baking Powder Biscuits. Add 2 tablespoons of sugar to the flour mixture and substitute cream or half-and-half for the milk. Roll out and cut as directed.

Berry Cobbler

2 packages (10 ounces each) frozen berries, thawed
¼ cup shortening
½ cup sugar
1 cup flour
2 teaspoons baking powder

$\frac{1}{2}$ cup milk
$\frac{1}{2}$ teaspoon vanilla

Drain the thawed berries in a small colander, reserving up to 1 cup of the juice. Set aside.

In a medium bowl, cream together shortening and sugar. In a separate bowl, combine flour and baking powder. Add to the creamed mixture alternately with the milk and vanilla. Mix well.

Pour the batter into a greased 9-inch-square pan. Spoon the berries over the top of the batter, distributing evenly. Pour the reserved juice over the batter and berries.

Bake in a preheated 350° oven for 45 to 50 minutes. Serve warm or at room temperature with whipped cream or ice cream.

Serves 6 to 8.

Royal Cheesecake

Cheesecake is great for potlucks. In addition to its sublime taste, it travels well and is easy to serve.

Crust:

1 cup finely ground walnuts
1 cup finely crushed vanilla wafers
1 cup finely crushed graham crackers
1 teaspoon cinnamon
$\frac{1}{2}$ cup sugar
3 tablespoons melted butter or margarine

Filling:

6 eggs
$\frac{3}{4}$ cup sugar
2 packages (8 ounces each) cream cheese, softened
1 package (3 ounces) cream cheese, softened
8 tablespoons flour

Although some cracking of cheesecake is inevitable, it can be minimized. Avoid drafts: Never unnecessarily open the oven door during baking, especially during the first 30 minutes. Upon removal from the oven, run a spatula around the outside of the cake, allowing it to pull away from the sides of the pan during the cooling process.

$1\frac{1}{2}$ *cups sour cream*
$1\frac{1}{2}$ *tablespoons lemon juice*

Stir together the ground walnuts, vanilla wafers, and graham crackers. Stir in the cinnamon and sugar. Pour in the melted butter or margarine; stir to combine. Press along the bottom and sides of a well-buttered 10-inch springform pan.

In a large bowl, beat the eggs and sugar. Add the cream cheese and beat well. Beat in the flour, sour cream, and lemon juice. Pour into the crust and bake in a preheated 325° oven for 60 minutes or until top is firm and golden. Turn off the oven and let the pie cool in the oven for 1 hour. Remove from oven; chill thoroughly for 24 hours before serving.

Serves 12 to 16.

Variations:

- Sour Cream Topping: Just before the cheesecake is done baking, beat together 2 cups sour cream, $\frac{1}{2}$ cup sugar, and 1 teaspoon vanilla. Take cheesecake out of oven, pour this mixture over it, and return to oven for about 8 minutes.
- Fruit-Topped Cheesecake: Top the baked cheesecake with a can of any pie filling. Cherry, blueberry, and peach work especially well.
- Crust Variations: Replace graham crackers or both graham crackers and vanilla wafers with chocolate wafers or gingersnaps.
- Chocolate Cheesecake: Make the crust with chocolate wafers and stir $\frac{2}{3}$ cup miniature chocolate chips into the cheesecake batter.
- Almond Cheesecake: Replace the ground walnuts with ground almonds. Replace lemon juice with 2 teaspoons vanilla. Top with the Sour Cream Topping and sprinkle on $\frac{3}{4}$ cup of sliced almonds.

When cutting cheesecake, always dip your knife into hot water to lessen the tendency of the cheesecake to stick to the knife. Cheesecake, by the way, freezes well, making it a good choice for baking ahead.

Chocolate-Orange Cheesecake

Chocolate and orange is a favorite flavor combination. Not only is this duo in the cheesecake itself, but the garnish of chocolate whipped cream topped with mandarin oranges also features this delicious flavor combination.

Crust:
2 cups crushed chocolate wafers
$\frac{1}{4}$ cup sugar
$\frac{1}{4}$ cup melted butter or margarine
1 tablespoon grated orange rind

Filling:
4 eggs
$\frac{3}{4}$ cup sugar
1 carton (8 ounces) sour cream
2 packages (8 ounces each) cream cheese, softened
$\frac{1}{3}$ cup flour
3 ounces unsweetened baking chocolate, melted
1 teaspoon vanilla
1 tablespoon grated orange rind
$\frac{1}{4}$ teaspoon orange flavoring

Garnish:
$\frac{1}{2}$ pint whipping cream
2 tablespoons confectioners' sugar
1 tablespoon cocoa powder
$\frac{1}{2}$ teaspoon vanilla
  mandarin orange sections, drained

Grease a 10-inch springform pan well with butter or margarine. In a medium bowl, combine the crushed chocolate wafers, sugar, melted butter or margarine, and orange rind. Press this mixture into the springform pan to make a crust. Set aside.

In a separate bowl, beat together the eggs and sugar until creamy. Add sour cream and beat until smooth, then beat in the cream cheese and flour.

Divide the filling between two bowls. To the first, add melted baking chocolate and vanilla; stir until mixed in well. To the second bowl, add orange rind and orange flavoring; stir until mixed in.

Layer these mixtures into the crust; swirl with a knife to form a marble pattern. Bake in a preheated 325° oven for 1 hour. Turn off the heat and allow the cheesecake to cool in the oven for an additional hour. Cool thoroughly before serving.

To make the topping, beat the whipping cream until slightly firm. Add confectioners' sugar, cocoa, and vanilla; beat until stiff. Top cheesecake with this chocolate cream and garnish with mandarin orange sections. You may also cut the cake into serving pieces first and then top each with a spoonful of the chocolate cream and a mandarin orange section.

Serves 12 to 16.

Icebox Millionaire Pie

Unbelievably rich and creamy, this recipe serves 15 to 24, depending on the generosity of your slices.

Crust:
1 cup crushed vanilla wafers
2 tablespoons melted butter or margarine
2 tablespoons granulated sugar

Filling:
3 cups confectioners' sugar
$\frac{3}{4}$ cup butter or margarine, softened

3 eggs
  dash of salt
$\frac{1}{4}$ teaspoon vanilla

Topping:
$1\frac{1}{2}$ cups heavy cream
$\frac{3}{4}$ cup confectioners' sugar
1 can (20 ounces) crushed pineapple, drained
$\frac{3}{4}$ cup chopped pecans

Stir together the crushed vanilla wafers, 2 table-spoons melted butter or margarine, and the granulated sugar. Pat in the bottom of a buttered, 9- by 13- inch pan.

Cream the confectioners' sugar and butter or margarine. Add eggs, salt, and vanilla; beat until light and fluffy. Spoon on top of the crumb mixture.

Whip cream until almost stiff; beat in confectioners' sugar. Fold in the pineapple and pecans. Spoon on top of the other mixture in the pan. Chill at least 4 hours or overnight.

Makes 15 large or 24 medium servings.

Frozen Banana Split Dessert

This is a bit of work to make, but it is worth it. It can be made ahead and, since it serves 24 to 30, it makes a great dessert for a summer barbecue.

Crust:
$\frac{3}{4}$ cup crushed graham crackers
$\frac{1}{4}$ cup melted butter or margarine

Filling:
2 or 3 bananas
$\frac{1}{2}$ gallon vanilla ice cream
1 cup chopped nuts

Wash the tops of cans before opening them in order to avoid contaminating the contents with substances inadvertently deposited on the exteriors, e.g., pesticides.

1 cup chocolate chips
$\frac{1}{2}$ cup butter or margarine
2 cups confectioners' sugar
1$\frac{1}{2}$ cups evaporated milk
1 teaspoon vanilla

Topping:
1 carton (16 ounces) frozen nondairy whipped topping,
   thawed
   chopped nuts for garnish
   maraschino cherries for garnish

In a small bowl, stir together the crushed graham crackers and butter or margarine. Press this mixture into the bottom of an 11- by 15-inch pan. Slice bananas lengthwise and layer over the crust. Spread the ice cream $\frac{1}{2}$-inch thick over bananas; sprinkle with chopped nuts. Freeze until firm.

Melt the chocolate chips and the $\frac{1}{2}$ cup butter or margarine. Add confectioners' sugar, evaporated milk, and vanilla. Cook over medium heat, stirring constantly, until thick and smooth. Cool and pour over the ice cream. Freeze until firm.

Spoon whipped topping on top and add nuts and maraschino cherries for garnish. Freeze at least 10 minutes before serving.

Serves 24 to 30.

Lemon Dream Dessert

Crust:
$\frac{1}{2}$ cup butter or margarine, softened
1 cup flour
1 cup finely chopped walnuts or pecans

Filling:
1 package (8 ounces) cream cheese, softened
1 cup frozen nondairy whipped topping, thawed
1 cup confectioners' sugar

Chocolate should be melted slowly over hot water—never over direct heat since it burns so easily. Remove it from heat before completely melted and stir until smooth. If it should tighten (become stiff and dry), add a dab of vegetable shortening.

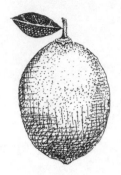

1 teaspoon lemon juice
2 packages (3¾ ounces each) *instant lemon pudding*
3½ cups milk

Topping:
1½ cups frozen nondairy whipped topping, thawed
½ cup finely chopped walnuts or pecans

Place the butter or margarine, flour, and walnuts or pecans in a medium bowl and blend well. Pat into a 9- by 13-inch baking pan. Bake in a preheated 350° oven for 20 minutes or until golden brown. Remove from oven and allow to cool.

In a medium bowl, beat cream cheese until fluffy. Add whipped topping, confectioners' sugar, and lemon juice; beat. Spread this mixture over the crust. Make lemon pudding according to package directions, using 3½ cups milk. Spread over cream cheese mixture. Spread whipped topping over pudding; sprinkle nuts on top. Allow to chill about 24 hours.

Makes 16 large or 24 medium servings.

· · · Cookies and Bars · · ·

Snickerdoodles

Cookies with the crackle of a cinnamon and sugar pattern on top. Wonderful with cold lemonade.

1 cup butter or margarine, softened
1½ cups sugar
2 eggs
2¾ cups flour
2 teaspoons cream of tartar

1 teaspoon baking soda
$\frac{1}{4}$ teaspoon salt
3 tablespoons sugar mixed with 3 tablespoons cinnamon

Cream together the butter or margarine, sugar, and eggs. In a separate bowl, stir together the flour, cream of tartar, baking soda, and salt. Stir this into sugar mixture; combine well. Form dough into balls about the size of walnuts. Roll each in cinnamon and sugar mixture and bake on an ungreased cookie sheet in a preheated 400° oven for 8 to 10 minutes.

Makes 5 dozen.

Snowballs

These are wonderful Christmas cookies.

$\frac{3}{4}$ cup butter or margarine, softened
$\frac{1}{2}$ cup sugar
2 teaspoons vanilla
1 egg
2 cups flour
$\frac{1}{2}$ teaspoon salt
$\frac{1}{3}$ cup chopped pecans
$\frac{1}{2}$ cup semisweet chocolate chips
   confectioners' sugar

Beat together the butter or margarine and sugar. Add vanilla and egg; beat again.

In a small bowl, stir together the flour and salt. Add this to the batter and mix in well. Stir in the nuts and chocolate chips. Roll into balls and bake in a preheated 350° oven for 15 to 20 minutes. Cool, then roll in confectioners' sugar.

Makes 3 dozen.

Spice Sugar Cookies

1 cup butter or margarine, softened
2 cups sugar
2 eggs
$\frac{2}{3}$ cup milk
5 cups flour
$\frac{1}{4}$ teaspoon salt
1 teaspoon cream of tartar
1 teaspoon baking soda
1 teaspoon nutmeg
$\frac{1}{2}$ teaspoon cinnamon

Beat together the butter or margarine and sugar. Add eggs and milk; beat again. In a separate bowl, stir together the flour, salt, cream of tartar, baking soda, nutmeg, and cinnamon. Add this to the batter and mix well. Chill dough for several hours. Take out a little at a time, roll out, and cut with cookie cutters. Bake on an ungreased cookie sheet in a preheated 375° oven for 10 minutes.

Makes 5 to 7 dozen cookies.

Cookie Exchange
Get together with several of your friends and neighbors and form a cookie barter to reduce the amount of baking for the holidays. Have each person bake his or her favorite cookie, but triple or quadruple the amount, then trade with others in the group. Everyone ends up with the best baked cookies from each person's repertoire.

Amish Sugar Cookies

These are one of the easier sugar cookies because they are drop cookies—you don't have to chill the dough and cut the cookies out.

1 cup granulated sugar
1 cup confectioners' sugar
1 cup butter or margarine, softened
1 cup vegetable oil
2 beaten eggs
1 teaspoon vanilla
1 teaspoon butter flavoring (optional)
$4\frac{1}{2}$ cups flour

1 teaspoon baking soda
1 teaspoon cream of tartar
   confectioners' or granulated sugar for topping

Combine the sugars, butter or margarine, and vegetable oil in a medium bowl; beat until well blended. Beat in eggs, vanilla, and butter flavoring.

In a separate bowl, stir together the flour, baking soda, and cream of tartar. Combine the two mixtures. Drop teaspoonfuls of dough on an ungreased cookie sheet. Flatten with a fork. Bake in a preheated 375° oven for 10 to 12 minutes. Remove from oven and dust tops with granulated or confectioners' sugar.

Makes 6 dozen.

Ranger Cookies

A little bit of everything goes into these cookies.

1 cup granulated sugar
1 cup firmly packed brown sugar
1 cup butter or margarine, softened
2 eggs
1 teaspoon vanilla
2 cups flour
1 teaspoon baking soda
$\frac{1}{2}$ teaspoon salt
$\frac{1}{2}$ teaspoon baking powder
2 cups regular or quick-cooking rolled oats
1 package (6 ounces) semisweet chocolate chips
$\frac{1}{2}$ cup chopped nuts

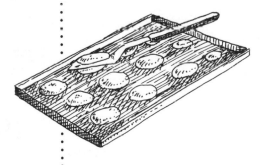

Cream together the sugars and the butter or margarine. Add eggs and vanilla; cream again.

In a separate bowl, stir together the flour, baking soda, salt, and baking powder; stir into the sugar mixture. Add the rolled oats, chocolate chips, and nuts. Drop by teaspoonfuls on a lightly greased cookie sheet. Bake in a preheated 375° oven for 12 to 15 minutes or until lightly browned.

Makes 7 dozen.

Peanut Butter Cookies

$\frac{1}{2}$ cup peanut butter
$\frac{1}{4}$ cup butter or margarine, softened
$\frac{1}{2}$ cup firmly packed brown sugar
$\frac{1}{2}$ cup granulated sugar
1 egg
1 cup flour
1 teaspoon baking soda

Cream together the peanut butter and butter or margarine. Add the sugars and the egg; beat in. In a separate bowl, stir together the flour and baking soda, then add to the peanut-butter mixture. Combine well. Drop by spoonfuls on a lightly greased cookie sheet. Press the tines of a fork on top of each cookie. Bake in a preheated 350° oven for 10 to 15 minutes.

Makes $4\frac{1}{2}$ dozen.

If the bottoms of cookies are browning too rapidly, slip an extra cookie sheet underneath.

Molasses Cookies

These are very moist, soft cookies, with that old-fashioned molasses flavor.

1 tablespoon vinegar
1 cup milk
$1\frac{1}{2}$ cups sugar
1 cup butter or margarine, softened
$\frac{1}{2}$ cup molasses
1 teaspoon vanilla
4 cups flour

2 teaspoons baking soda
1 cup chopped raisins

Stir the vinegar into the milk and allow to sit about 30 minutes or until thickened. In a medium bowl, beat together the sugar and the butter or margarine. Add molasses and vanilla and beat again. Pour in the thickened milk and beat in well.

In a separate bowl, stir together the flour and baking soda. Add to the other mixture and stir until well combined. Stir in raisins. Drop by spoonfuls onto a greased cookie sheet and bake in a preheated 350° oven for 7 to 10 minutes or until done.

Makes 4 to 5 dozen.

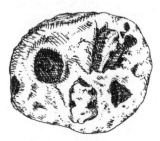  

Chocolate Chip Cookies

The quintessential American cookie. You may make this with many variations, some of which are given below.

⅔ cup butter or margarine, softened
1 cup granulated sugar
1 cup firmly packed brown sugar
2 eggs
2 teaspoons vanilla
2¼ cups flour

1 teaspoon baking soda
1 teaspoon salt
1 cup chopped walnuts
1 package (6 ounces) semisweet chocolate chips

Cream together the butter or margarine and sugars. Add eggs and vanilla; beat well.

In a separate bowl, stir together the flour, baking soda, and salt. Stir this into the butter mixture. Add nuts and chocolate chips. Drop by spoonfuls onto a lightly greased cookie sheet. Bake in a preheated 350° oven for 10 to 12 minutes or until very lightly browned.

Makes 4 dozen.

Variations:
• Substitute $\frac{1}{2}$ cup macadamia nuts and $\frac{1}{2}$ cup coconut for the nuts.
• Substitute peanut butter chips for the semisweet chocolate chips.
• Substitute mint chocolate chips for the semisweet chocolate chips and coconut for the nuts.
• Substitute milk chocolate chips for the semisweet chocolate chips and pecans for the walnuts.

Oatmeal Cookies

1 cup butter or margarine, softened
1 cup granulated sugar
1 cup firmly packed brown sugar
2 eggs
1 teaspoon vanilla
1 tablespoon milk
2 cups regular rolled oats
$1\frac{1}{2}$ cups flour
$\frac{1}{2}$ teaspoon salt
$\frac{1}{2}$ cup chopped walnuts
$\frac{1}{2}$ cup raisins

Cream the butter or margarine and sugars. Beat in the eggs, vanilla, and milk. Stir in the rolled oats.

In a separate bowl, stir together the flour and salt; add to butter mixture. Mix in the walnuts and raisins. Drop by teaspoonfuls on an ungreased cookie sheet. Bake in a preheated 375° oven for 10 to 12 minutes or until very lightly browned.

Makes 5 dozen.

Date and Nut Bars

Rich and delicious, yet they contain no shortening.

2 eggs
½ cup sugar
1 teaspoon vanilla
½ cup flour
½ teaspoon baking powder
½ teaspoon salt
½ cup chopped walnuts
1 cup chopped pitted dates
  confectioners' sugar

Beat the eggs until foamy. Mix in the sugar and vanilla.

In a separate bowl, stir together the flour, baking powder, and salt. Stir this into the egg mixture. Add walnuts and dates. Spread in a well-greased 8- by 8-inch baking pan. Bake in a preheated 325° oven for 30 minutes. Remove from oven and dust with confectioners' sugar. Cut while still warm.

Makes 16 squares.

Fudge Brownies

1 cup sugar
⅓ cup cocoa
⅓ cup melted butter or margarine
2 eggs
1 teaspoon vanilla
¼ teaspoon salt

$\frac{3}{4}$ cup flour
$\frac{1}{2}$ teaspoon baking powder
1 cup chopped nuts

Mix together the sugar and cocoa; add melted butter or margarine and beat. Add eggs and vanilla and beat again.

In a separate bowl, stir together the salt, flour, and baking powder. Add this to the batter and mix. Stir in nuts. Spread batter in a greased 8- by 8-inch baking pan. Bake in a preheated 350° oven for 25 minutes. Cut into squares when cool.

Makes 16 squares.

Lemon Squares

These are a great addition to any cookie platter. Their tangy, refreshing flavor contrasts well with heavier cookies.

$\frac{1}{2}$ cup butter or margarine, softened
1 cup flour
$\frac{1}{4}$ cup confectioners' sugar
2 eggs
1 cup granulated sugar
$\frac{1}{2}$ teaspoon baking powder
$\frac{1}{4}$ teaspoon salt
2 tablespoons lemon juice

Blend together the butter or margarine, flour, and confectioners' sugar. Press into a well-greased 8- by 8-inch baking pan. Bake in a preheated 350° oven for 20 minutes.

In a small bowl, beat together the eggs, sugar, baking powder, salt, and lemon juice. Pour over the crust and bake for 22 minutes.

Makes 16 squares.

Submerging a lemon in hot water for ten to fifteen minutes before squeezing will yield almost twice the amount of juice without harming the flavor.

Blond Brownies

2 cups firmly packed brown sugar
⅔ cup butter or margarine, softened
2 eggs
2 teaspoons vanilla
2 cups flour
1 teaspoon baking powder
¼ teaspoon baking soda
1 cup semisweet chocolate chips

Cream the brown sugar and butter or margarine. Beat in the eggs and vanilla.

In a separate bowl, stir together the flour, baking powder, and baking soda. Add to the other mixture and combine well. Stir in chocolate chips. Spread in a well-greased 9- by 13-inch baking pan. Bake in a preheated 350° oven for 20 to 25 minutes. Allow to cool slightly and cut into bars.

Makes 24 bars.

Beverages

· · · Hot Beverages · · ·

Coffee for a Crowd

The rich, warm smell of coffee communicates welcome and hospitality. And coffee is the lifeblood of any community meal, be it church supper or block party. Yet even the most capable cook can be paralyzed at the thought of making coffee for a crowd. Serving good coffee doesn't need to be a mystery if you use the following guidelines. In fact, you may want to keep a copy of them with the coffee maker.

Making Coffee for a Crowd:

1. Use a large-capacity coffee maker. If you don't own one, they may be rented from party supply services.

2. Always start with a clean coffee maker and never brew less than three-quarters of the coffee maker's capacity.

3. Use fresh coffee.

4. Pick the right grind. In order for coffee to brew properly, the water needs to circulate freely around the coffee. Most large-capacity coffee makers are the electric percolator type which uses regular grind.

5. Use freshly drawn cold water.

6. For twenty-five servings, use $\frac{1}{2}$ to $\frac{3}{4}$ pound of coffee and 6 quarts of water; for fifty servings, use 1 to $1\frac{1}{2}$ pounds of coffee and 3 gallons of water. Many folks find it's easier to ignore the markings on the pot and instead use accurate measurements for coffee and water.

7. Coffee should be served immediately after brewing; this is when the flavor is at its peak. Also, coffee burns easily, a particular concern if you are using an electric coffee maker which keeps cooking the brewed coffee as long as it is plugged in. Using the manufacturer's guidelines for the coffee maker, schedule the coffee to be finished just a short time before it will be served. While in many communities, coffee is served only at the end of a meal, many other communities serve coffee before and with a meal. To be certain that you serve fresh coffee, you may wish to use more than one coffee maker and schedule one to be ready before the meal and one to be ready by dessert.

Coffee Buffet

To make coffee time extra special, prepare a coffee buffet at your next brunch. Set aside a serving table or part of an island or breakfast bar in the kitchen. On it place a large pot of regular coffee, some decaffeinated coffee, and if desired, some of the herb teas that are similar to coffee in taste.

For better-tasting coffee put several cups of vinegar through your coffee-maker once a month to clean the insides.

Use the same method to clear hard-water deposits from a teakettle.

Place an assortment of coffee cups and spoons beside the coffee pots. In addition to these basics, place small bowls of whipped cream, granulated sugar, brown sugar, honey, nutmeg, cinnamon, orange peel, chocolate curls, grated chocolate, cinnamon sticks, instant hot chocolate mix, and whatever else you may enjoy to flavor the coffee.

To give your guests some ideas of tasty combinations, letter the suggestions below on a sign and set it up next to the coffee pot.

Brazilian Coffee: coffee, 1 teaspoon instant hot chocolate mix, 1 cinnamon stick, whipped cream, and chocolate curls

Cappuccino: coffee, cream, ground nutmeg, cinnamon, and sugar

Coffee Borgia: coffee, 1 teaspoon instant hot chocolate mix, whipped cream, and grated orange peel

Mexican Coffee: coffee, cinnamon stick, whipped cream, grated chocolate

Spanish Coffee: coffee, brown sugar, whipped cream, nutmeg

Hot Tea for a Crowd

The easiest way to serve hot tea to a crowd is to supply hot water and a selection of tea bags, and let people make their own.

Use a large capacity coffee maker to heat the hot water. If you are serving only tea (no coffee), you will need about 2 to $2\frac{1}{2}$ gallons of hot water to serve 25 people, about 4 to 5 gallons to serve 50 people. This allows for some refills.

Try to use a coffee maker in which coffee has never been made. Coffee often leaves an oil residue in a coffee maker that will flavor the water, making tea taste like coffee.

Provide a variety of tea bags—black teas, herb teas, fruit teas, and other special teas—and let folks make whichever they like.

To make any coffee blend taste expensive, sprinkle two teaspoons of ground cinnamon over the ground coffee in your coffee maker before brewing. The cinnamon imparts an exotic yet almost imperceptible flavor to the coffee.

Old-Fashioned Hot Cocoa for a Crowd

Perfect for a chilly winter night.

$\frac{3}{4}$ cup cocoa
$1\frac{1}{2}$ cups sugar
   dash salt
$\frac{1}{2}$ cup nondairy creamer (powder), optional
2 cups hot water
1 gallon milk

Optional Toppings:
miniature marshmallows
whipped cream
chocolate shavings
cinnamon
nutmeg

Stir together the cocoa, sugar, and salt. If desired, add the coffee creamer—it will give the cocoa a creamier flavor, but it isn't essential. Add hot water and stir to combine. Boil 3 minutes. Add milk a bit at a time and heat through, stirring constantly, but not allowing cocoa to boil. Dip out into cups to serve and add a few miniature marshmallows on top. If you want to get fancy, you may also add a dollop of whipped cream and sprinkle with chocolate shavings, cinnamon, or nutmeg.

Makes about 25 servings.

Quick Wassail

One of the easiest versions ever for this favorite warming beverage.

No Time to Cook?
Your contribution could be:
- *a pound of freshly ground coffee, flavored with almond or vanilla for a special touch*
- *an assortment of gourmet tea bags*
- *a selection of flavored soda waters*
- *a gallon of fresh apple cider and a bundle of cinnamon sticks*
- *after dinner mints*

4 cups water
1 teaspoon whole cloves
2 2-inch pieces stick cinnamon
2 tablespoons instant 100% tea
2 cups apple juice
2 cups cranberry juice
$\frac{1}{3}$ cup honey
1 teaspoon butter

Place the water, cloves, and cinnamon in a large saucepan. Bring to a boil and simmer for 5 minutes. Add instant tea, apple juice, cranberry juice, and honey. Reduce heat and heat thoroughly, stirring to dissolve honey. Add butter and stir until melted.
Serves 6 to 8.

Creamy Spiced Tea

Spicy and creamy—the flavor is fantastic! This keeps for several days in the refrigerator and is good served hot or cold.

10 cups water
25 whole peppercorns
20 whole cloves
25 cardamom pods, broken open
4 cinnamon sticks
10 slices fresh ginger
3 black tea bags
5 cups milk
$\frac{2}{3}$ cup honey

Cardamom, the dried ripe seeds of the cardamom plant, is an aromatic spice that is part of every curry blend. It is a particularly favorite spice in Scandinavia, where it is used generously in baking.

Place the water, peppercorns, cloves, cardamom pods, cinnamon sticks, and ginger in a very large kettle. Bring to a boil, reduce heat, and simmer 20 minutes. Turn off heat, add tea bags, and steep for 8 minutes. Strain out spices and remove tea bags.

Add milk and honey and stir until honey dissolves.
Serve either hot or cold.

Serves 12.

Delta Tea

The slight touch of almond gives this hot tea a
very different taste. This is nice to serve for a tea or
dessert buffet.

10 cups water
3 black tea bags
1 cup sugar
1 can (6 ounces) frozen lemonade concentrate
1 teaspoon vanilla
1 teaspoon almond extract

In a large kettle, bring water to a boil. Add tea
bags, turn off heat, and allow tea to steep 5
minutes. Remove tea bags. Add sugar and stir until
dissolved. Add frozen lemonade, vanilla, and almond extract. Heat through, but do not boil.

Serves 12.

Hot Spiced Afternoon Tea

This is a lovely beverage to serve for a tea party
on a chilly winter afternoon.

16 cups water
1 teaspoon whole cloves
2 sticks cinnamon
10 regular tea bags
$1\frac{1}{4}$ cups sugar

1 cup orange juice
½ cup lemon juice

Place water, cloves, and cinnamon in a large kettle. Bring to a boil and boil for 7 minutes. Remove from heat, add tea bags, and allow to steep for 5 minutes. Strain out spices and tea. Add sugar, orange juice, and lemon juice and stir until sugar is dissolved. Return to heat. Do not allow to boil. Serve hot.

Makes about 25 punch-cup-size servings.

Hot Mulled Cider

So good on fall evenings and perfect for Halloween parties.

1 gallon apple cider
2 teaspoons whole cloves
2 teaspoons whole allspice
2 sticks cinnamon
  dash salt
1 cup firmly packed brown sugar

Place the apple cider in a large kettle. Add the cloves, allspice, cinnamon, and salt, and bring to a boil. Reduce heat and simmer 20 minutes. Strain out spices. Add brown sugar and stir to dissolve. Serve hot.

Serves 12 to 16.

· · · Cold Drinks · · ·

Iced Coffee

Iced coffee is becoming more and more popular these days.

To make iced coffee, use one of these methods:

1. Brew extra-strong coffee. Chill completely. Serve in tall glasses filled with ice cubes.

2. Brew regular-strength coffee. Serve in tall glasses filled with coffee ice cubes. To make coffee ice cubes: brew extra strong coffee, cool, pour into ice cube trays, and freeze.

Serve with sugar and cream. (Note: powdered creamer will not dissolve in cold coffee.)

Iced Tea

Iced tea is a very regional drink. Some parts of the country make it with only the barest hint of tea flavor; other parts of the country prefer it dark and strong, to withstand the diluting power of melting ice. This recipe produces a medium-strength tea. If you prefer a milder flavor, either reduce the amount of tea you use or increase the amount of cold water you add.

Make a tea concentrate by pouring 2 quarts of boiling water over 24 to 36 tea bags. Allow tea to steep about 5 minutes or to desired strength. Cool. Add 4 quarts cold water. Chill well. Pour into ice-filled glasses and serve with sugar and lemon.

Makes 25 servings.

Often the best thing to serve on a hot summer afternoon is water. Offer a variety of chilled mineral waters, plenty of ice, a selection of sliced fruits (lemons, oranges, limes) and fresh sprigs of mint. For the more adventurous, provide angostura bitters, lime juice, and grenadine syrup.

Sun Tea

Clear and delicious tea with absolutely no bitter taste. It has become so popular in some parts of the country that special gallon jars with little spigots are produced just for making the tea. The only caution is that you should allow 3–4 hours to do it.

1 gallon jar of water
16–20 regular-size tea bags

Place the tea bags in the water, put on a lid and set it in the sun for 3 to 4 hours. The heat from the sun brews the tea perfectly.
Makes 16 servings.

Garnish ideas:
- *fresh mint sprigs in lemonade, iced teas, and punches*
- *slices of lemon, lime, and orange for summer drinks*
- *wedges of pineapple, lemon, lime, or orange on appetizer picks*
- *float strawberries, ca-rambola stars, or lemon, lime, or orange slices on the top of a bowl of punch*
- *edible flowers, such as nasturtium blossoms, placed in drinking straws make elegant garnishes for tall glasses of iced tea or lemonade*

Lemonade

Nothing beats the real thing. My grandmother taught me to add a few oranges to lemonade. It adds a delicious subtle difference to the flavor.

2 cups sugar
4 cups water
    juice from 20 lemons (about 2 cups)
    juice from 3 oranges
16 cups cold water
    ice

Bring sugar and 4 cups water to a boil, stirring until sugar is dissolved. Cool thoroughly, then mix with the juices and 16 cups cold water. Serve over ice in tall glasses.
Makes about 12 servings.

Party Punch

Reconstitute any kind of frozen juice concentrate with club soda or lemon-lime soda pop instead of water. For example, try frozen limeade with lemon-lime soda pop for a Mexican dinner. Or mix frozen apple juice with club soda for a light summer luncheon.

Citrus Sherbet Punch

This is a nice traditional punch for an open house or reception.

3 cups boiling water
3 teaspoons instant 100% tea
1½ cups sugar
½ cups orange juice
¾ cup lemon juice
⅓ teaspoon lemon extract
½ teaspoon orange extract
1 liter chilled ginger ale
1 pint orange sherbet

Stir together boiling water, instant tea, and sugar. Stir until sugar is dissolved. Remove from heat. Add orange juice, lemon juice, and lemon and orange extracts. Chill thoroughly. Just before serving, pour into punch bowl, add ginger ale, and float scoops of sherbet on top.

Makes about 24 punch-cup servings.

Ice Rings
Ring molds make
dramatic ice rings
for punch bowls. For a
clear ice ring, use dis-
tilled water or boiled
(and cooled) water. Pour
water into the mold,
filling to about a depth of
¼ inch. Arrange fruit
pieces such as strawber-
ries, sliced citrus fruits,
seedless grapes, and mint
leaves, if desired in a
pattern in the water.
Freeze 1 hour. Fill the
mold with distilled wa-
ter, pouring carefully so
you don't disturb the
arrangement. Freeze sev-
eral hours or overnight.
To unmold, dip the mold
into warm water, invert
onto a plate, and care-
fully remove the mold.

Lime Punch

This is for a huge crowd; it makes 150 servings.

10 cups sugar
6 cups water
12 cups boiling water
6 packages (6 ounces each) lime-flavored gelatin
3 cans (12 ounces each) frozen orange juice
2 cans (12 ounces each) frozen lemon juice
3 quarts pineapple juice
1 bottle (1 ounce) almond extract
5½ quarts cold water

Boil together sugar and 6 cups water and stir until sugar is dissolved. Place the 12 cups of boiling water in a large kettle. Sprinkle lime gelatin on top, and stir until dissolved. Add the sugar solution. Stir in frozen orange juice concentrate, frozen lemon juice concentrate, pineapple juice, and almond extract. Just before serving, add the 5½ quarts of water.

Serves about 150 small punch-cup servings.

Currant Punch Sparkle

A bit tangy and tart, people never guess that currant jelly is the base for this punch.

12 cups boiling water
11 cups currant jelly
15 cups orange juice
4 cups lemon juice
6 bottles (2 liters each) chilled ginger ale

In a large bowl, slowly add boiling water to jelly and mix until jelly is dissolved. Add orange juice and lemon juice and stir. Chill well. Just before serving, add ginger ale.

Makes about 50 servings.

Pineapple Sherbet Punch

Whenever I think of bridal or wedding showers, I think of this punch. It is refreshing, pretty, and delicious.

2 cans (46 ounces each) orange-grapefruit juice
2 cans (12 ounces each) apricot nectar
2 bottles (2 liters each) ginger ale
2 quarts pineapple sherbet

Assemble this punch in the punch bowl, just before serving. Pour in one can of orange-grapefruit juice, one can of the apricot nectar, and one bottle of ginger ale. Spoon one quart of pineapple sherbet on top. If the punch bowl is very large, you may repeat the procedure; if not, simply refill it as necessary with the remaining ingredients.

Makes about 50 small punch-cup servings.

Mocha Punch

This is a rather different sort of punch, a cold milk punch. It is nice to serve for brunch.

2 cups water
1$\frac{3}{4}$ cups sugar
$\frac{1}{4}$ cup instant coffee
1 gallon milk
2 teaspoons vanilla

1 teaspoon rum or brandy extract (optional)
1 quart vanilla ice cream

Bring the water to a boil and add the sugar. Stir until dissolved. Add the coffee, turn off the heat, and allow to cool. At serving time, combine cooled coffee mixture with the milk and flavorings. Place in punch bowl and place scoops of vanilla ice cream on top.

Makes about 50 punch-cup-size servings.

Common Equivalents

Apples	1 pound = 3 cups sliced
	1½ pounds = 1 quart sliced
Banana	1 pound = 3 medium = 2½ cups sliced = 1¼ cup mashed
Bacon (diced and cooked)	1 pound, uncooked = 1½ cups, cooked
Beans, navy	1 pound dry = 2⅛ pounds, soaked and cooked = 6 cups
Berries	1 pint = 1¾ cups
Bread	1 slice crisp dry bread = ¼ cup fine bread crumbs
	1 slice fresh bread (sandwich-style) = ½ cup soft bread crumbs
Cabbage (shredded)	1 pound = 5½ cups
Carrots (grated)	1 pound = 3½ to 4 cups grated
Celery (diced)	1 pound = 4 cups
Cheese	
hard cheese (Parmesan or Romano)	1½ to 2½ ounces = ½ cup grated cheese
firm cheese (Cheddar, Swiss, Monterey Jack, American)	¼ pound = 1 cup lightly packed shredded cheese
blue	¼ pound = 1 cup crumbled
cottage	1 pound = 2¼ cups
cream	3 ounces = 6 tablespoons
Cherries	1½ pounds = 1 quart
Chicken	one 5-pound chicken (cooked and boned) = 1¼ pounds meat = 4 cups meat
Chocolate (milk, semisweet or unsweetened)	1 pound melted = 2 cups
	1 pound grated = 4 cups
	1 ounce grated = 4 tablespoons
Chocolate chips (semisweet or milk)	6 ounces = 1 cup
Cocoa	1 pound = 4 cups
Coconut	3½ ounce can, flaked = 1⅓ cups
	4 ounce can, shredded = 1⅓ cups

Cookies 2-inch vanilla wafers	24 wafers = 1 cup crumbs
2-inch chocolate wafers	18 wafers = 1 cup crumbs
Crackers saltines	28 crackers = 1 cup crumbs
graham crackers	16 squares = 1 cup crumbs
Cranberries	1 pound uncooked = 1 quart cooked
Cream, heavy	8 ounces = 1 cup unwhipped = 2 cups whipped
Cream, sour	8 ounces = 1 cup
Dates	1 pound, unpitted = 2½ cups
	1 pound, pitted = 3 cups
Eggs (hard cooked)	1 pound = 8 eggs = 3 cups, chopped
Egg whites	8 to 10 large = 1 cup
Egg yolks	12 to 14 large = 1 cup
Flour	
All-purpose	1 pound = 3½ cups
Cake	1 pound = 4½ cups
Whole wheat	1 pound = 3½ cups
Garlic	1 clove, mashed = ⅛ teaspoon garlic powder = ½ teaspoon garlic salt
Gelatin, unflavored	1 envelope = 1 tablespoon
Ginger	1 teaspoon grated fresh ginger root = ½ teaspoon ground ginger
Green peppers	1 pound = 7 medium = 3⅛ cups chopped
	5 ounces, chopped = 1 cup
Herbs	1 tablespoon fresh = 1 teaspoon dried
Honey	11 ounces = 1 cup
Jam or Jelly	1 pound = 1½ cups
Lemon	1 medium = 3 tablespoons juice
	1 medium = 1 tablespoon grated peel
Lettuce (broken or shredded)	1 pound = ½ gallon
Lime	1 medium = 2 tablespoons juice
Meat, ground (uncooked)	1 pound = 2 cups
Milk, evaporated	5⅓- or 6-ounce can = ⅔ cup
	13- or 14½-ounce can = 1⅔ cups
Mushrooms	3 ounces dry = 1 pound fresh
	6 ounces canned = 1 pound fresh
	½ pound fresh = 2½ cups fresh slices
Nuts	
almonds	1 pound in shells = 1 to 1¼ cups nutmeats
	1 pound shelled = 3 cups nutmeats

hazelnuts	1 pound in shells = 1½ cups nutmeats
	1 pound shelled = 3½ cups nutmeats
peanuts	1 pound in shells = 2 to 2½ cups nutmeats
	1 pound shelled = 3 cups nutmeats
pecans	1 pound in shells = 2½ cups nutmeats
	1 pound shelled = 4 cups nutmeats
walnuts	1 pound in shells = 2 cups nutmeats
	1 pound shelled = 4 cups nutmeats
Onion	1 large = ¾ to 1 cups chopped
	1 medium = ½ cup chopped
	1 pound = 3 to 4 large = 3 cups chopped
Orange	1 medium = ⅓ to ½ cup juice
	1 medium = 2 tablespoons grated peel
Parsley	3 ounces, chopped = 1 cup
Pasta	
macaroni	1 pound = 4 cups uncooked
	1 cup, uncooked = 2 to 2¼ cups cooked
noodles	1 cup, uncooked = 1¾ cup cooked
	1 pound, uncooked = 3½ quarts cooked
spaghetti	7 ounces, uncooked = 4 cups cooked
	1 pound, uncooked = 2¾ quarts
Peanut butter	1 pound = 1¾ cups
Peaches	2¼ pounds = 1 quart
Pears	2¼ pounds = 1 quart
Pickle relish	1 pound = 2¾ cups
Pickles	1 pound = 3 cups
Pineapple	
canned chunks or tidbits	1 pound = 2 cups
fresh	2 pounds = 2½ cups
Plums	2 pounds = 1 quart
Potatoes	
white	1 pound = 3 medium = 2½ diced = 2 cups mashed
sweet	1 pound = 3 medium
Raisins	1 pound = 3 cups loosely packed
Rice, long grained	1 cup uncooked = 3 cups cooked
	1 pound, uncooked = 2 cups uncooked = 6 to 8 cups cooked
Rolled oats	1 pound = 4¾ cups
Salmon, flaked	1 pound = 2 cups

Sauerkraut	1 pound = 2¼ cups
Sausage	1 pound small links = 16 to 17 links
Strawberries	1 quart whole = 2¼ cups crushed
Sugar	
granulated	1 pound = 2⅓ cups
brown, firmly packed	1 pound = 2⅓ cups
confectioner's	1 pound = 4 to 4½ cups
Syrup, maple	12 ounces = 1½ cups
Tomatoes	1 pound = 3 to 4 medium
	1 pound, diced = 1 pint
Whipped topping (frozen)	8 ounces = 3½ cups (thawed)
Yeast	1 envelope active dry = 1 tablespoon

Emergency Substitutions

1 teaspoon baking powder	½ teaspoon baking soda plus ⅔ teaspoon cream of tartar
1 package active dry yeast	1 compressed yeast cake
1 tablespoon cornstarch (as thickening)	2 tablespoons all-purpose flour
1 cup buttermilk or sour milk	Stir 1 tablespoon white vinegar or lemon juice into 1 cup milk and allow to stand 5 minutes.
1 cup buttermilk	1 cup yogurt
1 cup milk	Stir ⅓ cup nonfat dry milk into 1 cup water.
1 square (1 ounce) unsweetened chocolate	Mix 3 tablespoons cocoa with 1 tablespoon melted butter
1 can (1 pound) tomatoes	Simmer 2½ cups chopped, peeled tomatoes for about 10 minutes.
1 cup catsup	Mix 1 can (8 ounces) tomato sauce with ½ cup granulated sugar and 2 tablespoons white vinegar.
1 teaspoon Italian seasoning	¼ teaspoon each dry basil, marjoram leaves, oregano leaves, and thyme leaves
1 teaspoon pumpkin pie spice	½ teaspoon cinnamon, ¼ teaspoon ginger, ⅛ teaspoon cloves

Common Baking Pan Equivalents

If you don't have the pan size called for in a recipe, use this chart to find another equal in volume.

For 4 cups
8-inch round layer cake pan
9-inch pie pan
7⅜- by 3⅝-inch loaf pan
8-inch ring mold
1-quart casserole dish

For 6 cups
9-inch round layer cake pan
10-inch pie pan
8½- by 3⅝-inch loaf pan
1½-quart casserole dish

For 8 cups   8-inch square pan   11- by 7-inch baking pan
9- by 5-inch loaf pan
two 8-inch round pans
2-quart casserole dish

For 10 cups
9-inch square pan
11- by 7-inch baking pan
9-inch Bundt pan
2½-quart casserole dish
15- by 10- by 1-inch jelly-roll pan

For 12 cups and over
8-inch springform pan
two 9-inch round pans
10-inch Bundt pan
9-inch tube (or angel cake) pan
3-quart casserole dish
13- by 9- by 2-inch baking pan (15 cups)
10-inch tube (or angel cake) pan (18 cups)
14- by 10- by 2½-inch roasting pan (19 cups)

Can Sizes

Size	Weight	Approximate Contents
8 oz.	8 oz.	1 cup
picnic	10½ to 12 oz.	1¼ cups
12 oz. vacuum	12 oz.	1½ cups
No. 300	14 to 16 oz.	1¾ cups
No. 303	16 to 17 oz.	2 cups
No. 2	1 lb. 4 oz. or 1 pt. 2 fl. oz.	2½ cups
No. 2½	1 lb. 13 oz.	3⅓ cups
No. 10		12 to 13 cups

Equivalent Measures

Dash = 2 to 3 drops or less than ⅛ teaspoon

1 tablespoon = 3 teaspoons

2 tablespoons = 1 fluid ounce

¼ cup = 4 tablespoon = 2 fluid ounces

⅓ cup = 5 tablespoons + 1 teaspoon

½ cup = 8 tablespoons = 4 fluid ounces

⅔ cup = 10 tablespoons + 2 teaspoons

¾ cup = 12 tablespoons = 6 fluid ounces

1 cup = 16 tablespoons = 8 fluid ounces

1 pint = 2 cups = 16 fluid ounces = 1 pound

1 quart = 2 pints = 4 cups = 32 fluid ounces

1 gallon = 4 quarts = 8 pints = 16 cups

1 peck = 8 quarts

1 bushel = 4 pecks

Oven Temperature Guidelines

Very slow oven	250° to 300° F.
Slow oven	300° to 325° F.
Moderate oven	325° to 375° F.
Medium hot oven	375° to 400° F.
Hot oven	400° to 450° F.
Very hot oven	450° to 500° F.

Index

Acapulco Delight, 103–104
  quantity, 41
All-American Apple Pie, 304–305
  quantity, 43
All-American Pancakes, 49
All-American Yams, 177–178
All-Day Lentil Soup, 149
  quantity, 39
All-Purpose Rolls, 269–272
  quantity, 37
Almond Butter, 278–279
Almond Cheesecake, 325
Almonds
  almond butter, 278–279
  almond cheesecake, 325
  baklava, 321–323
  orange-almond salad, 210–211
Ambrosia Salad, 228
  quantity, 42
American Cheese Ball, 69
Amish Sugar Cookies, 332–333
  quantity, 40
Angel Biscuits, 274–275
  quantity, 40
Angel Chiffon Cake, 290–291
Antipasto Platter, 63–64
Appetizers
  American cheese ball, 69
  chili toasted nuts, 79
  clam dip, 71

crab avocado dip, 72
cucumbers stuffed with feta cheese, 64
deviled eggs, 65
dill dip, 71
easy guacamole, 74
hot beef dip, 72
layered tostada dip, 73–74
nuts and bolts, 78
scotch eggs, 66
spicy chicken wings, 76–77
three-cheese torte, 68
Apple-Chestnut Stuffing, 183
  quantity, 43
Apple-Cinnamon Puffs, 277
  quantity, 40
Apple Crisp, 320
  quantity, 38
Apple Pie, 304–305
Apple Pie Pancakes, 49
Apple-Raisin Cake, 291–292
Apples
  All-American apple pie, 304–305
    quantity, 43
  apple-chestnut stuffing, 183
    quantity, 43
  apple-cinnamon puffs, 277
    quantity, 40
  apple crisp, 320
    quantity, 39
  apple-raisin cake, 291–292

Apples (cont.)
  crumb-topped apple pie, 306
  deep-dish apple pie, 306
  English apple pie, 305
  French apple pie, 307
  German apple kuchen, 256
  Granny Smith cabbage slaw, 223
  hot mulled cider, 346
  New York Waldorf Mold, 220–221
  Waldorf salad, 226
    quantity, 37
Applesauce
  Johnny appleseed cake, 290
  red hot salad mold, 218
Apricot Nectar Mold, 215
Apricots
  apricot nectar mold, 215
  apricot sauce, 114
  hearty apricot bread, 245
Apricot Sauce, 114
Artichokes
  Greek shrimp sauté, 134
  Italian chicken with artichokes, 112
  lamb and artichokes, 130
  Salinas Valley artichoke spread, 70
Asparagus
  mushroom and asparagus brunch munch, 136
    quantity, 42
Aspic
  spicy aspic salad, 214
    quantity, 41
Assignment of Food, 24–25
Avocados, 72
  easy guacamole, 74
  layered tostada dip, 73–74
  Pacific crab-avocado dip, 72
  Southern California cobb salad, 197

Bacon
  bacon and broccoli salad, 198
  calico beans with beef, 103
  Georgia bacon-pecan spread, 73
  hoppin' John, 187–188
Bacon and Broccoli Salad, 198
Baked Brisket with Fruit, 84

Baked Ham, 122
  quantity, 38
Baked Onions, 171
Baked Rice, 186
Baked Sauerkraut, 179–180
Baked Sweet and Sour Chicken, 116
Baked Tortilla Chips, 61
Baked Ziti, 190–191
Baking Powder Biscuits, 268–269
Baklava, 321–323
  quantity, 39
Banana Bread, 237–238
Bananas
  banana bread, 237–238
  banana raisin bread, 266
  banana yeast bread, 265–266
  frozen banana split dessert, 328–329
    quantity, 41
Banana Pancakes, 50
Banana Raisin Bread, 266
Banana Yeast Bread, 265–266
Barbecued Beef, 86
  quantity, 41
Barbecued Green Beans, 163
Barbecued Ground Beef, 86
Barbecuing, 53–55
Basil-Parsley Butter, 279–280
Beans
  Acapulco delight, 103–104
  black bean soup, 148–149
  Boston baked beans, 162
    quantity, 38
  calico beans with beef, 103
  easy baked beans, 162–163
  layered tostada dip, 73–74
  marinated bean salad, 195
  red beans and rice, 187
  Rio Grande chili con carne, 100
    quantity, 40
  Sedona bean and pork burritos, 125–126
  Texas beans, 102
  see also Green Beans
Beef
  Acapulco delight, 103–104
    quantity, 41

Beef (*cont.*)
  baked brisket with fruit, 84
  barbecued beef, 86
    quantity, 41
  barbecued ground beef, 86
  beef-mushroom meat loaf, 98
  beef stock, 158–159
  beef stroganoff, 87
  berry-glazed meat loaf, 98–99
  calico beans with beef, 103
  cheesy meat loaf, 97–98
  Danish meatballs, 92–93
  Evie's barbecued brisket, 83
    quantity, 40
  German beef and noodle stew, 144
    quantity, 39
  Grass Valley Cornish pasty pie, 107
  gridiron casserole, 101–102
  grilled hamburgers, 54
  grilled steak, 51
  Hungarian goulash soup, 142–143
    quantity, 39
  Italian wedding soup, 151–152
  Kansas City hot beef dip, 72
  lasagna, 95–96
  oven stew, 89–90
  perfect pasta sauce, 52
  pineapple beef, 88–89
  porcupines, 94
  Rio Grande Chili Con Carne, 100
    quantity, 40
  seven-layer hot dish, 104–105
  shepherd's pie, 106
  sloppy Joes, 90
    quantity, 41
  sloppy Josés, 91
  South Side stuffed cabbage rolls, 99–100
  Spanish rice with beef, 101
    quantity, 39
  Sunday dinner pot roast, 81–82
    quantity, 37
  super taco platter, 105–106
    quantity, 41
  Swedish meatballs, 93–94
  Swiss steak, 87–88

  Texas beans, 102
  traditional meat loaf, 97
  Yorkville sauerbraten, 85
    quantity, 39
  zucchini lasagna, 96–97
German Beef and Noodle Stew, 144
  quantity, 39
Beef-Mushroom Meat Loaf, 98
Beef Stock, 158–159
Beef Stroganoff, 87
Beet and Spinach Salad, 207
Beets
  beet and spinach salad, 207
Berry Cobbler, 323–324
Berry-Glazed Meat Loaf, 98–99
Beverages
  Brazilian coffee, 342
    cappuccino, 342
  citrus sherbet punch, 349
  coffee Borgia, 342
  coffee for a crowd, 340–341
  creamy spiced tea, 344–345
    quantity, 43
  currant punch sparkle, 350–351
  delta tea, 345
  hot mulled cider, 346
  hot spiced afternoon tea, 345–346
    quantity, 42
  hot tea for a crowd, 342
  iced coffee, 347
  iced tea for 25, 347
  lemonade, 348
    quantity, 40
  lime punch, 350
  Mexican coffee, 342
  mocha punch, 351–352
    quantity, 42
  old-fashioned hot cocoa for a crowd, 343
  party punch, 349
  pineapple sherbet punch, 351
  quick wassail, 343–344
  Spanish coffee, 342
  sun tea, 348
Beverage Service, 30, 32, 37
Biscuits
  angel biscuits, 274–275

Biscuits (*cont.*)
    quantity, 40
  baking powder biscuits, 268–269
  drop biscuits, 269
Black Bean Soup, 148–149
Blackberry Jam Cake, 293–294
Blond Brownies, 339
Blue Cheese Dressing, 235
Blueberries
  blueberry cream mold, 216–217
    quantity, 42
  blueberry pie, 310
Blueberry Cream Mold, 216–217
  quantity, 42
Blueberry Pancakes, 50
Blueberry Pie, 310
Boiled Icing, 300
Boise Potato Soup, 154–155
Boston Baked Beans, 162
  quantity, 38
Boston Brown Bread, 242
  quantity, 38
Bran Muffins, 275–276
Brazilian Coffee, 342
Breads
  all-purpose rolls, 269–272
    quantity, 37
  angel biscuits, 274–275
    quantity, 40
  apple-cinnamon puffs, 277
    quantity, 40
  banana bread, 237–238
  banana raisin bread, 266
  banana yeast bread, 265–266
  Boston brown bread, 242
  Brethren's cheese bread, 238–239
  brown sugar bread, 241
  challah, 260–261
    quantity, 39
  cheesy corn bread, 243
    quantity, 40
  cranberry tea bread, 245–246
  date-nut loaf, 244
  dill bread, 259
    quantity, 38

  hearty apricot bread, 245
  herb-onion bread, 257
    quantity, 39
  holiday Greek bread, 264–265
    quantity, 39
  homemade oat bread, 263–264
    quantity, 39
  hot cross buns, 273–274
    quantity, 42
  Irish soda bread, 247
  Kentucky wheat bread, 267–268
  poppy seed bread, 239
  pumpkin date bread, 246–247
  rye-garlic rounds, 60
  Sally Lunn, 257–258
  strawberry breakfast bread, 240
    quantity, 42
  Swedish coffee braid, 262–263
  Swedish rye bread, 261–262
    quantity, 39
  walnut bread, 266–267
Brethren's Cheese Bread, 238–239
Broccoli, 166
Broccoli
  bacon and broccoli salad, 198
  broccoli and tomatoes, 165–166
    quantity, 38
  broccoli cheese rice, 186
  broccoli cheese soup, 146–147
  broccoli-rice quiche, 184–185
  broccoli supreme, 165
  Garden State vegetable medley, 166–167
  ham and cheese broccoli bake, 124
  ham and cheese brunch munch, 135
  herbed broccoli with Brussels sprouts and carrots, 164
Broccoli and Tomatoes, 165–166
  quantity, 38
Broccoli Cheese Rice, 186
Broccoli Cheese Soup, 146–147
Broccoli-Rice Quiche, 184–185
Broccoli Supreme, 165
Broiled Cake Topping, 300–301
Brown Sugar and Butter Icing, 301
Brown Sugar Bread, 241

Brunswick Stew, 150

Brussels Sprouts
   Garden State vegetable medley, 166–167
   herbed broccoli with Brussels sprouts and car-
      rots, 164

Buckwheat Pancakes, 49

Budget, 21–22

Bulgur Pilaf, 189

Bulgur Salad, 205–206

Butter
   almond butter, 278–279
   basil-parsley butter, 279–280
   dill-chive butter, 280
   orange butter, 278
   raspberry butter, 279
   spicy honey butter, 279
   strawberry butter, 278
   sunshine butter, 278

Buttermilk Custard Pie, 315–316
   quantity, 43

Buttermilk Pancakes, 49

Buttermilk Spice Cake, 294–295

Cabbage
   baked sauerkraut, 179–180
   South Side stuffed cabbage rolls, 99–100
   see also Cole Slaws, Red Cabbage

Cakes
   angel chiffon cake, 290–291
   apple-raisin cake, 291–292
   blackberry jam cake, 293–294
   buttermilk spice cake, 294–295
   carrot cake, 285
      quantity, 38
   chocolate pound cake, 284
   cocoa sheet cake, 286–287
   cocoa-swirl coffee cake, 255–256
   cupcakes, 297
   fruit basket upset coffee cake, 251–252
   Georgia peach-pecan coffee cake, 248–249
   German apple kuchen, 256
   German chocolate cake, 285–286
      quantity, 38
   gingerbread, 292–293
   graham streusel coffee cake, 252–253

   hazelnut cocoa cake, 295
   Johnny Appleseed cake, 290
   oatmeal cake, 281–282
      quantity, 40
   overnight coffee cake, 249–250
      quantity, 42
   pineapple upside-down cake, 288–289
   pound cake, 282–283
   quick cherry coffee cake, 253–254
   rhubarb cake, 289
   Scripture cake, 296–297
   seed cake, 283
   self-frosted date cake, 287–288
   sour cream coffee cake, 250–251
   see also Cheesecakes

Calico Beans with Beef, 103

Can sizes, 358

Capers, 70

Cappuccino, 342

Carambola, 208

Carambola
   spinach carambola salad, 208
      quantity, 40

Cardamom, 311

Carrot Cake, 285
   quantity, 38

Carrots
   carrot cake, 285
      quantity, 38
   carrots and walnuts, 168
      quantity, 38
   copper pennies carrot salad, 196–197
      quantity, 42
   herbed broccoli with Brussels sprouts and car-
      rots, 164
   scalloped carrots with cheese, 168–169
      quantity, 37
   sunshine salad, 216

Carrots and Walnuts, 168
   quantity, 38

Casseroles
   Acapulco delight, 103–104
      quantity, 41
   chicken spaghetti, 118
   Chinese chicken casserole, 113

Casseroles (*cont.*)
　deviled eggs with ham sauce, 139
　El Paso grits casserole, 184
　English pea casserole, 171–172
　Grass Valley Cornish pasty pie, 107
　gridiron casserole, 101–102
　　quantity, 41
　hot chicken salad, 117
　moussaka, 128–129
　　quantity, 38
　Portuguese cod, 130–131
　seven-layer hot dish, 104–105
　tuna, chile, and rice casserole, 132
　tuna noodle casserole, 131
Cauliflower
　cauliflower cheese soup, 146
　　quantity, 39
　fresh cauliflower soup, 145
Cauliflower Cheese Soup, 146
　quantity, 39
Celery
　New York Waldorf mold, 220–221
　Twin Cities celery hot dish, 169–170
　Waldorf salad, 226
　　quantity, 37
Challah, 260–261
　quantity, 39
Cheese
　Acapulco delight, 103–104
　American cheese ball, 69
　Brethren's cheese bread, 238–239
　broccoli cheese rice, 186
　broccoli cheese soup, 146–147
　cauliflower cheese soup, 146
　　quantity, 39
　cheese and onion pie, 138
　　quantity, 42
　cheese sauce, 135–136
　cheese straws, 60
　cheesy corn bread, 243
　　quantity, 40
　cheesy meat loaf, 97–98
　cheesy orange mold, 215
　chicken enchiladas supreme, 114–115
　cucumbers stuffed with feta cheese, 64

　El Paso grits casserole, 184
　fancy potatoes, 175
　great northern salmon cream cheese ball, 69
　ham and cheese brunch munch, 135
　massive macaroni and cheese, 189–190
　nacho cheese dip, 75–76
　Roquefort cheese dip, 70
　scalloped carrots with cheese, 168–169
　three-cheese torte, 68
　zucchini cheese bake, 182–183
Cheese and Onion Pie, 138
　quantity, 42
Cheesecake
　almond cheesecake, 325
　chocolate cheesecake, 325
　chocolate-orange cheesecake, 326–327
　fruit-topped cheesecake, 325
　royal cheesecake, 324–325
Cheese Curls, 226
Cheese Sauce, 135–136
Cheese Straws, 60
Cheesy Corn Bread, 243
　quantity, 40
Cheesy Meat Loaf, 97–98
Cheesy Orange Mold, 215
Cherries
　cherry cream topping for fresh fruit, 236
　cherry pie, 308
　　quantity, 38
　cranberry-cherry mold, 217–218
　　quantity, 42
　quick cherry coffee cake, 253–254
Cherry Cream Topping for Fresh Fruit, 236
Cherry Pie, 308
　quantity, 38
Chestnuts
　apple-chestnut stuffing, 183
　　quantity, 43
Chicken
　baked sweet and sour chicken, 116
　Brunswick stew, 150
　chicken baked in cream, 109
　　quantity, 38
　chicken enchiladas supreme 114–115
　　quantity, 39

Chicken (cont.)
  chicken potpie, 115–116
  chicken spaghetti, 118
  chicken stock, 157–158
  Chinese chicken casserole, 113
  Chinese chicken wings, 77
  country fried chicken, 108
    quantity, 40
  creamed chicken and biscuits, 119
  creamy tarragon-mushroom chicken, 109
  Gilroy chicken wings, 78
  hot chicken salad, 117
    quantity, 40
  Italian chicken with artichokes, 112
  Italian wedding soup, 151–152
  Mama's chicken-rice soup, 151
  orange-coconut chicken, 110
  smothered chicken, 111–112
  Southern California cobb salad, 197
  spicy chicken wings, 76–77
  Waldorf salad, 226
  wild rice and mushroom chicken, 110–111
    quantity, 41
Chicken Baked in Cream, 109
  quantity, 38
Chicken Enchiladas Supreme, 114–115
  quantity, 39
Chicken Potpie, 115–116
Chicken Spaghetti, 118
Chicken Stock, 157–158
Chiles, 103
Chiles
  nacho cheese dip, 75–76
  rice and green chiles, 185
  Santa Fe salsa, 75
Chili Con Carne, 100
  quantity, 40
Chili powder, 100
Chili Toasted Nuts, 79
Chinese Chicken Casserole, 113
Chinese Chicken Wings, 77
Chinese Pea Pods
  Garden State vegetable medley, 166–167
Chocolate, 329

Chocolate
  blond brownies, 339
  chocolate cheesecake, 325
  chocolate chip cookies, 335–336
    quantity, 41
  chocolate cream icing, 298
  chocolate glaze, 297–298
  chocolate mint pie, 318–319
    quantity, 40
  chocolate-orange cheesecake, 326–327
  chocolate pound cake, 284
  cocoa sheet cake, 286–287
  frozen banana split dessert, 328–329
  fudge brownies, 337–338
  German chocolate cake, 285–286
    quantity, 38
  German chocolate cake frosting, 298–299
  hazelnut cocoa cake, 295
  old-fashioned hot cocoa for a crowd, 343
  pecan chocolate chip pie, 319
  ranger cookies, 333–334
  self-frosted date cake, 287–288
  snowballs, 331
Chocolate Cheesecake, 325
Chocolate Chip Cookies, 335–336
  quantity, 41
Chocolate Chip Pancakes, 49
Chocolate Cream Icing, 298
Chocolate Glaze, 297–298
Chocolate Mint Pie, 318–319
  quantity, 40
Chocolate-Orange Cheesecake, 326–327
Chocolate Pastry, 303
Chocolate Pound Cake, 284
Chorizo, 74
Cilantro, 75
Cinnamon, 294
Cinnamon Rolls, 271
Citrus Sherbet Punch, 349
Clam and Mushroom Soup, 153
Clam Chowder, 154
  quantity, 39
Clam Dip, 71
Clams
  clam and mushroom soup, 153
  Nantucket clam dip, 71
  New England clam chowder, 154

Clams (cont.)
  quantity, 39
  red clam spaghetti sauce, 53
Cleanup, 33–35
Cocoa Sheet Cake, 286–287
Cocoa-Swirl Coffee Cake, 255–256
Coconut
  broiled cake topping, 300–301
  impossible coconut custard pie, 315
  orange-coconut chicken, 110
  white Christmas pie, 317–318
Coconut Custard Pie, 315
Coffee
  Brazilian coffee, 342
  Cappuccino, 342
  coffee Borgia, 342
  coffee buffet, 341–342
  coffee for a crowd, 340–341
  Mexican coffee, 342
  Spanish coffee, 342
Coffee Borgia, 342
Coffee Buffet, 341–342
Coffee for a Crowd, 340–341
Cold Vegetable Platter, 61–62
Cole Slaws
  confetti cole slaw, 222
    quantity, 42
  Granny Smith cabbage slaw, 223
    quantity, 38
  tangerine cole slaw, 223
    quantity, 38
Common Baking Pan Equivalents, 357
Common Equivalents, 353–356
Condiments, 29
Confetti Cole Slaw, 222
  quantity, 42
Cookie Exchange, 332
Cookies
  Amish sugar cookies, 332–333
    quantity, 40
  blond brownies, 339
  chocolate chip cookies, 335–336
    quantity, 41
  date and nut bars, 337
  fudge brownies, 337–338

  lemon squares, 338
    quantity, 42
  molasses cookies, 334–335
  oatmeal cookies, 336–337
  peanut butter cookies, 334
  ranger cookies, 333–334
    quantity, 41
  snickerdoodles, 330–331
  snowballs, 331
  spice sugar cookies, 332
Copper Pennies Carrot Salad, 196–197
  quantity, 42
Corn
  broccoli supreme, 165
  cheesy corn bread, 243
    quantity, 40
  corn on the cob, 54
  Nebraska corn pudding, 170
    quantity, 38
  creamed zucchini and corn, 182
Cornish Pasty Pie, 107
Corn on the Cob, 54
Country Fried Chicken, 108
  quantity, 40
Country Potato Salad, 193–194
  quantity, 40
Crab
  crab gazpacho, 152–153
    quantity, 39
  Minnesota wild rice and crab salad, 204–205
  Pacific crab-avocado dip, 72
  perch with crab and mushroom topping, 132–133
    quantity, 40
Crab-Avocado Dip, 72
Crab Gazpacho, 152–153
  quantity, 39
Cracked Wheat Salad, 205–206
Cranberries, 227
Cranberries
  berry-glazed meat loaf, 98–99
  cranberry-cherry mold, 217
    quantity, 42
  cranberry relish, 227
  cranberry tea bread, 245–246

Cranberries (*cont.*)
  eggnog-cranberry salad, 213
  fresh cranberry salad, 226–227
Cranberry-Cherry Mold, 217–218
  quantity, 42
Cranberry Relish, 227
Cranberry Tea Bread, 245–246
Cream Cheese Frosting, 299–300
Cream Cheese Spreads, 244
Creamed Chicken and Biscuits, 119
Creamed Zucchini and Corn, 182
Creamy Cucumber Dill Dressing, 234
Creamy Russian Dressing, 233
Creamy Slaw Dressing, 235
Creamy Spiced Tea, 344–345
  quantity, 43
Creamy Tarragon-Mushroom Chicken, 109
Croutons, 159
Crumb Piecrusts, 304
Crumb-Topped Apple Pie, 306
Crunchy Topped Sweet Potatoes, 178–179
Cucumbers
  cucumbers stuffed with feta cheese, 64
  sour cream and cucumbers, 200
    quantity, 40
Cucumbers Stuffed with Feta Cheese, 64
Cupcakes, 297
Currant Punch Sparkle, 350–351
Curried Mushroom Soup, 141–142
Curried Pecans, 80

Danish Meatballs, 92–93
Date and Nut Bars, 337
Date-Nut Loaf, 244
Dates
  date and nut bars, 337
  date-nut loaf, 244
  pumpkin date bread 246–247
  self-frosted date cake, 287–288
Decorations, 21–22, 29
Deep-Dish Apple Pie, 306
Delta Tea, 345
Deviled Eggs, 65
  quantity, 40
Deviled Eggs with Ham Sauce, 139

Dijon Basil Dressing, 231
Dill Bread, 259
  quantity, 38
Dill-Chive Butter, 280
Dill Dip, 71
Dinner Rolls, 270–271
Dips
  dill dip, 71
  easy guacamole, 74
  Georgia bacon-pecan spread, 73
  Kansas City hot beef dip, 72
  layered tostada dip, 73–74
  Nacho cheese dip, 75–76
  Nantucket clam dip, 71
  Pacific crab-avocado dip, 72
  Roquefort cheese dip, 70
  Santa Fe salsa, 75
Down East Ham Loaf, 123

Easy Baked Beans, 162–163
Easy Guacamole, 74
Easy Peanut Butter Pie, 316
  quantity, 41
Easy Scalloped Potatoes, 174
  quantity, 38
Eggnog-Cranberry Salad, 213
Eggplant
  moussaka, 128–129
Eggs
  deviled eggs, 65
    quantity, 40
  deviled eggs with ham sauce, 139
  Salinas Valley artichoke spread, 70
  Scotch eggs, 66
El Paso Grits Casserole, 184
Emergency Substitutions, 356
Enchiladas
  chicken enchiladas supreme, 114–115
    quantity, 39
English Apple Pie, 305
English Pea Casserole, 171–172
Equivalent Measures, 358–359
Equivalents
  baking pans, 357
  can sizes, 358
  foods, 353–356

Equivalents (*cont.*)
  measures, 358–359
  oven temperatures, 359
Evie's Barbecued Brisket, 83
  quantity, 40

Fancy Potatoes, 175
  quantity, 37
Fast Fruit Fluff, 230
Filberts, 295
Fish
  Great Northern salmon cream cheese ball, 69
  Greek Shrimp sauté, 134
  perch with crab and mushroom topping, 132–133
    quantity, 40
  Portugese cod, 130–131
  seafood rotini, 133
  tuna, chile, and rice casserole, 132
  tuna noodle casserole, 131
Five-Cup Salad, 229
  quantity, 38
Flan
  strawberry-topped flan, 320–321
    quantity, 39
Fluff Salads
  fast fruit fluff, 230
  orange stuff, 230
  Watergate salad, 229–230
French Apple Pie, 307
French Dressing, 234
French Onion Soup, 140
French Quarter Mushroom Soup, 141
  quantity, 39
Fresh Cauliflower Soup, 145
Fresh Cranberry Salad, 226–227
Fresh Strawberry Pie, 308–309
  quantity, 43
Frostings
  boiled icing, 300
  broiled cake topping, 300–301
  brown sugar and butter icing, 301
  chocolate cream icing, 298
  chocolate glaze, 297–298
  cream cheese frosting, 299–300

German chocolate cake frosting, 298–299
  seven-minute icing, 300
  sour cream topping, 325
  whipped cream, 301–302
Frozen Banana Split Dessert, 328–329
  quantity, 41
Frozen Fruit Salad, 228
  quantity, 40
Fruit Basket Upset Coffee Cake, 251–252
Fruit Packets, 55
Fruit Salads
  ambrosia salad, 228–229
    quantity 42
  cranberry relish, 227
  five-cup salad, 229
    quantity, 38
  fresh cranberry salad, 226–227
  frozen fruit salad, 228
    quantity, 40
  grilled fruit packets, 55
  mixed fruit bowls, 224–225
  Waldorf salad, 226
    quantity, 37
Fruit Shortcake, 323
Fruit-Topped Cheesecake, 325
Fudge Brownies, 337–338

Garden State Vegetable Medley, 166–167
  quantity, 43
Garlic Nuts, 80
Georgia Bacon-Pecan Spread, 73
Georgia Peach-Pecan Coffee Cake, 248–249
German Apple Kuchen, 256
German Beef and Noodle Stew, 144
  quantity, 39
German Chocolate Cake, 285–286
  quantity, 38
German Chocolate Cake Frosting, 298–299
German Potato Salad, 194
  quantity, 39
Gilroy Chicken Wings, 78
Ginger, 88
Gingerbread, 292–293
Gingersnap Gravy, 85
  quantity, 39
Glaze, 296

Goulash, 142–143
  quantity, 39
Graham Streusel Coffee Cake, 252–253
Granny Smith Cabbage Slaw, 223
  quantity, 38
Grass Valley Cornish Pasty Pie, 107
Great Northern Salmon Cream Cheese Ball, 69
Great Plains Corn-Potato Chowder, 156
Greek Shrimp Sauté, 134
Green Beans
  barbecued green beans, 163
  Italian green bean salad, 196
    quantity, 41
  marinated bean salad, 195
  nutty green salad, 208
  potluck green beans, 161
    quantity, 38
Green Peppers
  stuffed green pepper, 172–173
Gridiron Casserole, 101–102
  quantity, 41
Grilling, 53–55
Grits
  El Paso grits casserole, 184
Guacamole, 74

Ham
  baked ham, 122
    quantity, 38
  deviled eggs with ham sauce, 139
  down east ham loaf, 123
  ham and cheese broccoli bake, 124
  ham and cheese brunch munch, 135
Ham and Cheese Broccoli Bake, 124
Ham and Cheese Brunch Munch, 135
Hamburgers, 54
Harvest Squash Medley, 181
Hash-Brown heaven, 177
Hash Browns
  hash-brown heaven, 177
  party hash browns, 176
Hazelnut Cocoa Cake, 295
Hazlenuts, 295
Hearty Apricot Bread, 245

Herbed Broccoli with Brussels Sprouts and Carrots,
  164
Herb-Onion Bread, 257
  quantity, 39
Herbs, meanings of, 149
Holiday Greek Bread, 264–265
  quantity, 39
Homemade Oat Bread, 263–264
  quantity, 39
Honey Butter Baked Turkey, 120
  quantity, 43
Hoppin' John, 187–188
Hot Beef Dip, 72
Hot Chicken Salad, 117
  quantity, 40
Hot Cocoa, 343
Hot Cross Buns, 273–274
  quantity, 42
Hot dogs, 54
Hot Mulled Cider, 346
Hot Spiced Afternoon Tea, 345 346
  quantity, 42
Hot Tea for a Crowd, 342
Hot Wurst Salad, 201 202
Hungarian Goulash Soup, 142–143
  quantity, 39

Icebox Millionaire Pie, 327–328
Iced Coffee, 347
Iced Tea for 25, 347
Ice Rings, 350
Impossible Coconut Custard Pie, 315
Irish Soda Bread, 247
Italian Chicken with Artichokes, 112
Italian Green Bean Salad, 196
  quantity, 41
Italian Sausage Sauce, 52
Italian Vinaigrette Dressing, 232
Italian Wedding Soup, 151–152

Jicama, 199
Jicama Salad, 199
  quantity, 39
Johnny Appleseed Cake, 290

Kansas City Hot Beef Dip, 72
Kasha Pilaf, 189
Kentucky Wheat Bread, 267–268
Kitchen Equipment, 27–28
Kiwi
   spinach carambola salad, 208

Lamb
   Grass Valley Cornish pasty pie, 107
   lamb and artichokes, 130
   moussaka, 128–129
   Yorkshire hot pot, 128
Lamb and Artichokes, 130
Lasagna, 95–96
Layered Salad with Mayonnaise and Cheese Top-
   ping, 209–210
Layered Tostada Dip, 73–74
Lemon Dew Salad, 219–220
Lemon Dream Dessert, 329–330
Lemon-Egg Dressing, 231
Lemon Mayonnaise, 232
Lemon Squares, 338
   quantity, 42
Lemonade, 348
   quantity, 40
Lentil Soup, 149
   quantity, 39
Lime Punch, 350
Location, 21–22

Macaroni and Cheese, 189–190
Macaroni Salad, 203
Mama's Chicken-Rice Soup, 151
Mandarin Cream Jellied Salad, 218–219
Maple Pumpkin Pie, 312
   quantity, 43
Marinated Bean Salad, 195
Marinated Tomato Salad, 201
Marinated Vegetable Medley, 198–199
Mashed Potatoes, 175
Massive Macaroni and Cheese, 189–190
Meat Loaf
   beef-mushroom meat loaf, 98
   berry-glazed meat loaf, 98–99

   cheesy meat loaf, 97–98
   traditional meat loaf, 97
      quantity, 38
Menu, 21–28, 36–55
Mexican Coffee, 342
Minestrone á la Genovese, 143–144
   quantity, 39
Minnesota Wild Rice and Crab Salad, 204–205
Mint Dressing, 224
Mississippi Sweet Potato Pie, 313
   quantity, 43
Mixed Fruit Bowls, 224–225
   quantity, 42
Mocha Punch, 351–352
   quantity, 42
Molasses Cookies, 334–335
Molded Salads
   apricot nectar mold, 215
   blueberry cream mold, 216–217
      quantity, 42
   cheesy orange mold, 215
   cranberry-cherry mold, 217–218
      quantity, 42
   eggnog-cranberry salad, 213
   lemon dew salad, 219–220
   mandarin cream jellied salad, 218–219
   New York Waldorf mold, 220–221
   Pacific ginger pear mold, 220
   raspberry-honeydew mold, 221
   red hot salad mold, 218
   spicy aspic salad, 214
   sunshine salad, 216
Moussaka, 128–129
   quantity, 38
Muffins
   six weeks bran muffins, 275–276
      quantity, 38
   sunshine muffins, 276–277
      quantity, 42
Mushroom and Asparagus Brunch Munch, 136
   quantity, 42
Mushrooms
   beef-mushroom meat loaf, 98
   clam and mushroom soup, 153
   creamy tarragon-mushroom chicken, 109

Mushrooms (*cont.*)
  curried mushroom soup, 141–142
  French Quarter mushroom soup, 141
    quantity, 39
  mushroom and asparagus brunch munch, 136
    quantity, 42
  mushroom spaghetti sauce, 52
  perch with crab and mushroom topping, 132–133
    quantity, 40
  pork chops Italiano, 126
  wild rice and mushroom chicken, 110–111
    quantity, 41
  zucchini and mushroom brunch munch, 136
Mushroom Soup, 141–142
  quantity, 39
Mushroom Spaghetti Sauce, 52

Nacho Cheese Dip, 75–76
Nantucket Clam Dip, 71
Nebraska Corn Pudding, 170
  quantity, 38
New England Clam Chowder, 154
  quantity, 39
New York Waldorf Mold, 220–221
Nuts and Bolts, 78–79
Nutty Cakes, 49
Nutty Green Salad, 208
Nutty Pastry, 303

Oatmeal
  homemade oat bread, 263–264
  oatmeal cake, 281–282
    quantity, 40
  oatmeal cookies, 336–337
Oatmeal Cake, 281–282
  quantity, 40
Oatmeal Cookies, 336–337
Old-Fashioned Hot Cocoa for a Crowd, 343
Onions
  baked onions, 171
  cheese and onion pie, 138
    quantity, 42
  French onion soup, 140
  herb-onion bread, 257

Orange-Almond Salad, 210–211
Orange Butter, 278
Orange-Coconut Chicken, 110
Orange Curry Dressing, 233
Orange Rolls, 271
Oranges
  chocolate-orange cheesecake, 326–327
  mandarin cream jellied salad, 218–219
  orange-almond salad, 210–211
  orange-coconut chicken 110
  orange curry dressing, 233
  orange scones, 272–273
  orange stuff, 230
  pineapple-orange spinach salad, 209
    quantity, 40
  sunshine butter, 278
  sunshine muffins, 276–277
Orange Scones, 272–273
  quantity, 42
Orange Spice Pancakes, 49
Orange Stuff, 230
Organization, 21–35
Outdoor Cooking, 53–55
Oven Stew, 89–90
Oven Temperature Guidelines, 359
Overnight Coffee Cake, 249–250
  quantity, 42

Pacific Crab-Avocado Dip, 72
Pacific Ginger Pear Mold, 220
Pancakes, 48–51
Pancake Toppings, 50–51
Paper Goods, 29
Party Hash Browns, 176
Party Punch, 349
Pasta Salad Primavera, 203–204
  quantity, 42
Pasties, 107
Peaches
  Georgia peach-pecan coffee cake, 248–249
  peach pie, 311
Peach Pie, 311
Peanut Butter
  easy peanut butter pie, 316
    quantity, 41
  peanut butter cookies, 334

Peanut Butter (*cont.*)
   peanut butter cream pie, 316
Peanut Butter Cookies, 334
Peanut Butter Cream Pie, 316
Pears
   Pacific ginger pear mold, 220
Peas
   English pea casserole, 171–172
   split pea soup, 147–148
Pecan Chocolate Chip Pie, 319
Pecan Pie, 313–314
Pecans, 314
   curried pecans, 80
   Georgia bacon-pecan spread, 73
   Georgia peach-pecan coffee cake, 248–249
   pecan chocolate chip pie, 319
   pecan pie, 313–314
   pumpkin pecan pie, 314
Perch with Crab and Mushroom Topping, 132–
     133
   quantity, 40
Personnel, 21–22, 26, 28, 32
Pie Apples, 304
Pies
   All-American apple pie, 304–305
     quantity, 43
   blueberry pie, 310
   buttermilk custard pie, 315–316
     quantity, 43
   cheese and onion pie, 138
     quantity, 42
   cherry pie, 308
     quantity, 38
   chocolate mint pie, 318–319
     quantity, 40
   chocolate pastry, 303
   crumb piecrusts, 304
   crumb-topped apple pie, 306
   deep-dish apple pie, 306
   easy peanut butter pie, 316
     quantity, 41
   English apple pie, 305
   French apple pie, 307
   fresh strawberry pie, 308–309
     quantity, 43

   icebox millionaire pie, 327–328
   impossible coconut custard pie, 315
   maple pumpkin pie, 312
     quantity, 43
   Mississippi sweet potato pie, 313
     quantity, 43
   nutty pastry, 303
   peach pie, 311
   peanut butter cream pie, 316
   pecan chocolate chip pie, 319
   pecan pie, 313–314
   pumpkin pecan pie, 314
   raisin cream pie, 317
     quantity, 43
   strawberry cream pie, 309–310
   sweet potato pie, 313
   traditional pastry, 303
   water whip pastry, 302
   white Christmas pie, 317–318
Pineapple, 288
Pineapple
   blueberry cream mold, 216–217
   orange stuff, 230
   pineapple beef, 88–89
   pineapple-orange spinach salad, 209
     quantity, 40
   pineapple rolls, 272
   pineapple sherbet punch, 351
   pineapple upside-down cake, 288–289
   sunshine salad, 216
Pineapple Beef, 88–89
Pineapple-Orange Spinach Salad, 209
   quantity, 40
Pineapple Rolls, 272
Pineapple Sherbet Punch, 351
Pineapple Upside-Down Cake, 288–289
Planning, 21–27
Polish Sausage and Red Cabbage, 127
Poppy Seed Bread, 239
   quantity, 42
Porcupines, 94
Pork
   down east ham loaf, 123
   grilled hot dogs, 54
   pork chops Italiano, 126
     quantity, 41

Pork (*cont.*)
  Sedona bean and pork burritos, 125–126
  skillet pork chops and rice, 124
Pork Chops Italiano, 126
  quantity, 41
Portuguese Cod, 130–131
Potatoes
  Boise potato soup, 154–155
  country potato salad, 193–194
    quantity, 40
  easy scalloped potatoes, 174
    quantity, 38
  fancy potatoes, 175
    quantity, 37
  German potato salad, 194
    quantity, 39
  Great Plains corn–potato chowder, 156
  hash-brown heaven, 177
Potatoes
  hot wurst salad, 201–202
  party hash browns, 176
  potatoes primavera, 174–175
  potatoes with rosemary, 173–174
    quantity, 41
  shepherd's pie, 106
Potatoes Primavera, 174–175
Potatoes with Rosemary, 173–174
  quantity, 41
Potluck Green Beans, 161
  quantity, 38
Potpies
  chicken potpie, 115–116
    quantity, 38
Pound Cake, 282–283
Pumpkin
  maple pumpkin pie, 312
    quantity, 43
  pumpkin date bread, 246–247
  pumpkin pecan pie, 314
Pumpkin Date Bread, 246–247
Pumpkin Pecan Pie, 314

Quantity of Food, 26, 37–47
Quiche
  broccoli-rice quiche, 184–185

sausage quiche, 137
  quantity, 42
shrimp quiche, 137–138
  quantity, 42
Quick Cherry Coffee Cake, 253–254
Quick Wassail, 343–344

Raisin Cream Pie, 317
  quantity, 43
Raisin Sauce, 122–123
  quantity, 38
Raisins, 290, 317
Raisins
  apple-raisin cake, 291–292
  Boston brown bread, 242
  molasses cookies, 334–335
  raisin cream pie, 317
    quantity, 43
  raisin sauce for ham, 122–123
  Waldorf salad, 226
Ranger Cookies, 333–334
  quantity, 41
Raspberry Butter, 279
Raspberry-Honeydew Mold, 221
Red Beans and Rice, 187
Red Cabbage
  Polish sausage and red cabbage, 127
  red cabbage side dish, 167–168
    quantity, 39
Red Cabbage, 167–168
  quantity, 39
Red Clam Spaghetti Sauce, 53
Red Hot Salad Mold, 218
Rental Equipment, 28
Rhubarb
  rhubarb cake, 289
Rhubarb Cake, 289
Rice
  baked rice, 186
  broccoli cheese rice, 186
  broccoli-rice quiche, 184–185
  hoppin' John, 187–188
  Mama's chicken–rice soup, 151
  Minnesota wild rice and crab salad, 204–205
  porcupines, 94

Rice (*cont.*)
   red beans and rice, 187
   rice and green chiles, 185
   rice pilaf, 188
   skillet pork chops and rice, 124–125
   Spanish rice with beef, 101
     quantity, 39
   tuna, chile, and rice casserole, 132
   wild rice and mushroom chicken, 110–111
     quantity, 41
Rice and Green Chiles, 185
Rice Pilaf, 188
Rio Grande Chili Con Carne, 100
   quantity, 40
Rock Cornish Hens with Apricot Sauce, 113–114
Rocky Road Pancakes, 49
Rolls
   all-purpose rolls, 269–272
     quantity, 37
   cinnamon rolls, 271
   dinner rolls, 270–271
   hot cross buns, 273–274
   orange rolls, 271
   pineapple rolls, 272
   sticky buns, 271
Roquefort Cheese Dip, 70
Royal Cheesecake, 324–325
   quantity, 41
Rye-Garlic Rounds, 60

Saffron, 260
Salad Bars, 211–212
   quantity, 39
Salad Dressings and Toppings
   blue cheese dressing, 235
   cherry cream topping for fresh fruit, 236
   creamy cucumber dill dressing, 234
   creamy Russian dressing, 233
   creamy slaw dressing, 235
   dijon basil dressing, 231
   French dressing, 234
   Italian vinaigrette dressing, 232
   lemon-egg dressing, 231
   lemon mayonnaise, 232
   orange curry dressing, 233

Salads
   bacon and broccoli salad, 198
   beet and spinach salad, 207
   bulgur salad, 205–206
   copper pennies carrot salad, 196
     quantity, 42
   country potato salad, 193–194
     quantity, 40
   five-cup salad, 229
     quantity, 38
   German potato salad, 194
     quantity, 39
   hot chicken salad, 117
     quantity, 40
   hot wurst salad, 201–202
   Italian green bean salad, 196
     quantity, 41
   jicama salad, 199
     quantity, 39
   layered salad with mayonnaise and cheese topping, 209–210
   macaroni salad, 203
   marinated bean salad, 195
   marinated tomato salad, 201
   marinated vegetable medley, 198–199
   Minnesota wild rice and crab salad, 204–205
   nutty green salad, 208
   orange-almond salad, 210–211
   pasta salad primavera, 203–204
     quantity, 42
   pineapple-orange spinach salad, 209
     quantity, 40
   salad bars, 211–212
     quantity, 39
   sour cream and cucumbers, 200
     quantity, 40
   Southern California cobb salad, 197
   spicy aspic salad, 214
     quantity, 41
   spinach carambola salad, 208
     quantity, 40
   sunshine salad, 216
     quantity, 38
   tangy toss, 206–207
   Waldorf salad, 226
     quantity, 37

Salads (*cont.*)
  see also molded salads
Salinas Valley Artichoke Spread, 70
Sally Lunn, 257–258
Santa Fe Salsa, 75
Sauces
  apricot sauce, 114
  cheese sauce, 135–136
  perfect pasta sauce, 52–53
  raisin sauce, 122–123
Sauerbraten, 85
  quantity, 39
Sausage
  berry-glazed meat loaf, 98–99
  grilled sausage, 54
  hot wurst salad, 201–202
  Italian sausage sauce, 52
  lasagna, 95–96
  perfect pasta sauce, 52
  Polish sausage and red cabbage, 127
  sausage quiche, 137
    quantity, 42
  Scotch eggs, 66
  turkey sausage, 67
Sausage Quiche, 137
  quantity, 42
Scalloped Carrots with Cheese, 168–169
Scotch Eggs, 66
Scripture Cake, 296–297
Seafood Rotini, 133
Sedona Bean and Pork Burritos, 125–126
Seed Cake, 283
Self-Frosted Date Cake, 287–288
Setting Up, 30–33
Seven-Layer Hot Dish, 104–105
Seven-Minute Icing, 300
Shepherd's Pie, 106
Shopping, 28–29
Shortcake, 323
Shrimp
  Greek shrimp sauté, 134
  seafood rotini, 133
  shrimp quiche, 137–138
    quantity, 42
Shrimp Quiche, 137–138

  quantity, 42
Sign-up Sheets, 22, 24
Six Weeks Bran Muffins, 275–276
  quantity, 38
Skewers, 63
Skillet Pork Chops and Rice, 124–125
Sloppy Joes, 90
  quantity, 41
Sloppy Josés, 91
Smothered Chicken, 111–112
Snickerdoodles, 330–331
Snowballs, 331
Soup Garnishes, 145
Soups
  all-day lentil soup, 149
    quantity, 39
  beef stock, 158–159
  black bean soup, 148–149
  Boise potato soup, 154–155
  broccoli cheese soup, 146–147
  brunswick stew, 150
  cauliflower cheese soup, 146
    quantity, 39
  chicken stock, 157–158
  clam and mushroom soup, 153
  crab gazpacho, 152–153
    quantity, 39
  curried mushroom soup, 141–142
  French onion soup, 140
  French Quarter mushroom soup, 141
    quantity, 39
  fresh cauliflower soup, 145
  Great Plains corn-potato chowder, 156
  Hungarian goulash soup, 142–143
    quantity, 39
  Italian wedding soup, 151–152
  Mama's chicken-rice soup, 151
  minestrone á la Genovese, 143–144
    quantity, 39
  New England clam chowder, 154
    quantity, 39
  split pea soup, 147–148
  tuna chowder, 157
Sour Cream and Cucumbers, 200
  quantity, 40

Sour Cream Coffee Cake, 250–251
Sour Cream Topping, 325
Southern California Cobb Salad, 197
South Side Stuffed Cabbage Rolls, 99–100
Soy Sauce, 113
Spaghetti, 51–53
Spanish Coffee, 342
Spanish Rice with Beef, 101
   quantity, 39
Spice Sugar Cookies, 332
Spices, meanings of, 149
Spicy Aspic Salad, 214
   quantity, 41
Spicy Chicken Wings, 76–77
Spicy Honey Butter, 279
Spinach –
   beet and spinach salad, 207
   pineapple-orange spinach salad, 209
      quantity, 40
   spinach carambola salad, 208
      quantity, 40
   spinach squares, 180
Spinach Carambola Salad, 208
   quantity, 40
Spinach Squares, 180
Split Pea Soup, 147–148
Squash
   harvest squash medley, 181
Steak, 54
Stews
   Brunswick stew, 150
   German beef and noodle stew, 144
      quantity, 39
   oven stew, 89–90
   Yorkshire hot pot, 128
Sticky Buns, 271
Strawberries
   fresh strawberry pie, 308
      quantity, 43
   strawberry breakfast bread, 240
      quantity, 42
   strawberry cream pie, 309–310
   strawberry-topped flan, 320–321
      quantity, 39
Strawberry Breakfast Bread, 240

   quantity, 42
Strawberry Butter, 278
Strawberry Cream Pie, 309–310
Strawberry-Topped Flan, 320–321
   quantity, 39
Stuffed Cabbage Rolls, 99–100
Stuffed Green Peppers, 172–173
Stuffed Shells, 191–192
Sugar Glaze Frosting, 274
Sun Tea, 348
Sunday Dinner Pot Roast, 81–82
   quantity, 37
Sunshine Butter, 278
Sunshine Muffins, 276–277
   quantity, 42
Sunshine Salad, 216
   quantity, 38
Super Taco Platter, 105–106
   quantity, 41
Swedish Coffee Braid, 262–263
Swedish Meatballs, 93–94
Swedish Rye Bread, 261–262
   quantity, 39
Sweet Potatoes
   crunchy topped sweet potatoes, 178–179
   Mississippi sweet potato pie, 313
      quantity, 43
   whipped sweet potatoes, 179
      quantity, 42
Sweet Potato Pie, 313
Swiss Steak, 87–88

Tabouleh Salad, 205–206
Tangerine Cole Slaw, 223
   quantity, 38
Tangy Toss, 206–207
Tea
   creamy spiced tea, 344–345
      quantity, 43
   delta tea, 345
   hot spiced afternoon tea, 345–346
      quantity, 42
   garnishes, 348
   hot tea for a crowd, 342
   iced tea for 25, 347

Tea (*cont.*)
  sun tea, 348
Tea for a Crowd, 342
Texas Beans, 102
Themes, 21–22
Three-Cheese Torte, 68
Tomatoes
  broccoli and tomatoes, 165–166
    quantity, 38
  marinated tomato salad, 201
  turkey and tomato brunch munch, 136
Traditional Meat Loaf, 97
  quantity, 38
Traditional Pastry, 303
Tuna
  seafood rotini, 133
  tuna, chile, and rice casserole, 132
  tuna chowder, 157
  tuna noodle casserole, 131
Tuna, Chile, and Rice Casserole, 132
Tuna Chowder, 157
Tuna Noodle Casserole, 131
Turkey
  honey butter baked turkey, 120
    quantity, 43
  turkey and tomato brunch munch, 136
  turkey delight, 121
  turkey sausage, 67
Turkey and Tomato Brunch Munch, 136
Turkey Delight, 121
Turkey Sausage, 67
Twin Cities Celery Hot Dish, 169–170

Vanilla Pancakes, 50
Vanilla Sugar, 228
Vegetable Kabobs, 55
Vegetables and Side Dishes
  All-American yams, 177–178
  antipasto platter, 63–64
  apple-chestnut stuffing, 183
    quantity, 43
  baked onions, 171
  baked rice, 186
  baked sauerkraut, 179–180
  baked ziti, 190–191

barbecued green beans, 163
Boston baked beans, 162
  quantity, 38
broccoli and tomatoes, 165–166
  quantity, 38
broccoli cheese rice, 186
broccoli-rice quiche, 184–185
broccoli supreme, 165
bulgur pilaf, 189
carrots and walnuts, 168
  quantity, 38
cold vegetable platter, 61–62
country potato salad, 193–194
  quantity, 40
creamed zucchini and corn, 182
crunchy topped sweet potatoes, 178–179
cucumbers stuffed with feta cheese, 64
easy baked beans, 162–163
easy scalloped potatoes, 174
  quantity, 38
El Paso grits casserole, 184
English pea casserole, 171–172
fancy potatoes, 175
  quantity, 37
Garden State vegetable medley, 166–167
  quantity, 43
German potato salad, 194
  quantity, 39
harvest squash medley, 181
hash-brown heaven, 177
herbed broccoli with Brussels sprouts and carrots, 164
hoppin' John, 187–188
kasha pilaf, 189
massive macaroni and cheese, 189–190
Nebraska corn pudding, 170
  quantity, 38
party hash browns, 176
potatoes primavera, 174–175
potatoes with rosemary, 173–174
  quantity, 41
potluck green beans, 161
  quantity, 38
red beans and rice, 187
red cabbage, 167–168

Vegetables and Side Dishes (*cont.*)
   quantity, 39
   rice and green chiles, 185
   rice pilaf, 188
   scalloped carrots with cheese, 168–169
      quantity, 37
   sour cream and cucumbers, 200
      quantity, 40
   spinach squares, 180
   stuffed green peppers, 172–173
   stuffed shells, 191–192
   Sunday dinner pot roast, 81–82
   Twin Cities celery hot dish, 169–170
   vegetable kabobs, 55
   whipped sweet potatoes, 179
      quantity, 42
   zucchini cheese bake, 182–183

Waldorf Salad, 226
   quantity, 37
Walnut Bread, 266–267
Walnuts
   apple raisin cake, 291–292
   baklava, 321–323
   broiled cake topping, 300–301
   carrots and walnuts, 168
      quantity, 38
   date and nut bars, 337
   harvest squash medley, 181
   New York Waldorf mold, 220–221

three-cheese torte, 68
Waldorf salad, 226
   quantity, 37
walnut bread, 266–267
Wassail, 343–344
Water, 347
Watergate Salad, 229–230
Watermelon Basket, 225
Water Whip Pastry, 302–303
Whipped Cream, 301–302
Whipped Sweet Potatoes, 179
   quantity, 42
White Christmas Pie, 317–318'
Wild Rice, 204
Wild Rice and Mushroom Chicken, 110–111
   quantity, 41

Yams
   All-American yams, 177–178
Yorkshire Hot Pot, 128
Yorkville Sauerbraten, 85
   quantity, 39

Zucchini
   creamed zucchini and corn, 182
   zucchini and mushrooms brunch munch, 136
   zucchini cheese bake, 182–183
   zucchini lasagna, 96–97
Zucchini and Mushroom Brunch Munch, 136
Zucchini Cheese Bake, 182–183
Zucchini Lasagna, 96–97